THE
COMPLETE
STORY

Arthur Gent

The Crowood Press

First published in 2011 by
The Crowood Press Ltd
Ramsbury, Marlborough
Wiltshire SN8 2HR

www.crowood.com

British Library Cataloguing-in-Publication Data
A catalogue record for this book is available from the British Library.

ISBN 978 1 84797 246 0

Typeset and designed by D & N Publishing, Baydon, Wiltshire.

Printed and bound in Singapore by Craft Print International Ltd.

Contents

Preface

I first became involved with motorcycles while serving in the Royal Air Force at RAF Honington in the 1950s when I purchased a 98cc James machine from Ronald Whitney, who was to become a lifelong friend. Ron became my best man, and we have kept in touch ever since. A succession of James and BSA machines followed until I was posted to Cyprus; on return I bought one of Alec Issigonis' Minis, and left the motorcycling scene for some considerable time.

I became involved with motorcycles again in the 1980s, but not to any great extent. While we were spending Christmas with our daughter Christine and son-in-law, Nigel, at RAF Scampton, I and my son Andrew managed to get a Suzuki running that had been seized up. We went for a meal with Nigel's friend Mark, and after relating the story of the Suzuki, Mark offered me the motorcycle that was lying outside his house covered with snow. Some time later I borrowed a trailer and went to fetch the motorcycle, and it turned out to be a 1958 Francis-Barnett Cruiser 80. It had originally belonged to Mark's father, but Mark and his brother had stripped everything heavy from it and used it off road. When time permitted, and with the help of my son Andrew, by now a qualified electrical/mechanical engineer, we rebuilt the Cruiser, and I still own it and take it to local shows. My passion for motorbikes rekindled, I ended up with two Cruiser 80s, two Falcon 87s and a 1948 Merlin L51; however, I sold one Cruiser and one Falcon and so am left with only three machines.

One of the first things I did was to join the Francis-Barnett Owners' Club; eventually I took over maintaining the *Club Register of Owners' Machines*. It soon became apparent that many members either did not know which model they owned, or had identified it incorrectly, probably because a lot of the older machines, particularly the pre-war ones, came with little or no paperwork. Before I could suggest the correct identity of a machine I had to research the marque extensively, building up an index of the models; this helped to some extent, and when I became librarian and had the manuals to hand, the task became easier. An A5-size manuscript book was produced of the index, which also included copies of sales literature to help in identifying machines. Jeff Venning, the then Club Chairman, put forward the idea of a book relating to the history of Francis-Barnett based on this information. Unfortunately it did not get off the ground at that time, but Jeff must take the credit for planting the seed that eventually flourished.

The book is not intended to be a workshop manual, but a compendium of the company and its machines. The specification information has been gleaned from annual sales brochures, instruction manuals, spare parts lists and road test reports. It is not possible to state that the specification for a particular machine is such and such unless it is said, for example, that according to the instruction book for the 1958 Cruiser 80, the specification is this. In many instances an advance announcement was made, giving specifications; a pre-production model could then be given to the Press for a road test, when they could come up with another set of specifications. If the machine went into production, which it did not always, it appeared in an annual sales brochure with another set of specifications – and then there are the specifications in the instruction manual given to the new owner. Should the machine remain in production over a period of time, there is a distinct possibility that each year's model has a slightly different specification than previous years. There is also the possibility that the original owner might have specified an alternative to the standard part; for example, it is known of a particular machine that according to its specification, it had a Villiers 8E engine fitted, but the purchaser requested and had the Villiers 7E engine instead.

The only thing that may have been altered is the conversion of imperial measurements to metric. Francis-Barnett used a variety of methods to show the metric equivalent over the years, from the nearest 5mm to the nearest 1/10mm, with some wildly inaccurate calculations. The conversion has been standardized to the nearest millimetre. Gallons and pints have been converted to litres – but what is the conversion for a specification of 'nearly two gallons'? It is suggested that the metric measurements should be used as a guide only, and recalculated if required to be used.

Arthur Gent

The machine shown here has been immaculately restored and modified to make it road legal. It is unique in having no name and no model number, and is one of only three built to compete in trials competitions. A new capacity class of 125–175cc was announced for the 1954/55 International Six Day Trial (ISDT). Francis-Barnett decided to enter a team of 172cc machines, which Ernie Smith prepared using modified 197cc cylinders with a reduced bore of 50mm. The team was Ernie Smith (MHP 469), George Fisher (MHP 470) and Dick Kemp (MHP 471). The machine was displayed at the FBOC AGM, 2010.

CHAPTER ONE

The Francis & Barnett Company Ltd

The Origins of the Coventry Motorcycle Industry

Coventry, an ancient city associated with the county of Warwickshire, is situated in the area once covered by the Forest of Arden; it is now a city and metropolitan borough in the county of the West Midlands. Some believe that Coventry is so named because it was thought to have been built on a settlement that grew up around a Saxon nunnery or convent founded by St Osburga around AD 700, and so took its name from the old word *coventre*, meaning a settlement built around a convent.

In the Middle Ages, Coventry became one of the most important cities in England through its connection with the wool trade. Later, blanket weaving, ribbon making and the textile industry were its main trades, as listed in seventeenth-century records. In the eighteenth and nineteenth centuries it became an important centre for watch and clock manufacture, on a par with Prescot and Clerkenwell; the earliest clock in Coventry's Herbert Museum is Samuel Watson's, made for Charles II in 1680. In the census of 1851, over 750 heads of households were employed in the watch trade industry. Coventry then went on to be a centre for the manufacture of sewing machines, cycles, motorcycles and motor cars.

From Clock Making to Cycles

James Starley was born in about 1830 in Sussex; as a young man he moved to London. He eventually worked in a sewing machine business managed by Joshua Turner. In the early 1860s Turner and Starley moved to Coventry, and in 1863 founded the European

Sewing Machine Company. The reason given for locating to Coventry was the pool of skilled employees from the watch-making industry, who were able to undertake the intricate work of sewing machine manufacture. Because of the difficulties in expanding their sales of sewing machines, the company diversified into the manufacture of *vélocipèdes* in 1868. This was followed by a change of name in 1869, to the 'Coventry Machinists' Company'.

James Starley brought about several improvements to the basic *vélocipède* while working for the company, in addition to the improvements he made to the sewing machine. In 1871 he set up his own sewing machine manufacturing company with William Borthwick Smith – Smith, Starley & Co. – at St Agnes' Works, Hale Street, Coventry. They manufactured the Europa sewing machine patented by Starley earlier that year. At the same time he was collaborating with William Hillman on designs for cycles. In 1872 he was joined in Coventry by his nephew, John Kemp Starley, who found employment with Haynes and Jefferis, manufacturers of the James Starley-designed Ariel cycle. In 1878 he became a cycle manufacturer with William Sutton in the business of Starley and Sutton; in 1886 this was renamed 'J. K. Starley & Co. Ltd'.

Starley's claim to fame was as the manufacturer of the Rover Safety Cycle introduced in 1885, with a triangulated frame, both wheels of the same diameter, and chain driven. Within two years he had perfected the design that changed cycling forever, and in 1896 changed the name of his company to the Rover Cycle Company. He died of heart failure in 1901, at the early age of forty-six.

Lea Francis motorcycle (Richard Lea and Graham Francis). (Courtesy CTM)

John Kemp Starley's Rover Safety Cycle, the forerunner of the modern bicycle. (Courtesy Coventry Transport Museum)

In 1878, his uncle James Starley began working in the cycle business, Starley Bros, which he helped to establish with his sons. His inventions made cycles more practical and easier to use, and so they became more popular. He died in 1881, and is remembered as the 'father of the cycle industry'. He was buried in the London Road Cemetery where his grave is sadly neglected for someone who played such an important role in Coventry's history.

The 'Made in Coventry Motoring Association (MICMA)' website lists in excess of 250 companies manufacturing cycles in Coventry, including A. Barnett & Co., Lea-Francis Ltd, and Francis & Barnett Ltd (from 1919).

The first production two-wheeled motor vehicle referred to as a 'motorcycle' was the Hildebrand and Wolfmuller machine manufactured in Munich. It was actually referred to as a *motorrad* in Germany, which is German for motorcycle; Hildebrand and Wolfmuller patented the name in 1894. In 1895, the Hildebrand and Wolfmuller motorcycle was demonstrated by M. J. Schulte of the Triumph Cycle Company at the Coventry Cycle Stadium, with a view to building it under licence in England; however, this did not materialize.

Several of Coventry's cycle manufacturers turned their attention to the motorcycle and subsequently to the motor car, or went straight to manufacturing motor cars. One of these was the Rover Company, started by John Kemp Starley, that produced the first Rover motorcycle in 1903, followed by car production a year later. Another was a partnership of Richard H. Lea and Gordon I. Francis, set up in 1895 at Day's Lane producing cycles. The partnership was put on a more legal footing in 1896 when the Lea & Francis Ltd Company was formed. It was around this time that the firm moved to Lower Ford Street, Hillfields, in Coventry.

In 1903, they tried their hand at motor car manufacture and designed a 3-cylinder car, which was not commercially successful. Then in 1911 they built their first motorcycle, powered by a 3.5bhp J. A. Prestwich (JAP) V-twin, and offered to the public in 1912 priced at £69 10s. Their most notable client was George Bernard Shaw. Cycle production ceased in about 1920, and motorcycle production in about 1924 when they concentrated on the manufacture of motor cars.

Another firm was that of A. Barnett & Co. Ltd, although it was not established until 1912; the proprietor was Arthur Barnett, one of the driving forces behind Francis & Barnett Ltd.

Francis & Barnett Ltd

Francis & Barnett Ltd was registered in 1919 with three directors: Arthur Barnett, Arthur's son-in-law Gordon I. Francis, and Gordon's father, Graham I. Francis. The company was set up in part of the old Hillman factory they had acquired, used for the manufacture of munitions during the war, and previously used for the manufacture of the Bayliss-Thomas 'Excelsior', the first-ever British production motorcycle. Francis-Barnett manufactured motorcycles in Coventry over a longer time period than any other company, and of all the companies that originated in Coventry, only Triumph continued in production longer than Francis-Barnett.

The Founders of the Company

Mr Arthur Barnett, 1863–1937
Mr Barnett started his career as a clerk with the Singer Motor Company, and rose to become one of the directors of that company in 1912. In that year he also set up his own company under the name of A. Barnett & Co. Ltd, in Coventry, to manufacture the Invicta bicycle and later the Invicta motorcycle. The Invicta motorcycles, produced at the West Orchard factory, became available to the public in 1913; they were fitted with the 269cc two-stroke Villiers engine with petroil lubrication and a chain-driven magneto. Two versions were available, both fitted with druid forks, one belt-driven and the other fitted with a Jardine two-speed gear and chain-cum-belt drive. These were followed by 346cc and 678cc sv JAP-engined machines, plus a 499cc sv Abingdon-engined machine.

By 1923 production was reduced to machines with a 292cc and a 346cc four-stroke engine, and a 247cc Villiers two-stroke engine. 1924 continued with four-strokes only, then in 1925 a 147cc AZA two-stroke-engined machine was added; 1925 was the final year that the Invicta was produced. The 1917 *Red Book* shows two 2.5bhp machines (one with a two-speed gearbox) at £36 15s and £44 2s 6d respectively, a 2.75bhp JAP-engined machine at £48 5s, a 3.5bhp machine with three-speed gearbox, countershaft and kick-start at £65 2s 6d, and a 5/6bhp 2-cylinder machine with three-speed box, countershaft and kick-start at £75 7s 6d.

In 1919 Arthur joined forces with his son-in-law, Gordon I. Francis, to set up the firm of Francis & Barnett Ltd in Lower Ford Street, Coventry. When the Clarendon Pressing & Welding Co. Ltd became part of Francis & Barnett, he became the chairman and joint managing director of that firm.

Mr Barnett was involved with organizations both nationally and locally, becoming the senior vice president of the British Cycle and Motor Cycle Manufacturers' and Traders' Union Ltd, and for many years the chairman of the Coventry Provident Permanent Building Society.

Invicta motorcycle (A. Barnett & Son Ltd).
(Courtesy CTM)

Mr Barnett was chairman and managing director of Francis & Barnett Ltd, and on his death at the age of seventy-four was described as a pioneer of the cycle industry; he had been in failing health for some months. The funeral service was held at Coventry Cathedral.

On his death, his son Eric Arthur Barnett took over his mantle at Francis & Barnett Ltd and became sales director. Unfortunately on 30 November 1961 Eric was involved in a road traffic accident while crossing a road and died from his injuries. This was to prove a significant setback in local resistance to AMC policies, and the resistance was never the same again.

Mr Gordon Inglesby Francis, 1889–1972
Mr Gordon Francis was born in 1889 in the United States, but moved to Coventry with his parents when he was three months old; he was the eldest of five children, the others being Hilma, Bernard, Ulyth and Ethne. He resided and had his business interests in the Coventry area, apart from service in the Army Service Corps (now the RASC) during World War I. He was promoted to Temp. Captain with seniority from 11 September 1916, and Hon. Captain on being invalided from the army through ill health on 24 May 1917. While serving in the army he found that the welded frame of their motorcycles was liable to fracture under rough riding conditions, and it was largely as a result of his experience of motorcycle repairs at army bases that he introduced the revolutionary bolted triangulated frame, put on the market in 1923.

In the 1911 census Gordon Francis was recorded as lodging at 30 Welford Place, Coventry, the residence of the Parker sisters, and his occupation given as 'manager of iron foundry'; unfortunately it does not include the owners of the foundry. The first International Six Days Trial was held from 18 to 23 August 1913 at Carlisle, and listed as a recipient of a gold medal is G. T. Francis – probably a misprint for G. I. Francis – on a Lea Francis; N. Lea was awarded silver and bronze medals, also on a Lea Francis – this is presumably Norman Lea, son of Richard Lea. It is quite probable that this is when Gordon obtained his experience of motorcycles, which stood him in such good stead whilst serving in the Army Service Corps during World War I.

Francis married Annie Elizabeth Barnett, the daughter of Arthur Barnett, on 9 May 1916 at Christ Church, Coventry. Following the war he formed the motorcycle manufacturing partnership, Francis & Barnett Ltd, with his father-in-law in 1919. Francis retired as joint managing director of Francis & Barnett Ltd. in 1960; he remained on the board of directors and as technical consultant to the firm. He also remained on the board of the parent company, Associated Motor Cycles Ltd.

Gordon and Annie's son, also named Gordon (1922–2008), was a highly rated motor sports press photographer based in the West Country. The Somerton Classic Club holds an annual race for the Gordon Francis Memorial Trophy in his honour. Many of the photographs in Andy Westlake's book *Off-Road Giants* are by Gordon.

Graham Inglesby Francis, 1861–1940
The third founder of the company was Mr Graham Francis. He was born in Islington in 1861, the son of George Baggett Francis, a wholesale druggist, and Sarah Inglesby Butt. Graham had three siblings: William, ten years his senior – also a wholesale druggist, and later employed by Lea & Francis Ltd – and two sisters, Ellen and Edith. Although not involved in the day-to-day running of Francis & Barnett Ltd, he was a director because of his financial investment. He is best known for his association with Richard Henry Lea in the Lea & Francis Company.

Graham Francis began his career as an engineering apprentice, and being primarily concerned with machine tools, spent a considerable time abroad, both in Europe and the USA. While in America he was employed by the Brown & Sharpe Manufacturing Company of Providence, Rhode Island, a well known and influential firm in the machine tool industry during the nineteenth and twentieth centuries. One of his personal books, now in the possession of the Francis-Barnett Owners' Club, is signed and dated 'G. I. Francis, Providence, Rhode Island, USA – May/86'. On his return to England, one of his appointments was as works manager of the Coventry-based firm, Auto Machinery Company Ltd.

Some Company History

A large part of the firm's records and documents was destroyed as a result of the bombing of Coventry during

Coventry Cathedral after World War II. (Courtesy FBOC)

World War II. Coventry was very heavily bombed on the night of 14 November 1940, with a great loss of life; the German attack was code-named Operation *Moonlight Sonata*, and because of the widespread destruction a new word was coined by the Germans – 'coventrieren', meaning 'to totally destroy'. This was not the only occasion Coventry was attacked, as the bombers returned again in April 1941.

One of the myths that is constantly repeated is that the factory was razed to the ground in the Coventry blitz. In fact there were four factories run by Francis-Barnett in Coventry, and according to Gordon Francis they ceased the production of motorcycles during World War II, and instead built tubular trolleys for use by the Bristol Aircraft Company in their factories. Two of the Francis & Barnett factories were badly damaged in air raids, but were back in production within a fortnight, albeit under tarpaulin roofs. A small team of mechanics was retained to undertake repairs to War Department motorcycles under the supervision of J. H. (Joe) Goddard, the service manager.

It was J. H. Goddard who suggested that, in his view, a number of Francis-Barnett owners had only a

J. H. (Joe) Goddard, service manager. (Courtesy FBOC)

hazy idea as to who had made their machines. Some letters had started 'Dear Sir or Madam', others 'Dear Madam', while others were even more cautious and had started 'To Whom It May Concern' – and had left it at that. Whether it was thought that there was something of a feminine touch in the design of the first really ultra lightweight bike is not quite known, although it is a fact that these machines did make a strong appeal to ladies – indeed, at one time a lady's dress guard was an optional extra.

Joe Goddard spent forty years of his life working for Francis-Barnett; Mr Dono was his predecessor and mentor, George Goodyear his first boss and works manager, Bill King he referred to as the designer and brains of the firm, absolutely indefatigable, and Dick Shade the inveterate road tester. Last but not least there was Stanley Wright, the repair shop manager, whom he described as his closest colleague and who happily found the solution to every problem. Goddard went on to say that in many ways these men were the backbone of the firm.

One of the tasks undertaken by Mr E. A. Barnett was to reconstruct a *Competitions Record Book* – and on the first page went George Brough, designer of the world-famous Brough Superior. It appears that 'GB' was once an ardent Francis-Barnett fan, and the book records him as finishing first in the 250cc class in the East Midland Centre ACU hill climb held on 24 August 1921. On the same page are the names of Gordon I. Francis and Eric A. Barnett, both of whom took part in numerous events in the 1920s. Eric Barnett enjoyed riding, and when sales director he always wanted first-hand experience – besides which he was a no mean trials rider as well.

Another name in the book was that of W. A. King, designer of several Francis-Barnett machines. J. W. Moxon was as well known among the golfing fraternity as motorcycling: he lived in Ludlow and played golf for the county. At the time motorcycling was not looked down upon as it was to be later. Geoffrey Jones went on to become managing director of Villiers Engines. Also included was the legendary T. G.

Stanley Wright, workshop repair manager. (Courtesy FBOC)

(Tommy) Meeten; it was said that he knew more about Francis-Barnetts than anybody, even those at the works. Ultimately he formed his own highly successful business at Shannon Corner, New Malden.

Early Production Models

There has been much confusion over the designation of early production models. The model numbering system appears to have come into existence around 1925/26 and was allied to the triangular frame machines. Until then, a description relating to either the horsepower or the cubic capacity of the engine was used, or a description such as 'Light Sporting Model' or 'TT Model 350cc' to convey to the reader the type of machine it was. Fortunately, a 'code word' was used for most of the machines, which helps to identify the early unnumbered models. It is therefore possible to surmise that the triangulated frame machines with the 147cc Villiers two-stroke engines were from 1926:

ZARABOUT – Model No. 1
ZARALLON – Model No. 2
ZARCHECK – Model No. 3
ZARELECT – Model No. 4.

The model numbering system was brought into use in the 1926 season, and the numbers indicated the machines that were available that year. Model Nos 1, 2 and 3 can be traced back to the original 1923 models, and Model No. 4 to 1925 – and the latter was not the fourth machine produced with the triangulated frame and 147cc Villiers engine, but one of five machines carried forward from 1925, the other being the 1.75HP Sports Model (ZARSPEED), which became Model No. 5 in 1926.

Prior to the model numbering system, the 'code word' is the only common denominator whereby a machine can be traced from one year to the next. Where a 'code word' was used, it has been included in the specifications charts from the early JAP and Villiers-engined machines up to the 1926 Model No. 5. Interestingly, three of the 269cc Villiers-engined machines, Model Nos A, B and C, had the name of a plant as a 'code word'; these were aubretia, begonia and euphorbia.

It is obvious that from time to time machines were built to individual specifications for such riders as Tommy Meeten. These were mainly for those competing in trials, time trials and suchlike, and were not included in the general run of model numbers. The company also built a limited number of machines of a type, for example to test in competitions, and to let the Press road test them. There are cases where the road test of a machine, or the report of a trial, appeared in the motorcycle press of the day, yet the machine in question never went into production. If seen in isolation, the reader of the report could easily conclude that the machine was a production machine. This practice continued throughout the life of the company, with the prime example of three 172cc machines being built for the works trials team in 1954.

From 1928, some of the models were given names, such as, for example, Pullman, Empire and Dominion for models 10, 12 and 16. Then in 1931 the names of birds of prey were introduced, Black Hawk, Falcon, Merlin, Kestrel and Condor among them. Other bird names were Lapwing, Plover, Seagull, Snipe and Fulmar. Non-bird names used were Cruiser, Stag and Red Stag, the last two being powered by four-stroke engines.

In 1931, a letter prefix was introduced to the frame number: 'A' for the 1931 model year, then 'B', 'C' and so on, followed later by a second letter, which appears to denote the frame type rather than the model type, as some were used for more than one model. The letters 'I', 'U' and 'X' were omitted; also left out were the war years 1941 to 1945, therefore 1940 was 'K' and 1946 'L'. The letter 'A' was used again in 1959 and ran through until 1966, with the letter 'I' being used for that year. After World War II, a suffix was added to the frame number to indicate that the colour was other than the standard colour scheme. Thus if the suffix was 'B' and the machine was normally black, it indicated that the colour was blue. However, if the colour was normally, say, Arden Green, then 'B' would indicate that the machine left the factory painted black.

In 1947 the company amalgamated with Associated Motor Cycles Ltd (AMC), owners of the AJS Matchless machines; AMC then took over the James Cycle Company in 1951.

The Factory Layout

Broadly speaking, the Francis-Barnett factory was built in a U shape around a central yard, which served to receive and unload raw materials and also to dispatch finished machines to the separate packing department in nearby Priory Street, where Francis-Barnett had some 10,000sq ft (929sq m) of the old Triumph works, bombed during the war. At Lower Ford Street there was about 21,000sq ft (1,951sq m) of factory space, and the company also operated a subsidiary concern, the Clarendon Pressing & Welding Co. Ltd, in another part of the city. Even in 1951 shortages of materials were causing a problem with regard to future developments; nevertheless the management had great hopes for the future, and production was some 30 per cent greater than for 1950.

In the 1950s, all factory operations were directed from the materials control office, which supervised the intake of raw materials, the allocation of materials to machines and finished parts to assembly operations, and also decided the sequence of assembly and the priority of work according to availability of materials and parts. This triple control enabled the work staff to be employed most efficiently and economically. Limitations of space in the factory and other considerations called for the solving of material handling problems in a way different from the more usual conveyor systems. Such parts as frame tubes, lugs and so on, were issued from the stores in deep steel containers, designed to nest together when empty to save space. This enabled the bins to be handled easily by special wheeled trucks, and with these an operative could move more than 3cwt of material with no difficulty at all. From Lower Ford Street, finished machines were taken to the Priory Street works already mentioned, for packing and dispatch with part of the machine card still attached to the model. Here, wheeled trolleys and tables were used wherever possible to minimize handling effort. With their wide export experience, Francis-Barnett packing methods were of a high standard, and their export cases, lined with waterproof paper, displayed

Staff at No. 2 Works, Osborne Road. Left to right: Bill King, Stan Wright, Joe Goddard, Jonny Roberts (works rider), unknown, Bill Jilks, Dick Kendle, Ron Morley, Percy Wills, Hector Chamberlain, Les Gascoigne, John Hall, Horace Dagley. Unfortunately no one knew the names of the ladies. (Courtesy FBOC)

George Briggs, service department foreman. (Courtesy FBOC)

Percy Wills, experimental technician. (Courtesy FBOC)

the same care in securing every component firmly as was taken in the manufacture of the machines.

Priory Street works also contained the service department and the service stores, where spare parts were packed and dispatched. A series of nesting trays was used for making up and collecting individual orders.

Frequent references have been made to the many ingenious fittings and handling containers in use at this works, and all of these were made by the subsidiary company, Clarendon Pressing & Welding Co. Ltd. Francis & Barnett Ltd decided early on to concentrate on the purely cycle side of motorcycle manufacture and employ proprietary engine units. This meant that all their design energies could be devoted to the one side, as they were not hampered by engine problems, and in consequence set out to make more of the component parts than many other makers did.

The Clarendon Works

The Clarendon works were established in 1929, producing petrol tanks, mudguards, number plates, silencers, powerbike engine shields, and any other motorcycle parts, as well as all the trays, trolleys and

containers used in the Lower Ford works. As the capacity of the works was by no means fully absorbed by their own internal demands, they undertook many other presswork projects, and welded commissions for firms in the motor, artificial silk and a variety of other trades.

At this branch factory, like the main works, a central control room organized all material and production planning. It had its own well equipped toolroom for producing the wide variety of dies and tools used. There is a short clip of 1min 7sec on the internet of petrol tanks being manufactured at the Clarendon works in 1956. The website is www.macearchive.org/media.html?title=974 and the description of the film is as follows:

The film shows production work on petrol tanks for Francis-Barnett motorcycles at their subsidiary factory, Clarendon Pressing and Welding on Clarendon Street in Earlsdon, Coventry. We see the tank being welded and trim-fitted, and decorative paint applied. We then see the completed tank fitted to a Falcon 74 motorcycle on the production line at Francis Barnett's main factory in Lower Ford Street, Coventry. It is ridden out of the factory by Dick Shade.

LEFT: Unknown. Appears to be building a competition machine. (Courtesy FBOC)

BELOW: Bill King, Hector Chamberlain (experimental technician), Percy Wills, Horace Dagley (designer and works rider). (Courtesy FBOC)

The Manufacturing Process

The system of machine building at this period always followed the same format. The first operation was to place the frame in a jig and reamer all bushes and fixtures. Next the forks were added, and the frame placed on a wheeled trolley for its journey round the track. Here the Villiers engine was added, and when this was completed, a machine card was attached securely to the frame. This stayed on the model throughout all successive stages right to final inspection and dispatch, the tester's report being written on it in addition to all other information regarding assembly. Different coloured cards were used according to the type of model.

Ingenious rubber-padded tubular racks alongside the track held mudguards, while petrol tanks were carried in special metal containers from the time they were made at the Clarendon works, through painting, lining and stores to the final assembly operation, these containers being so designed that they could be stacked and handled without any danger to the finish of the petrol tank itself.

Wheels were built up in another sub-assembly bay, which had two truing machines of dial type, one dial showing the truth on the diameter, and another truth sideways as the wheel was rotated. A good true wheel could be built very quickly with the minimum of training for the operators.

Completed machines were lifted off their trolleys by an overhead hoist and underwent inspection and road test. Final rectification and inspection was a very thorough business at Lower Ford Street, and six experienced mechanics were employed full time on this, a high proportion of the total works force as compared with many other factories at that time. Finally, the model was bench tested under its own power, an extracting plant disposing of exhaust fumes.

As regards the engine, in 1956 the AMC combine announced the production of their own Vincent Piatti-designed, single-cylinder, two-stroke engine and gearbox, to be used by James and Francis-Barnett. Piatti was an Italian, as the name suggests; he designed the Piatti scooter, built under licence in the UK by Cyclemaster Ltd. However, the new AMC engine brought many warranty claims from customers, and a loss of confidence in the machines. Other factors aggravated the situation, including the high development costs of the new engine. In 1961, AMC announced that they were to cease assembling their engines, and this would be carried out in future by Villiers. The engines assembled by Villiers were denoted by having the letter 'V' included in the engine prefix, as V15T, V20T and so on. However, Villiers engines were used again: the Mark 2T and Mark 4T in the Cruisers 89 and 91, the Mark 32A in the Trials 92, the Mark 36A in the Scrambler 93 and the Starmaker in the Scrambler 94.

The Merger of James and Francis-Barnett

In the early 1960s AMC found themselves in financial difficulties, and in 1962 the Coventry factories of Francis & Barnett were closed, and production moved to the James factory at Greet in Birmingham. The last new machine designed and produced in Coventry was the Fulmar 88 of 150cc priced at £137.

As a result of the merger of James and Francis-Barnett at Greet, Gordon Francis became a director of the James Company, and Mr C. S. Summerton, the managing director of the James Company, became a director of Francis & Barnett. The design section of Francis-Barnett, headed by W. A. King, moved to Greet to coordinate a joint James and Francis-Barnett design team; Bill King designed most of the prewar bikes with Gordon Francis, a designer of no mean ability. Unfortunately the move was not a happy one for Bill King, and he was eventually made redundant. J. H. Goddard, service manager, also moved to Greet to coordinate a combined service department, but eventually left for Reliant. George Denton, sales manager of Francis & Barnett at the time, said: 'The Greet factory had the capacity for efficiently producing greater numbers of machines in one factory than Francis & Barnett were able to produce in their Coventry factories.'

Noteworthy Company Employees

Besides Joe Goddard and Bill King, other employees are worthy of mention. Ken Clark joined the company in 1949 and worked with Bill King in the Design Department, which was situated in premises purchased in the Earlsdon area of Coventry and known as No. 3 factory. The machine shop, detail parts assembly

The prototype Fulmar being ridden by design draughtsman Tony Wright. (Courtesy FBOC)

Hector Chamberlain working on the Fulmar. (Courtesy FBOC)

and the Experimental Department were also situated at the site. In an interview with the late John Goodberry and his wife Jean (FBOC), Ken told them that Mr Francis was extremely shy, a bit autocratic, and adverse to change.

FBs had always been finished in black and gold, but Bill and Ken felt a change was needed, and that is how the famous Arden Green came about, as in certain lights it looked black. Ken Clark was involved in all the machines up to and including the all-enclosed Cruiser, Model No. 84. He also said that Mr Francis used to come and see him quite often, and that they were a good team. He had a drawing board with the Cruiser detail on it, with the various parts picked out in colour, which made it look like a map of the London Underground. One day Mr Francis came in and said, 'Very pretty – point out Earls Court and I'll go from there!'

The 1956 Francis-Barnett sales brochure depicted a young lad riding a new Plover 73 ahead of workers leaving a factory. That lad was a young engineering apprentice, Colin Dean, who started at Francis-Barnett in 1950 at the age of nineteen. In 1956 he joined the Test

ABOVE: Percy Wills working on the Fulmar. (Courtesy FBOC)

BELOW: Road test of the prototype Fulmar, ridden by Tony Wright. (Courtesy FBOC)

Section, when Falcon 74 and Cruiser 75 were the models being built. The Plover 73, built by James, was to be introduced, and Colin was asked to ride one out of the Alvis Car Factory: the idea was for him to ride off as they opened the gates to let the workers out. Then in 1957 the chief tester, Dick Shade, had a serious road accident: he was off work for months and never rode again, and as a result of this Eric Levison, the works manager, asked Colin if he would take over the Test Section, which he agreed to do. The Cruiser 80, with the AMC single cylinder 249cc engine, was introduced in 1957, and Colin had to ride it for 500 miles (800km).

Road testing took place all year round, the only exception being if it was too icy to stay on the bike. A typical road test for Colin was as follows: he would take a bike as it came off the track, then check and fill the chain case and gear oil level, put fuel into the tank, fit the test plates and fire up the engine. Then out of the factory door, off to the right along Ford Street and into second or third gear, and hands off to check the steering. Change down for the traffic lights at Gosford Street junction, across the lights into Vequery Street and right at the end up to the top of Gulson Road Hill, then left on to London Road, past the cemetery on the right, and down the hill to the entrance drive of Whitley Hospital. There he would check and adjust the carburettor setting, adjust the front and rear brakes, and return to the works noting any faults on the way. Back at the works the steering head adjustment would be checked, and the tyres and wheels for run out, the bike would be given an all-over visual check, and then he would make out the test report sheet.

Colin left the firm in 1962, but he met up with Joe Goddard again at Reliant, where Joe was the spares manager.

Peter Sheen was sales office manager from 1959 to 1965, and director general of the Motor Cycle Industry Association.

Another long-serving stalwart was Vincent (Vince) Carroll (1930–97); he joined the firm in 1950 at the same time as Colin Dean, and was the office manager for a considerable period of time.

The other important side of the firm comprised the works riders: names such as Derek Adsett, Vic Ashford, David Clegg, Bill Faulkner, George Fisher, Bob Haines, Max King, Bill Martin, Peter Marr, Ray Peacock, Mike Ransom, Jackie Rees, Johnny Roberts,

Some Works Registration Numbers and their Riders

Registration	Rider
KJW 923	Jack Botting
KWK 170	Brian Martin
LWK 164	Olga Kevelos
LWK 254	E. W. Smith
LWK 324	Arthur Shutt
MWK 499	George Fisher
UWK 562	E. W. Smith
VWK 554	Sid Wicken
WWK 488	Arthur Dovey
ODV 200	Max King
MHP 469	E. W. Smith
MHP 470	George Fisher
MHP 471	Dick Kemp
YRW 134	George Fisher
VRW 750	Arthur Shutt
VOC 588	Jim Sandiford
VWK 554	Sid Wicken
VWK 562	Ernie Smith
VWK 563	Bill Faulkner
	Jackie Rees
JKV 16	Brian Martin
YKV 772	Jim Sandiford
OEL 990	David Martin
SDU 626	Dick Kemp
SDU 628	Ray Peacock
SDU 629	Ernie Smith
SOR 337	Triss Sharp
320 ADV	Ian Williamson
305 AKV	Ian Williamson
	Bill Martin
	Peter Gaunt
306 AKV	Johnny Roberts
	Derek Adsett
	(Mick Andrews)
307 AKV	Mick Ransom
837 ARW	Johnny Roberts
258 AWK	Horace Dagley
	Derek Adsett

Jimmy Sandiford, Triss Sharp, Arthur Shutt, E. W. Smith, Ian Williamson come to mind, and of course Ernie Smith the competitions manager. Other names can be found in the panel [*above*] that lists the works registration numbers and their riders. No doubt there

Left to right: Tony Denton (son of George Denton) and Colin Dean, chief works tester. (Courtesy FBOC)

must have been many more, and the author apologises for not including them.

The Competitions Department

The Competitions Department was located in a large wooden shed in part of the old Triumph works in Priory Street, which had been taken over by Francis-Barnett after World War II. The Development and Testing Department was situated at Osborne Road, Earlsdon. 1951 was the first full year for the works trials team, which consisted of Jack Botting, Alan Greenway and Brian Martin. The Falcon 59 and the Falcon 60, the first postwar competition models, were shown at the 1951 Earls Court Show in the standard finish of black with gold lining and lettering.

Ernie Smith joined the company as competitions manager and works rider in 1953, and completed the trio of George Fisher and Arthur Strutt. George Denton also joined the company in 1953 as sales manager.

Arthur Shutt (1925–97) was a member of the Francis-Barnett works trials team from 1953 to 1959. He was the mainstay of the team in the 1950s, and worked closely with George Fisher and Ernie Smith to improve the machines, particularly in the field of electrics, where he was an expert. Arthur's best ride was his outright win in the Scott Trial in 1953, riding a rigid Francis-Barnett of 197cc. Arthur, together with George Fisher, will always be remembered as one of the Francis-Barnett aces, who really lifted the lightweight trials bike revolution to another level. Arthur is recorded as having won the Richmond Motor Club's Scott Trial in 1953 on a Francis-Barnett, the first small machine win.

Francis-Barnett entered a team in the 1954/55 ISDT on machines with a 172cc engine and a four-speed gearbox. The reduction in engine size was made using a modified cylinder from the 197cc engines with a 55mm bore instead of the normal 59mm. The team consisted of Ernie Smith, who prepared the machines,

ABOVE: Mick Ransom, works rider. (Courtesy FBOC)

BELOW: Mick Ransom, works rider. (Courtesy FBOC)

George Fisher and Dick Kemp, who collected a manufacturers' gold medal. The team was also awarded the T. G. Meeten Trophy by the British Two-Stroke Club (BTSC) for the year's outstanding performance by two-stroke riders. Dick Kemp did not join the works trials team until 1957, but in the meantime he was supported by the company with a 197cc machine, some parts and expenses.

In 1956 the team was given new machines with Arden Green frames and silver tanks, but still using the Villiers 7E engines.

In 1958 George Fisher left the team and was replaced by Ray Peacock. This season began the period of the AMC engines, but these were low-powered and far too heavy and wide, and let down the excellent frame and Norton Roadholder forks. At 270lb (122.5kg) the machines were around 50lb (22.7kg) heavier than the competition with a Greeves at 230lb (104kg) and a Dot at 220lb (100kg), and both using the Villiers 9E engine, which was never used by Francis-Barnett in a production model.

Mick Ransom on the Devil's Staircase section, Mordart Peninsular, in the 1962 Scottish Six Day Trial. (Courtesy FBOC)

TOP: Horace Dagley, designer and works rider. (Courtesy FBOC)

BOTTOM: Horace Dagley, designer and works rider. (Courtesy FBOC)

LEFT: *Horace Dagley, designer and works rider. (Courtesy FBOC)*

BELOW: *Private entrant David Dunnicliffe carries out running repairs. (Courtesy FBOC)*

Ian Williamson on the Devil's Staircase section, Mordart Peninsular, in the 1962 Scottish Six Day Trial. (Courtesy FBOC)

Mick Ransom has been extremely helpful in naming the riders and the sections; he also told me the following about the Devil's Staircase in 1962:

At this time, the only way to reach Kinlochmoidart and Glenuig was by the old drovers' track or by sea. We used to come down the section on the outward run to the lunch stop at Salen, and at one point ran on the beach. Then after the stop we used the Devil's Staircase as a section on the way back – previously sidecars were also in the trial and had to use the same track. When you see some of the drops and the narrowness, I take my hat off to the sidecar boys, although Jack Oliver, who won one year, had his mother in the chair. In those days sidecars were huge, wide and heavy compared to today's outfits. The Staircase run was done on a Thursday in 1962; I remember, because on that day I did not lose any marks for the whole day.

Each year I go back to ride in the pre-'65 two-day event at Kinlochleven on my original Barnett; I shall be seventy-four in June, and first rode an Ariel 500 HT in 1957. Each year we try to make this pilgrimage to see the Staircase – and it hasn't changed much. There is now a fine road round to Kinlochmoidart from Lochailort; thereafter it goes into single track as far as Strontium. Maureen and I occasionally used to sit on the hotel wall at Salen, where we had the lunch stop, and imagined all the hustle and bustle of 210 riders milling around. Nowadays I cheat and ride round the Moidart on my KTM 690 Enduro, which develops 63 BHP from a single, something only dreamed of in the 1960s – the 500 Manx Norton would have loved that power! This year the organizing club had a pre-'72 run round the Moidart, starting from Kinlochleven, and of course had to visit the Staircase, around 120 miles.

The 33rd International Six Day Trial (ISDT) was held at Garmisch Partenkirchen in Austria, and is remembered for the torrential rain that caused numerous problems for both the event organizers and the competitors. Triss Sharp competed in the 1958 ISDT on a full works machine and obviously conquered the conditions, winning a gold medal. For this feat, Francis-Barnett presented Triss with a pair of gold cufflinks embossed with an enamelled FB logo.

In 1962, Ian Williamson and Johnny Roberts were joined by Mick Ransom, just as the team went back to Villiers engines, with the iron-barrelled Mark 32A being fitted into the works bikes. Three new machines were built in the Design and Development Department at Osborne Road by Percy Wills and Hector Chamberlain for the 1962 Scottish Six Days' Trial; they had new frames and Norton forks. It was a clean sweep in the 1962 Reliance Trial, with Mick coming first, Ian second and Johnny third; in addition Mick won the 201–250cc cup. The 149cc Fulmar was second in its class, with Derek Adsett gaining a first class award.

When AJS and Matchless ceased production of their heavyweight trials machines (350cc) in 1964, some of the AJS riders were given Francis-Barnett two-strokes repainted red and rebadged as James. The rebadged 306 AKV was given to Mick Andrews, who had the nickname of 'Magical'. Already the James and Francis-Barnett catalogues were showing identical trials machines. The team carried on through 1965 and into 1966, when the end finally came. (For more detailed information *see* Ian Williamson's *The Francis-Barnett Trials Teams – Competitions Reference Library, Volume 1*.)

ABOVE: *Derek Adsett, works rider on the Fulmar 258 AWK. (Courtesy FBOC)*

LEFT: *The late Jonny Roberts on the 1962 FB, Hawk's Nest section, Derbyshire. (Courtesy FBOC)*

OPPOSITE TOP: *Left to right: Mike Ahern (FBOC member), Tony Denton and Tony Wright, design draughtsman 1960–63. (Courtesy FBOC)*

OPPOSITE BOTTOM: *Derek Adsett, works rider on the Fulmar 258 AWK. (Courtesy FBOC)*

ABOVE: *258 AWK, the Fulmar Special freshly painted. (Courtesy FBOC)*

306 AKV, which had several riders. (Courtesy FBOC)

307 AKV, which goes hand-in-glove with Mick Ransom. (Courtesy FBOC)

As with the competition machines, the ranges of James and Francis-Barnett roadster machines were integrated and were very similar, with mainly only the badges and colour to distinguish them, James being maroon and Francis-Barnett Arden Green. In addition, spares catalogues included both James and Francis-Barnett machines, although the cover used a much smaller font size for the Francis-Barnetts as if they were inferior; however, they were, in fact, almost identical.

Derek Adsett fixing the Fulmar 258 AWK. (Courtesy FBOC)

The Collapse of AMC

In 1963, Norton was joined by the other marques owned by AMC. Also in 1963, Associated Motor Cycles Ltd set up a new company, Suzuki (Great Britain) Ltd, to import Suzuki motorcycles into the UK. In the last three months of 1963 approximately 18,000 machines were imported by AMC and distributed from their Birmingham distribution centre set up in the James factory in Greet. So while British-made machines were going out the front door, the Japanese-made Suzuki was going out the back door.

But on 4 August 1966, the production of Francis-Barnetts ceased as AMC themselves collapsed. After Manganese Bronze took over the remnants of AMC, it absorbed Villiers in 1967 and set up the Norton-Villiers combine; however, this was short-lived and went into liquidation in 1974. It was reformed as Norton-Villiers-Triumph with financial help from the government, but this organization also went into receivership shortly afterwards.

Michael Jackson competing on a 225cc FB in the 1958 French Grand Prix, Cassel. (Courtesy M. Jackson)

Michael Jackson competing on a 197cc FB at Budleigh Salterton, Devon in 1956. (Courtesy M. Jackson)

Gwen Wickham at the end of the 1952 Scottish Six Day Trial. (Courtesy Gwen White)

Gwen Wickham has a precautionary dab in the 1952 Scottish Six Day Trial. (Courtesy Gwen White)

The Aftermath: Keeping the Living Legend Alive

There are several organizations dedicated to keeping British motorcycles of the past alive and running. For the two-stroke machine the three best known ones are probably the Vintage Motor Cycle Club (VMCC), the British Two-Stroke Club (BTSC) and of course the Francis Barnett Owners' Club (FBOC). The VMCC and the BTSC cater for more than one marque, while the FBOC by definition is solely for Francis-Barnett machines. The other thing they have in common is the fact that they are all limited companies.

The Vintage Motor Cycle Club

The VMCC is by far the largest of the three clubs: today it has in excess of 16,000 members, and is affiliated with other like-minded clubs world wide. Its roots go back to 1946 when a group of enthusiastic riders met at the Lounge Café, Hog's Back, in Guildford with the purpose of forming a motorcycle club for owners of

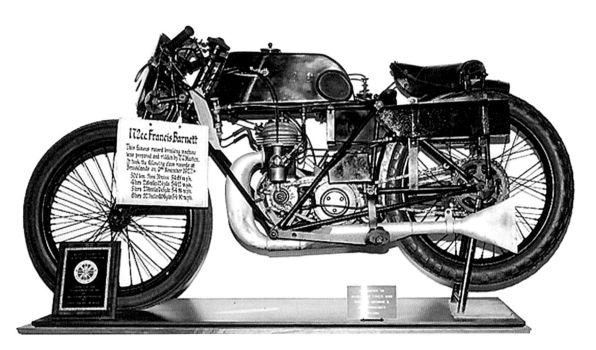

T. G. (Tommy) Meeten's 172cc Francis Barnett Special in the Brooklands Museum. (Courtesy FBOC)

machines manufactured up to and including 1930. Membership was initially restricted to those owning machines, whether solos or sidecar combinations, manufactured prior to 31 December 1930. It now has over eighty territorial sections and a handful of non-territorial sections within the UK, and well over 1,000 events are organized annually. Some of the best known are the annual Banbury Run, which still holds true to the founding spirit as the run is only open to machines manufactured prior to 1931; the 1000 Bike Rally held at Mallory Park in July; the TT Rally held on the Isle of Man in June; and the West Kent International Rally in August.

The members' benefits are quite considerable, including a monthly club journal, a not inconsiderable library, clothing, spares, and also the marque specialists, of which there are over 180 residing in the UK and overseas.

The British Two-Stroke Club

This is the oldest of the three clubs, although like the FBOC it had a short period when it was defunct, before being resurrected. The club – in full it calls itself the 'British Club for Motorcycles Powered by Two-Stroke Engines' – was originally formed in 1929 by a group of enthusiastic riders to promote the cause of two-stroke machines in sport. Two-stroke machines were usually small compared with four-stroke machines, with which they were grouped at competitions.

T. G. Meeten, normally a Francis-Barnett rider, was instrumental in setting up the club, which originally was centred at Tommy's motorcycle shop in Dorking and then later at Meeten's Motorcycle Mecca at Shannon Corner, New Malden, also in Surrey. The BTSC was defunct during World War II, but was restarted after the war, albeit with a more socially based structure. It has widened its base to include not only machines of British manufacture, but all makes of two-stroke-powered machines imported into the UK during their production. Like the others, it is a national club with several regional sections.

In 2003, while listing the club's trophies for insurance purposes, the Francis-Barnett Challenge Trophy came to light. At that time no one knew the history of the trophy, except what was on the shield itself. The shield was presented to the British Two-Stroke Club by Francis & Barnett Ltd, with L. Sheaf on a 246cc Levis being the first winner in March 1930 and the last one B. Jackson in 1953.

The Francis-Barnett Owners' Club

By far the youngest of the three clubs, the FBOC was formed in May 1955, with Mr G. J. Privett as the

The late John Goodberry, publicity officer FBOC. (Courtesy Mrs J. Goodberry)

honorary secretary. Meetings were held at the community centre in Greenford every other Tuesday evening, with the annual visit to the Coventry factory as the highlight of the year. The club was wound up when Francis-Barnett ceased trading, and unfortunately the club records from that period no longer exist.

Moving on twenty years, to May 1986, the club was reformed in Bristol by Mr and Mrs David Furze and Mr and Mrs Frank Gardner, with a club magazine entitled *The Directory*, first published bi-monthly, and then quarterly from 1987. John Harding joined the committee in 1987 and has been a committee member continuously since that year. He is the club technical secretary and validating officer for the marque. The current membership fluctuates between 500 and 600 members, with ex-works staff being awarded honorary membership.

TOP RIGHT: *Strumpshaw steam engine rally: the author's Cruiser 80, Tony Wood's Falcon 87, Jack Horwood's Falcon 87 and Des Heckle's Overseas Falcon 65.*

RIGHT: *Rod Buckenham on his Cruiser 80 at a FBOC East of England section meeting.*

BOTTOM LEFT: *Mark Bradshaw starts out on his first run with the newly restored Merlin 52 at a FBOC East of England section meeting, Leiston 2010.*

BOTTOM RIGHT: *Mike Daykin on his Cruiser 75, with the Villiers 2T engine replacing the original 1H engine, at a FBOC East of England section meeting, Leiston 2010.*

LEFT: Jack Lloyd (at rear) discussing the finer points of his 1933 Falcon 31 at the Battlesbridge Show 2009.

MIDDLE LEFT: FBOC committee 2000. Back row: Tony Woods, membership secretary; author, librarian and registrar; John Baker, events organizer. Middle row: Keith Young, regalia officer; John Harding, technical secretary and validating officer; Jeff Venning, chairman. Front row: Moira Woods, treasurer; Sue Dorling, general secretary; Jean Goodberry, editor. (Courtesy FBOC)

MIDDLE RIGHT: Des Heckle, Jack Lloyd and Ted Lloyd at Battlesbridge Show 2009.

BOTTOM: Line-up of FBs at the FBOC East of England section meeting at March, Cambridgeshire.

Banbury Run 2002: Tony Woods' Lapwing and Trevor Wells' Model 9. (Courtesy FBOC)

FBOC chairlady, Sue Dorling, presenting ex-works rider Brian Martin with his honorary membership certificate at the Bristol Show 2010. (Courtesy FBOC)

FBOC East of England section meeting 2006 at the Long Shop Museum, Leiston.

FBOC stand, Founders' Day. Left to right: Norman Clarke, Mike Ahern, Geoff Hearn, Les Heaton, Ted Lloyd. (Courtesy Mrs J. Goodberry.)

Ted Lloyd (106) at the Banbury Run. (Courtesy FBOC)

Possibly one of the best known members of the club was the late Barry Appleby, the excellent cartoonist whose family 'The Gambols' featured in the press – and still does. From time to time he drew a cartoon for the club magazine featuring 'the Barnetts'. Few realized that he had been a keen motorcyclist from the age of sixteen, and on his death in 1996 the 1924 Francis-Barnett he owned was donated to the Haynes International Motor Museum, Yeovil, where it is on display.

The club AGM was held in varies locations in conjunction with other events, such as Ross-on-Wye autojumble, and Cheltenham racecourse. In 1994, what was billed as the club's 'Inaugural Big Show' included a display of machines, and autojumble stalls in addition to the AGM, and was held at Beale Park near Reading. The venue then gravitated towards the Midlands, first moving to Stanford Hall, then Hagley;

it is currently at The Heritage Motor Museum, Gaydon, in Warwickshire. The substance of the meeting remains the same, with the show of machines, autojumble, fun run and AGM. There is no typical member, excepting that they all love their Fanny Bs: some want to restore their machines to pristine condition and win prizes, others to restore them to the condition they left the factory, and still others to ride them, making modifications to the brakes, and fitting items such as indicators and modern tyres to increase the safety level of riding the fifty plus-year-old motorcycles in today's traffic.

Members' benefits include the magazine, a library supplying reprinted copies of Francis-Barnett and Villiers manuals, dating and validating services, technical advice, spares and sourcing parts, and – possibly the most important – assistance, advice and encouragement in restorations from other like-minded members.

Russia trip trio. Left to right: Mike Goulding, Jeff Venning (trip organizer) and Mike Ahern. Jeff and Mike Ahern made it to Red Square, but Mike Goulding's forks gave up in Smolensk and he had to return to the UK. (Courtesy FBOC)

FBOC trophies. (Courtesy FBOC)

The club magazine, *The Directory*, is a quarterly magazine free to all members; in the early 1990s it contained around twenty pages, and the latest editions thirty-two pages. The content and layout have changed considerably over the years, to what is now a very professional-looking magazine. This was due mainly to the efforts of Jean Goodberry, who took over as editor in 1995, and her husband John who was appointed publicity officer in 1999 and held the post until his untimely death in 2008. John is reputed to have been the one who coined the phrase 'Keeping alive the living legend'. John and Jean's reports on the staff, who played a key role in the company, were excellent pieces of journalism, and together with John's photography, uplifted the magazine to a higher level. I quote from John's obituary, written by Tony Wright (honorary member and ex-FB employee): 'We Francis-Barnett enthusiasts owe a lot to the likes of John Goodberry. Let the spirit live on!'

The club attends many of the national shows and several of the territorial sections attend local shows or organize meetings themselves.

The pre-war climbs up Snowdon and Ben Nevis, and Mrs Meeten's ride round Britain, were described as stunts in some quarters at the time they took place, and probably the author thought along the same lines. What changed my mind were the intrepid riders of Francis-Barnetts who have undertaken trips abroad to Moscow, Gibraltar, Norway, Germany and UK – trips such as Land's End to John O'Groats; I would not call these trips stunts, but rather a challenge or having the spirit of adventure to undertake such arduous trips on a motorcycle that was probably advertised as a 'commute to work' bike.

CHAPTER TWO

Manufacturing Seasons 1920–1929

The 1920 Season

The original model announced in March 1920 had a conventional brazed frame, and a 2.75bhp side-valve, four-stroke engine of 292cc. The engine was supplied by J. A. Prestwich & Co. Ltd and coupled to a two-speed Sturmey-Archer gearbox. The transmission was chain-cum-belt (a combination of primary chain and rear belt drive).

The Francis-Barnett did not supersede the Invicta model of A. Barnett & Co., but was complimentary to it. The Invicta and Francis-Barnett models existed side by side for some time; both shared the same frame design, and even the style of the Francis-Barnett name was similar to that of the Invicta, including the under-line flourish.

For the Francis-Barnett, the emphasis even in those days was on quality and refinement with attention to detail; to scan through an old catalogue may mean little today apart from an occasional reminiscence, yet when one reads such a specification as 'toe guards to footboards, an undershield, saddle tank, cast alumini-um chain case and a host of other mentionable fea-tures', it makes one realize that the later machines were the fruition of the seeds sown then. The price listed in *Motor Cycle* was 84 guineas, a considerable sum of money in 1920.

The 1921 Season

In 1921 there were quite a number of changes in both the machines themselves and the availability of alter-native machines. An advertisement of the time stated:

Invicta advertisement.

We have introduced improvements which appeal to the discriminating buyer, and which, added to excellent work-manship, lend an undeniable distinction to the machine. Features include: Quick Action Chain Adjustment; Quick

Machine Specifications

Model	2.75bhp (Zaraband, Zaraluxe)	2.5bhp (Zacastra, Zacadual)	2.75bhp (Zaratrice, Zaraflexo)
Manufacturing year	1920–1922	1921	1922
Engine	JAP single-cylinder, air-cooled, side-valve four-stroke; silencer with extension pipe	Villiers single cylinder, air-cooled two-stroke with double silencer	JAP single-cylinder, air-cooled, side-valve four-stroke; silencer with extension pipe
Bore and stroke	70 × 76mm	70 × 70mm	70 × 76mm
Capacity	292cc	296cc	292cc
Lubrication	Hand pump inside tank	Best & Lloyd semi-automatic sight drip-feed lubricator	Hand pump inside tank
Ignition	High tension magneto	Flywheel magneto	High tension magneto
Carburettor	Brown and Barlow	Amac	Brown and Barlow
Primary drive	Chain	Chain	Chain
Final drive	Belt Dunlop	Belt Dunlop	Belt Dunlop
Gearbox	Sturmey-Archer two-speed, clutch and kick-starter	Single or Sturmey-Archer two-speed, clutch and kick-starter	Sturmey-Archer three-speed, clutch and kick-starter
Frame	Special design, straight tubes		Special design, straight tubes
Suspension front	Brampton bi-flex	Brampton bi-flex	Brampton bi-flex
Suspension rear	Rigid	Rigid	Rigid
Wheels front and rear	26 × 2.25in	26 × 2.25in	26 × 2.25in
Tyres front and rear	26 × 2.25in Dunlop	26 × 2.25in Dunlop	26 × 2.25in Bates
Brake front	Bowden hand	Bowden hand	Bowden hand
Brake rear	Foot-operated on belt rim	Foot-operated on belt rim	Foot-operated on belt rim

General Specifications

Fuel tank capacity	Nearly 2gal (9ltr)	Nearly 2gal (9ltr)	Nearly 2gal (9ltr)
Oil tank capacity	3 pints (1.7ltr)	3 pints (1.7ltr)	3 pints (1.7ltr)
Dry weight	Standard model 188lb (85kg), de luxe model 195lb (88kg)	Single-speed model 152lb (69kg), two-speed model 174lb (79kg)	Standard model 188lb (85kg), de luxe model 195lb (88kg)

Action Rear Brake Adjustment by cam-faced nut; Saddle Tank affording large capacity; Detachable Aluminium Chain Case; Footboards combined with Toe Shields and Undershield in one unit; Effective Mudguards with large valances; complete outfit of high-grade Tools.

The four-stroke range consisted of two 292cc JAP-engined machines with Sturmey-Archer two-speed gear, clutch and kick-starter; a Standard Model at 85 guineas and a De Luxe Model with M-L 'Maglita' combined ignition and lighting set, complete with

THE FRANCIS-BARNETT 2¾ H.P. MODEL
With Two-Speed Gear, Clutch and Kick-Starter.

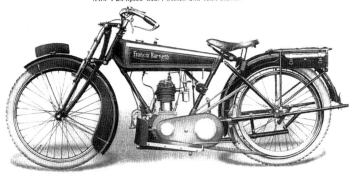

STANDARD MODEL   -   -   -   -   -   PRICE **85 GUINEAS**

DE LUXE MODEL, with M-L "Maglita" combined Ignition and Lighting Set. complete with Electric Head Lamp and Tail Lamp, and with Leg Shields   PRICE **100 GUINEAS**

LEFT: 1921 four-strokes.

BELOW: 1921 two-strokes.

THE FRANCIS-BARNETT 2½ H.P. TWO-STROKE MODEL

PRICE– Single Speed Model   -   -   -   -   -   **66 GUINEAS**

PRICE—Two Speed Model with Clutch and Kick-Starter   -   **78 GUINEAS**

electric head lamp and tail lamp, and with leg shields at 100 guineas. The colour finish was of black enamel; the tank was lined and the bright parts plated.

Finally there was the start of an unbroken run of Villiers-powered machines. The first two-stroke employed was a 269cc Villiers engine with magneto in flywheel. According to Cyril Grange in *The Book of Villiers Engine*, the Mark I, II and III, and some Mark IV models had the ordinary chain-driven horseshoe-type magneto, while the later Mark IV and all Mark V engines were fitted with Villiers flywheel magnetos. This tends to suggest that it was the later Mark IV or Mark V engines that were used by Francis-Barnett. They were available as a single speed at 66 guineas, or as a two-speed with clutch and kick-starter at 78 guineas. The colour finish was identical to the four-stroke models.

Since this was the first unit to come out of the factory with a two-stroke Villiers engine, it can be said that this machine was the forerunner of lightweight two-stroke motorcycles, which gained in popularity every day. The cost of these motorcycles was extremely high, however, and only the very well off were able to afford them.

The 1922 SEASON

The two JAP-engined machines continued in production in 1922 and were joined by a third, the Sporting Model with a 346cc JAP engine, described as having a long exhaust pipe. The prices of the first two had been reduced to £73 for the Standard Model and to £88 for the De Luxe Model; the Sporting Model was £85, and £90 for a specially tuned Speed Machine. A combination was available, based on the Sporting Model with the gearing suitably reduced, the Grindley Lightweight Sports Sidecar with cover-all apron being specified. The price of £104 included a four-point attachment.

There were three 269cc Villiers-engined machines for 1922, designated Model A, single speed, priced at £50; Model B, single speed with Villiers' engine-shaft clutch, priced at £52 10s; and Model C, two-speed with clutch and kick-starter, priced at £62. The engines were probably the later Mark IV or the Mark V, which were fitted with the Villiers flywheel magneto. The ordinary chain-driven horseshoe-type magneto was available to order.

THE FRANCIS-BARNETT 2½ H.P. TWO-STROKE MODEL

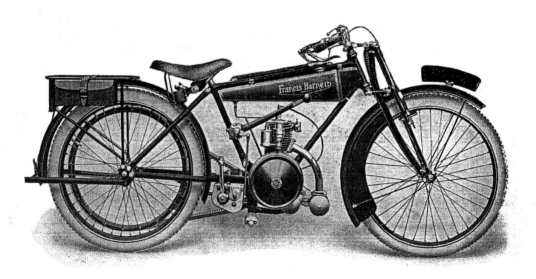

1922 models A, B and C: Aubretia, Begonia and Euphorbia.

Machine Specifications

❖

Model	2.5bhp Model A (Aubretia)	2.5bhp Model B (Begonia)	2.5bhp Model C (Euphorbia)
Manufacturing year	1922	1922	1922
Engine	Villiers single-cylinder, air-cooled two-stroke with double silencer	Villiers single-cylinder, air-cooled two-stroke with double silencer	Villiers single-cylinder, air-cooled two-stroke with double silencer
Bore and stroke	70 × 70mm	70 × 70mm	70 × 70mm
Capacity	269cc	269cc	269cc
Lubrication	Best & Lloyd semi-automatic sight drip-feed lubricator	Best & Lloyd semi-automatic sight drip-feed lubricator	Best & Lloyd semi-automatic sight drip-feed lubricator
Ignition	Flywheel magneto	Flywheel magneto	Flywheel magneto
Carburettor	Amac, Brown & Barlow or Senspray	Amac, Brown & Barlow or Senspray	Amac, Brown & Barlow or Senspray
Primary drive	Brampton or Coventry chain	Brampton or Coventry chain	Brampton or Coventry chain
Final drive	Belt Dunlop	Belt Dunlop	Belt Dunlop
Gearbox	Single speed	Single speed with Villiers engine shaft clutch	Sturmey-Archer two-speed, clutch and kick-starter
Frame	Special design, straight tubes	Special design, straight tubes	Special design, straight tubes
Suspension front	Brampton bi-flex	Brampton bi-flex	Brampton bi-flex
Suspension rear	Rigid	Rigid	Rigid
Wheels front and rear	26 × 2.25in	26 × 2.25in	26 × 2.25in
Tyres front and rear	26 × 2.25in	26 × 2.25in	26 × 2.25in
Brake front	Bowden hand	Bowden hand	Bowden hand
Brake rear	Foot-operated on belt rim	Foot-operated on belt rim	Foot-operated on belt rim

General Specifications

Fuel tank capacity	Nearly 2gal (9ltr)	Nearly 2gal (9ltr)	Nearly 2gal (9ltr)
Oil tank capacity	3 pints (1.7ltr)	3 pints (1.7ltr)	3 pints (1.7ltr)
Dry weight	130lb (59kg)	133lb (60kg)	150lb (68kg)

The 1923 Season

The range for 1923 included the following JAP-powered machines: the Light Sporting Model of 292cc, a 350cc Sports Model, a 350cc Touring Model and a 350cc Sports Combination all with a 346cc engine, a 250cc TT Model and a 350cc TT Model, both fitted with Competition engines. All models had undergone detailed improvements, and with the exception of the 1922 chain-cum-belt model, all were chain-driven.

The 350cc Sports machine, fitted with semi-T.T. handlebars of new design, gave a slightly better riding position. The black tank, now lettered and lined in gold, and 2.5in Dunlop tyres, were standardized. A

'Built like a bridge', as used on numerous occasions in advertisements.

new type of cast-aluminium silencer of very pleasing appearance was fitted, and the exhaust and tail pipes projected into this to form baffles. A Webb front brake was fitted, and the powerful dummy belt-rim type brake on the rear wheel was retained.

On the 350cc touring model, combined aluminium footboards and leg-shields were standardized, while the toolbag was now accommodated between the saddle tube and rear mudguard. Wide, domed guards were fitted with valances in the case of the tourist models. The T.T. machines were supplied with either 250cc or 350cc Special JAP engines, and had narrow guards and Brampton forks but no carrier fitted. Sturmey-Archer gearboxes were a standard feature on all the new models.

The Sports Combination was listed at £85, the 350cc Sports at £70, and the 350cc Touring Model at £72. The Light Sports two-speed of 292cc was listed at £62, or with three-speed gear at £64. The 1922 chain-cum-belt model could be obtained for £60, while the special T.T. models were £75 for the 350cc and £73 for the 250cc engine.

Prejudices die hard, and then, as indeed today, there was a preference for four-stroke engines as opposed to the two-stroke, and it needed courage, conviction and hard cash to give the lightweight two-stroke motorcycle the prominence it came to enjoy. Necessity, however, is the mother of invention, so as the high cost of production prevented sales following World War I, the need to produce a cheaper machine was a pressing requirement. Such thoughts paved the way for the first machine having a triangulated frame, which was a complete breakaway from any previous motorcycle design. The frame comprised seven pairs of tubes, six pairs of which were straight, and the one pair taking the gearbox were bent. The ends of the tubes were simply flattened, linered and drilled.

A most worthy feature at the time was the ease and compactness with which the machine could be built either at home or overseas. Literally thousands of these machines were shipped, completely dismantled, to South Africa, and reassembled by local labour. A regular monthly shipment was also exported to Japan. The dismantled parts occupied little shipping space as compared with other makes of machine, and there was therefore a saving in freight charges which was reflected in the selling price abroad. There were no

Francis-Barnett

A New Standard of Value in Light Sidecar Combinations—Three-Speeds—Chain Drive

THE FRANCIS-BARNETT T.T. MODEL. 350 c.c.

¶ PRICE, including Special J.A.P. 346 c.c. Competition Engine, specially tuned for speed **£75**
(The Specification is published in the complete Catalogue). Carriage Paid

THE FRANCIS-BARNETT T.T. MODEL. 250 c.c.

¶ PRICE, including Special J.A.P. 250 c.c. Competition Engine, specially tuned for speed ; otherwise identical with above machine - - - - Carriage Paid **£73**

THE FRANCIS-BARNETT 350 c.c. SPORTS COMBINATION.

A serviceable and compact Runabout capable of a wide range of work. The 350 c.c. Sports Model is employed, with the gear suitably reduced. The complete specification of the cycle is given on page 1. The price includes Four-point attachment and overall apron.

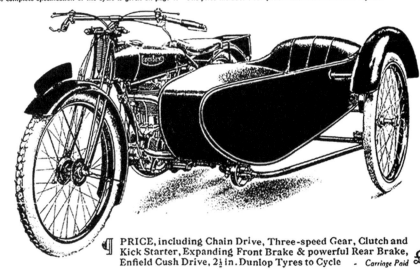

¶ PRICE, including Chain Drive, Three-speed Gear, Clutch and Kick Starter, Expanding Front Brake & powerful Rear Brake, Enfield Cush Drive, 2½ in. Dunlop Tyres to Cycle - Carriage Paid **£85**

W. W. CURTIS, LTD., COVENTRY.

1923 advertisement for 350cc and 250cc TT Models and 350cc Sports Combination.

Machine Specifications

Model	2.75bhp Sporting Model (Zarasport)	350cc Touring Model (Zaratourer)	Light Sporting Model
Manufacturing year	1922–24	1923–24	1922–23
Engine	JAP single-cylinder, air-cooled, side-valve four-stroke;long exhaust pipe with aluminium silencer	JAP single-cylinder, air-cooled, side-valve four-stroke; long exhaust pipe with aluminium silencer	JAP single-cylinder air-cooled, side-valve four-stroke; long exhaust pipe with aluminium silencer
Bore and stroke	70 × 90mm	70 × 90mm	70 × 76mm
Capacity	346cc	346cc	292cc
Lubrication	Hand pump inside tank, sight drip feed to order	Hand pump inside tank, sight drip feed to order	Hand pump or sight drip feed to order
Ignition	ML or Fellows magneto	ML or Fellows magneto	ML or Fellows magneto
Carburettor	Brown & Barlow	Brown & Barlow	Brown & Barlow
Primary drive	Renold chain 0.3125in	Renold chain 0.3125in	Renold or Coventry 0.25in
Final drive	Renold chain 0.31in	Renold chain 0.31in	Renold or Coventry 0.31in
Gearbox	Sturmey-Archer three-speed	Sturmey-Archer three-speed	Sturmey-Archer two-speed or three-speed
Gearbox ratios	5.9; 8.8; 17.2:1	5.9; 8.8; 17.2:1	
Frame	Special design, straight tubes	Special design, straight tubes	Special design, straight tubes
Suspension front	Brampton bi-flex	Brampton bi-flex	Brampton bi-flex
Suspension rear	Rigid	Rigid	Rigid
Wheels front and rear	26 × 2.25in		
Tyres front and rear	26 × 2.5in Bates' heavy type	26 × 2.5in Dunlop	26 × 2.5in Dunlop
Brake front	Webb's expanding hub brake	Webb's expanding hub brake	Webb's expanding hub brake
Brake rear	Foot brake on rear wheel	Foot brake on rear wheel	Foot brake on rear wheel
Hub front			
Hub rear	Enfield cush hub	Enfield cush hub	Enfield cush hub

General Specifications

Fuel tank capacity	Nearly 2gal (9ltr)	1.5gal (6.8ltr)	1.5gal (6.8ltr)
Oil tank capacity	3 pints (1.7ltr)	3 pints (1.7ltr)	3 pints (1.7ltr)
Dry weight	190lb (86kg)	205lb (93kg)	Not known

ABOVE: Rolling chassis showing the triangulated frame.

RIGHT: Triangulated frame inside a golf bag at the Ardingly Show, 2009.

brazed or welded parts in the frame head or forks at all; only the eyes were brazed into the rear stand. When the frame was taken to pieces it could be carried about in a golf bag.

Is it any wonder that the slogan used by the firm for many years was 'Built like a Bridge', with the Firth of Forth bridge shadowing all advertising at that time. There can be no doubt that many motorcyclists started with a machine of this description, and indeed several such machines still survive.

Zarabout, Zarallon and Zarcheck

Initially, three machines were offered for sale with the 147cc Villiers Mark VIIC engine in 1923. The first was a basic two-speed machine, belt-driven but without clutch or kick-starter; the second was a two-speed machine also belt-driven but including clutch and kick-starter; and the third was also two-speed with clutch and kick-starter, but with chain drive.

The instructions for starting the plain two-speed model were as follows: turn on the petrol and flood the carburettor by depressing the plunger. Push the machine off the stand and engage low gear. Stand over the machine and lift the release valve lever, and

paddle the machine forwards; when the engine is turning over freely, drop the valve lever and the engine will fire. Similarly, when changing gear up or down, lift the release valve lever and move the gear lever.

The construction of the steering head reversed all preconceived ideas at this point, in as far as the tank tube's head spindle, between the top and bottom tubes, remained stationary, while the head, itself a casting, moved round with the handlebars and forks. Cup and cone bearings were used for the steering head, a principle from which there had been no departure even on later machines, apart from autocycles.

Another unique feature was the design of the front forks. Still fully triangulated, these were used in conjunction with a three-leaf laminated spring in the shape of a letter 'C', which later on was supplemented by a rubber buffer fitted inside the spring itself.

The handlebars were adjustable and fastened to the steering head by two clips; the same type of clips were used to fasten the engine's 'V'-shaped engine plates, and then to the footrest tube separating the footrests. So satisfactory was this frame that a guarantee against breakage was given for all time.

'C' spring with rubber insert.

Both wheels were quickly detachable, having knock-out spindles which passed though hollow tubes in the hubs on which the cones were mounted. Conforming once again to the interchangeability of parts, the same cups, cones and balls were used in the wheels as in the steering head, and only two sizes of nut were used for building the frame.

Both brakes operated on the belt rim – the handbrake on the outside of the 'V' section, and the footbrake on the inside. A further noteworthy feature was the footbrake adjustment, in that the rod connection pedal to shoe could be positioned in one of three holes, thus varying the effective length of the rod, and taking up wear as it occurred in the brake blocks themselves.

The triangulated framed motorcycles were first shown at the 1923 Olympia Show, and as a centre-piece, Gordon Francis had a special all nickel-plated model with leg-shields and lighting. The basic model was priced at £25, although in some advertisements it is shown as £27. With the various configurations that were available, and the many factory-fitted extras to order, is it not surprising when nearly a century later there is great difficulty in trying to decide exactly which model has been recently unearthed?

The first of the run of engines used with a capacity of 147cc was the Villiers Mark VIIC with a bore and stroke of 55 × 62mm. The letter prefix for this engine number was 'L'. The cylinder was of one piece, the gudgeon pin at first fixed with split pins, but replaced later by a fully floating type.

Lighting from the top pole magneto was reliable, using alternating current wired in series. Bulbs, head

An early machine with belt-cum-chain drive, as found by Keith Clarke. (Courtesy Keith R. Clarke)

Machine Specifications

Model	1.5bhp (Zarabout)	1.5bhp (Zarallon)	1.5bhp (Zarcheck)
Manufacturing year	1923–25	1923–25	1923–25
Engine	Villiers Mark VIIC single-cylinder, air-cooled two-stroke	Villiers Mark VIIC single-cylinder, air-cooled two-stroke	Villiers Mark VIIC single-cylinder, air-cooled two-stroke
Number prefix	L	L	L
Bore and stroke	55 × 62mm	55 × 62mm	55 × 62mm
Capacity	147cc	147cc	147cc
Lubrication	Petroil	Petroil	Petroil
Ignition	Villiers flywheel magneto	Villiers flywheel magneto	Villiers flywheel magneto
Carburettor	Villiers	Villiers	Villiers
Primary drive	Chain	Chain	Chain
Final drive	Belt	Belt	Chain
Gearbox	Two-speed, no clutch*	Albion two-speed or three-speed	Albion two-speed or three-speed; 1925 two-speed only
Gearbox ratios	6.75; 10.75:1	6.75; 10.75:1	6.75; 10.75:1
Gearbox ratios optional	6.75; 10.5; 16:1	6.75; 10.5; 16:1	6.75; 10.5; 16:1
Frame	Fully triangulated, weldless steel tubing	Fully triangulated, weldless steel tubing	Fully triangulated, weldless steel tubing
Suspension front	Link action with 'C' spring	Link action with 'C' spring	Link action with 'C' spring
Suspension rear	Rigid	Rigid	Rigid
Wheels front and rear	24in knock-out spindle	24in knock-out spindle	24in knock-out spindle
Tyres front and rear	24 × 2in Hutchinson cord	24 × 2in Dunlop cord	24 × 2.25in Dunlop cord
Brake front	None	None	None
Brake rear	Left foot and right hand, acting on rear wheel	Left foot and right hand, acting on rear wheel	Right foot and right hand, acting on rear wheel

General Specifications

Fuel tank capacity	1.5gal (6.8ltr)	1.5gal (6.8ltr)	1.5gal (6.8ltr)
Dry weight	Standard model 100lb (45kg) *Two-speed with clutch, two-speed with clutch and kick-starter, or three-speed with clutch and kick-starter	126lb (57kg) Includes electric lighting, leg-shields and luggage carrier	136lb (62kg)

and rear, were double-centre contact type, 6v. 5amp in front, 4v 3watt at the back.

The carburettor was at first the famous Mills, later to be taken over and developed by Villiers.

One could reflect still further on such a machine, but at least mention must be made of the fact that in 1923 it was decided to make a film showing just how it was built. It took place in a film studio in London, with the clock showing in the background. It took exactly twenty minutes to build completely, after which, without any fuss, a road test was immediately undertaken without incident. Speed was 35/40mph (56/64km/h) and petrol consumption 150mpg (1.9ltr/100km).

It was inevitable that for such unconventional designs there must be unusual forms of advertising, and so it was. Following the filmed build that was achieved in record time, all sorts of petrol consumption tests were officially recorded.

The 1924 Season

The first three machines with the 147cc Villiers two-stroke engine were joined by a fourth for the 1924 season. Whereas the other machines used the Villiers Mark VIIC engine, this one used the 147cc Villiers Mark VIIIC engine, with the same bore and stroke of 55 × 62mm as the Mark VIIC. The machine was basically the same as the model with the 'code word' Zarcheck, and in 1925 the only difference between them was that Zarcheck had the Albion two-speed gear, and Zarchain the Albion three-speed gear, and was priced at £34.

A machine without a 'code word' was advertised for sale as the 1.5bhp two-stroke model, with the advertisement giving details of the English Six Days' Trial model of 1923, and inferring that this model took part and was awarded a Certificate of Merit. The machine had the same specification as the basic model,

The 1924 basic triangulated model.

with the two-speed gear, clutch and kick-starter, but included electric headlight, leg-shields and luggage carrier for the price of £33. The advertised price for the basic model as above was £30, the electric headlight was £1 10s, leg-shields £1 and a luggage carrier 10s, making a total of £33, the same as the English Six Days' Trial model.

Two four-strokes continued in production, the 350cc Touring Model (2.75bhp Touring Model) priced at £65, and the 350cc Sports Model (2.75bhp Sporting Model) priced at £63, both with the 346cc Jap engine.

Hire purchase was brought in to make the machines affordable to a larger number of the public. The deposit was one-third of the full invoice value for 1.5bhp models and one-quarter for 350cc models, with twelve monthly payments and the APR at approximately 8.75 per cent. Even so, the monthly payment required was probably the average weekly wage.

Showing the foot-operated brake shoe on the inside of the dummy wheel, and the hand-brake shoe on the outside.

The 1924 Six Days' Trial model.

Francis-Barnett

1½ H.P. TWO-STROKE MODEL

Illustrated with Complete Equipment, showing Kick-Starter, Leg Shields, Carrier, &c.

THE ENGLISH SIX DAYS' TRIAL, 1923.

THROUGHOUT the English Six Days' Trial, the performance of the 1½ h.p. Francis-Barnett was watched with intense interest by vast numbers. The Trial was one of the most strenuous ever organised. Included in the route were some of the severest hills in Yorkshire, Derbyshire, Wales, The Cotswolds and the Chilterns, while on the sixth day a speed test of about 70 miles was undergone at Brooklands. Day after day the little Francis-Barnett won unstinted praise. Its climbing of such gradients as Rosedale Chimney and Alms Hill was generously acclaimed, and in the prolonged speed test at Brooklands it concluded a magnificent demonstration of efficiency by lapping at over 36 m.p.h. and was awarded a Certificate of Merit.

Registered Design No. 694755.

PRICE : Including Two-Speed, Clutch and Kick-Starter, Electric Head Light, Leg Shields and Luggage Carrier - **£33**

N.B.—Electric Lighting must be ordered with the machine, as otherwise an alteration to the flywheel magneto is necessary.

Delivered Carriage Paid to any Railway Station in Great Britain.

The 1925 Season

The 'Fanny B'

In 1925 another 147cc Villiers-engined machine joined the stable, with the 'code word' Zarelect; it was this machine that became Model No. 4 in 1926. It continued in production until 1929, and in 1930 became the updated Model No. 4B. The original 1925 model had two-speed gear, clutch and kick-starter, electric lighting, leg-shields and luggage carrier, all for the sum of £31. Outside the works, the Model 4 was affectionately referred to as 'Fanny B', and because it was always referred to as 'she' in letters and conversation, one would have thought that 'Fanny' was her Christian name. Later, 'Fanny B' became a generic name covering the marque, rather than one individual model.

Sports Model No. 5 'Zarspeed'

Despite always being progressive in outlook, the need for a 'sportier' machine was making itself felt. Although

by now, 1925, the use of all-chain drive, a three-speed gearbox, clutch and kick-starter was standard, pride of place was given to a 'Sports Model', later to be referred to as 'Model No. 5'. This machine was indeed a real step forwards, having a capacity of 172cc with a bore of 57.15mm and stroke of 67mm; the cylinder was again the fixed-head type. Two exhaust ports connected with short pipes leading into a cylindrical expansion chamber in front of the crankcase, and the outlet was via a long pipe to the rear of the machine. The exhaust note was sporty – in fact a little too much so at times.

Lubrication was by a Best & Lloyd drip-feed pressure pump mounted on the oil compartment of the petrol tank on the right-hand side – perfectly satisfactory as long as it was remembered to depress the plunger when it got to the top. The flow was regulated by a knurled adjuster, and the early pump had a tubular glass down the nose of the outside of the oil tank through which it was possible to see the drips. This type of pump was superseded by one with the same action, but where the sight feed was visible when riding.

Ted Lloyd's immaculate Model 3, first registered 1 January 1925.

Machine Specifications

◆

Model	1.5bhp (Zarchain)	1.5bhp (Zarelect)	1.75bhp Sports (Zarspeed)
Manufacturing year	1924–25	1925	1925
Engine	Villiers Mark VIIIC single-cylinder, air-cooled two-stroke	Villiers Mark VIIIC single-cylinder, air-cooled two-stroke	Villiers Sports single-cylinder, air-cooled two-stroke
Number prefix	W	W	TL
Bore and stroke	55 × 62mm	55 × 62mm	57.15 × 67mm
Capacity	147cc	147cc	172cc
Lubrication	Petroil	Petroil	Sight drip-feed
Ignition	Villiers flywheel magneto	Villiers flywheel magneto	Villiers flywheel magneto
Carburettor	Mills or Amac; 1925 – Mills	Villiers	Sports Amac two-lever
Primary drive	Renold chain 0.5 × 0.25in	Renold chain 0.5 × 0.25in	Renold chain 0.5 × 0.25in
Final drive	Renold chain 0.5 × 0.25in	Renold chain 0.5 × 0.25in	Renold chain 0.5 × 0.25in
Gearbox	Albion two-speed or three-speed 1925 three-speed only	Albion two-speed	Albion three-speed
Gearbox ratios	6.75; 10.75:1	6.75; 10.75:1	5.8; 8.5; 13.5:1
Gearbox ratios optional	6.75; 10; 16:1	6.75; 10.5; 16:1	
Frame	Fully triangulated, weldless steel tubing	Fully triangulated, weldless steel tubing	Fully triangulated, weldless steel tubing
Suspension front	Link action with 'C' spring	Link action with 'C' spring	Link action with 'C' spring
Suspension rear	Rigid	Rigid	Rigid
Wheels front and rear	24in knock-out spindle	24in knock-out spindle	24in knock-out spindle
Tyres front and rear	24 × 2.25in Hutchinson cord	24 × 2.25in Dunlop cord	24 × 2.25in Dunlop cord
Brake front	None	None	None
Brake rear	Right foot and right hand, acting on rear wheel	Right foot and right hand, acting on rear wheel	Right foot and right hand, acting on rear wheel

General Specifications

Fuel tank capacity	1.25gal (5.7ltr)	1.5gal (6.8ltr)	1.5gal (6.8ltr)
Oil tank capacity	Not known	Not known	2.5 pints oil (1.4ltr)
Dry weight	138lb (63kg)	Not known	147lb (67kg)
		Includes electric lighting, leg-shields and luggage carrier	

The 172cc Sports model advertisement.

Albion three-speed counter-shaft gearboxes were used, and Senspray carburettors were specified. It could be said that Model No. 5 was of a type that came into its own for competition purposes; it was competing in races such as the Six Days' Stock Trial and the Scottish Six Days with measurable success – but still more power was needed. The chain adjustment front and rear was quite unorthodox. The gearbox was mounted on steel plates extending from the crankcase to the chain-stay frame tubes – with the introduction of all chain drive the bent tubes gave place to the provision of a further triangle. A short tube from the saddle terminated to join up with the short tube leading from the back wheel on either side. The Albion gearbox was suspended by means of two 0.375in studs

screwed into the gearbox case and thereby attached to the rear engine plates by top and bottom steel clamps. There was then a trunnion between the engine plates to accommodate a screwed eye bolt, which in turn was fitted over the front gearbox-holding stud. Thus front chain adjustment was varied by sliding the gearbox along the engine plates and locking the adjuster on the side of the trunnion. Additional support was later provided by a reinforced malleable casting above the steel clamps, and an auxiliary support strap which extended from the side of the gearbox on the KS side to the chain stay frame stud.

Rear chain adjustment was by means of a jockey sprocket. From the rear of the engine plates and distanced along the chain stay frame stud, two jockey plates were suspended, each having three holes connected by two slots. The jockey sprocket was eccentrically mounted in the bottom hole until chain adjustment was no longer possible, after which the sprocket was moved into the next hole, and so on. This method of chain adjustment was continued until 1931.

The 1926 Season

An Improved Zarspeed

Model No. 5 (Zarspeed) was continued into 1926 virtually unaltered, but was supplemented by an improved edition of the Villiers 172cc Super Sports engine. The bore and stroke remained the same at 57.15 × 67mm and the piston remained unaltered, still being cast iron with a fully floating gudgeon pin. Experience was showing, however, that increased power from the engine was taking its toll of the gudgeon pin bushes, and it became necessary to make changes in the design.

In 1926, the Villiers Company fitted bronze bushes for the first time, and this completely stopped the wear at this point – an innovation which was part of the Villiers piston design from then on. There was much to be said for the new engine, which together with the first Villiers middleweight carburettor was a good combination.

The engine had a cylinder barrel with an aluminium detachable head. The carburettor was fitted to the cylinder by means of a swan-neck induction manifold,

1928 Model 5. (Courtesy FBOC)

and for the first time provision was made for varying the ignition. As was common to all Villiers units, the magneto was located by means of a split steel bush in the armature plate mounted on the crankcase bush. A long grub screw extended through the armature plate, and when this was tightened judiciously it closed the split bush on to the crankcase. Care was needed, however, otherwise on the one hand it would be impossible to move the armature plate and thereby vary the ignition timing, at the same time distorting the crankcase bush itself, or on the other hand too much slack would make the armature plate wobble, creating a varying gap at the contact breaker points.

Also at this time a change was made in the contact breaker spring. Originally brass springs were used, but the increase in rpm was taking its toll, and rocker 'float' was remedied by the specification of steel springs, which subsequently were increased still further in strength, as the rpm on later types of engine dictated.

Power was stepped up considerably by the provision of unusual exhaust pipes: a new theory was being tried out in expanding the gases as quickly as possible. Consequently the size of the exhaust ports and flanges was increased, and the pipes then took the shape of bulbous attachments, nicknamed 'Oxford bags', which were the vogue at the time. These expansion chambers were made from steel pressings separately constructed, each Oxford bag terminating immediately below the crankcase. From this point there was a length of steel tube, to which was fitted on each side of the machine a small tubular silencer. While it was considered that this method of exhausting the machine provided more power, it most certainly provided more noise, and it became the preoccupation of the design department to deal with each – first separately and then collectively.

In 1926 there was also a departure from beaded-edge tyres, and a move in favour of low-pressure balloon tyres on 19 × 3in well-base rims. This may well have been commonplace in the 1950s, but much was made at that time of the added riding comfort such tyres provided.

Machine Specifications

	1.5bhp No. 1 (Zarabout)	1.5bhp No. 2 (Zarallon)	1.5bhp No. 3 (Zarcheck)
Model	1.5bhp No. 1 (Zarabout)	1.5bhp No. 2 (Zarallon)	1.5bhp No. 3 (Zarcheck)
Manufacturing year	1926	1926	1926–29
Engine	Villiers Mark VIIIC single-cylinder, air-cooled two-stroke	Villiers Mark VIIIC single-cylinder, air-cooled two-stroke	Villiers Mark VIIIC single-cylinder, air-cooled two-stroke
Number prefix	W	W	W
Bore and stroke	55 × 62mm	55 × 62mm	55 × 62mm
Capacity	147cc	147cc	147cc
Lubrication	Petroil	Petroil	Petroil
Ignition	Villiers flywheel magneto	Villiers flywheel magneto	Villiers flywheel magneto
Carburettor	Villiers	Villiers	Villiers
Primary drive	Chain	Chain	Renold chain 0.5 × 0.25in
Final drive	Belt .625 × 66.25in	Belt	Renold chain 0.5 × 0.25in
Gearbox	Albion two-speed clutch and kick-starter; three-speed to order	Albion two-speed clutch and kick-starter; three-speed to order	Albion two-speed clutch and kick-starter; three-speed to order
Gearbox ratios	6.75; 10.75:1	6.75; 10.75:1	6.75; 10.75:1
Gearbox ratios optional	6.75; 10.5; 16:1	6.75; 10.5; 16:1	6.75; 10.5; 16:1
Frame	Fully triangulated, weldless steel tubing	Fully triangulated, weldless steel tubing	Fully triangulated, weldless steel tubing
Suspension front	Link action with 'C' spring	Link action with 'C' spring	Link action with 'C' spring
Suspension rear	Rigid	Rigid	Rigid
Wheels front and rear	24in knock-out spindle	24in knock-out spindle	24in knock-out spindle
Tyres front and rear	24 × 2in Dunlop cord	24 × 2in Dunlop cord	24 × 2.25in Dunlop cord
Brake front	None	None	None
Brake rear	Left foot and right hand, acting on rear wheel	Left foot and right hand, acting on rear wheel	Right foot and right hand, acting on rear wheel

General Specifications

1929 specifications

	1.5bhp No. 1 (Zarabout)	1.5bhp No. 2 (Zarallon)	1.5bhp No. 3 (Zarcheck)
Fuel tank capacity	1.5gal (6.8ltr)	1.5gal (6.8ltr)	1.63gal (7.4ltr)
Oil tank capacity	Not known	Not known	Not known
Overall length	Not known	Not known	77.25in (1,962mm)
Overall width	Not known	Not known	29.25in (743mm)
Wheelbase	Not known	Not known	47.63in (1,210mm)
Ground clearance	Not known	Not known	6.5in (165mm)

Machine Specifications *continued*

Model	1.5bhp No. 1 (Zarabout)	1.5bhp No. 2 (Zarallon)	1.5bhp No. 3 (Zarcheck)
Seat height (min.)	Not known	Not known	26.75in (679mm)
Dry weight	110lb (50kg)	126lb (57kg) Includes electric lighting, leg-shields and luggage carrier	144lb (65kg)

The 175cc four-stroke Model No. 6.

175 c.c. FOUR-STROKE MODEL, No. 6.

175 c.c. CHAIN DRIVE.

To meet the demand for a Light Four-Stroke Motor Bicycle, we have introduced the 175 c.c. model illustrated. The engine is of robust construction ; it is furnished with an outside flywheel, has roller bearing to the big end, and the valve mechanism is of generous proportions. The bearing surfaces throughout are of ample size.

This machine has been subjected to exhaustive tests on the road, and we offer it to our clients with confidence that it will give thoroughly reliable service.

Registered Design No. 694755.

PRICE : Including Three-Speed Gear, Clutch and Kick-Starter, Terry Saddle, etc.   -   -   **£34 15s.**

Code Word : " ZARFIELD."

EXTRAS TO ORDER : Acetylene Head Lamp and Generator, 17/- ; 10 in. Bulb Horn, 6/6 ; Leg Shields, 15 - ; Carrier 10 -
24" ; 21" Dunlop Heavy Cord Tyres, 25 -.

Super-Sports and Four-Strokes

One machine that may not have gone into general production was the Super-Sports Model 8 exhibited at Olympia, in September 1925. The prototype(s) were successfully entered into competitions, in the Colmore Cup Trial in February 1926, awarded the Walker Cup and souvenir and gold medal, and in the Victory Cup Trial awarded gold and silver medals. The company appeared to go for the next generation of Super-Sports models, the No. 9, three of which had already seen success in the ascent of Snowdon on 12 July, and which had an improved specification over Model 8.

In 1926 there was also a further venture into the four-stroke field. Retaining the famous triangulated frame and interchanging entirely with previous frame design, a 175cc JAP four-stroke made its appearance. With a 60mm bore and 62mm stroke, outside flywheel and roller-bearing big end and an Amac or Binks carburettor, the design was intended to appeal to riders who would not be wooed by Villiers two-stroke engines but who were interested in the frame layout.

Simultaneously a larger engine was tried out: conforming to previous frame theory it was fundamentally the same as the smaller engined machine but with

Machine Specifications

	1.5bhp No. 4 (Zarelect)	1.75bhp Sports No. 5 (Zarspeed)	1.75bhp Sports No. 5 (Zarspeedal)
Model	1.5bhp No. 4 (Zarelect)	1.75bhp Sports No. 5 (Zarspeed)	1.75bhp Sports No. 5 (Zarspeedal)
Manufacturing year	1926–29	1926–27	1928–29
Engine	Villiers Mark VIIIC single-cylinder, air-cooled two-stroke	Villiers Sports single-cylinder, air-cooled two-stroke	Villiers Sports single-cylinder, air-cooled two-stroke
Number prefix	W	TL	TL
Bore and stroke	55 × 62mm	57.15 × 67mm	57.15 × 67mm
Capacity	147cc	172cc	172cc
Lubrication	Petroil	Sight drip feed	Automatic
Ignition	Villiers flywheel magneto	Villiers flywheel magneto	Villiers flywheel magneto
Carburettor	Villiers	Sports Amac two-lever	Villiers
Primary drive	Renold chain 0.5 × 0.25in	Renold chain 0.5 × 0.25in	Renold chain 0.5 × 0.25in
Final drive	Renold chain 0.5 × 0.25in	Renold chain 0.5 × 0.25in	Renold chain 0.5 × 0.25in
Gearbox	Albion two-speed clutch and kick-starter; three-speed to order	Albion three-speed	Albion three-speed
Gearbox ratios	6.75; 10.75:1	5.8; 8.5; 13.5:1	6.2; 10.5; 18.75:1
Gearbox ratios optional	6.75; 10.5; 16:1	1927; 6.2; 9.1; 14.5:1	6.2; 9.00; 14.5:1
Frame	Fully triangulated, weldless steel tubing	Fully triangulated, weldless steel tubing	Fully triangulated, weldless steel tubing
Suspension front	Link action with 'C' spring	Link action with 'C' spring	Link action with single compressed spring
Suspension rear	Rigid	Rigid	Rigid
Wheels front and rear	24in knock-out spindle	24in knock-out spindle	24in knock-out spindle
Tyres front and rear	24 × 2.25in Dunlop cord	24 × 2.25in Dunlop cord	24 × 2.50in Dunlop cord
Brake front	None	None	Internal expanding
Brake rear	Right foot and right hand, acting on rear wheel	Right foot and right hand, acting on rear wheel	Internal expanding

General Specifications

	1929 specifications		*1929 specifications*
Fuel tank capacity	1.63gal (7.4ltr)	1.5gal (6.8ltr)	1.63gal (7.4ltr)
Oil tank capacity		2.5 pints oil (1.4ltr)	Separate oil tank 4 pints (2.3ltr)
Overall length	77.25in (1,962mm)		79.25in (2,013mm)

Machine Specifications *continued*

Overall width	29.25in (743mm)		31in (787mm)
Wheel base	47.63in (1,210mm)		49.63in (1,260mm)
Ground clearance	4.75in (120mm)		4.75in (120mm)
Seat height (min.)	26.75in (679mm)		27in (686mm)
Dry weight	157lb (71kg) Includes electric lighting, leg-shields and luggage carrier	147lb (67kg)	179lb (81kg)

larger diameter tubing and of increased overall size to accommodate the 350cc JAP engine with a 70mm bore and 90mm stroke, again fitted with an Amac carburettor. This design did not receive the support that was expected, notwithstanding the specification, which was lavish at the time.

Link-action front forks made their debut, together with Webb internal expanding front and rear brakes. The triangular soldered petrol tank so characteristic of Francis-Barnetts for many years was retained, and

the bike's appearance was enhanced by the fitting of a hand-operated, drip-feed oil pump made by Best & Lloyd, but fitted inside the oil compartment of the petrol tank – on the smaller 175cc four-stroke machine the pump was fitted on the outside.

Mechanical oil pumps were yet to come – which leads to some extent into our next model. The 175cc model was priced at £34 15s, and the 350cc model at £41 15s. Despite being in the annual sales catalogue, doubts have been raised as to whether these two

350 c.c. FOUR-STROKE MODEL, No. 7.

350 c.c. CHAIN DRIVE.

WE invite particular attention to this new model, which we have designed to meet the requirements of our customers for a well-equipped 350 c.c. Touring Machine at a strictly moderate price. The specification is a generous one, including 27″ × 2·75″ Dunlop Cord Tyres and Internal Expanding Brakes to both wheels, which are of the detachable and interchangeable type.

The fork is of special design, with a single compression spring, permitting vertical movement. The steering of the machine at all speeds is absolutely steady.

Registered Design No. 694755.

PRICE : Including Three-Speed Gear, Clutch and Kick-Starter and 27′ × 2⅛″ Dunlop Cord Tyres- - - **£41 15s.**

Code Word : " ZARTOURIST."

EXTRAS: Best and Lloyd Mechanical Pump, 20/- ; Lucas No. 63 Horn, 10.6 ; Lucas No. 442 Acetylene Lamp Set, 45/- ; Lucas No. 344 Acetylene Tail Lamp Set, 13 - ; Leg Shields, 25/- ; Terry Saddle, 27,6.

Delivered Carriage Paid to any Railway Station in Great Britain.

The 350cc four-stroke Model No. 7.

The 172cc Model No. 8.

1 3/4 HP SUPER SPORTS MODEL, No. 8.
172 c.c.
Colmore Cup Trial, February, 1926; Awarded Walker Cup and Souvenir and Gold Medal.
Victory Cup Trial, March, 1926; Awarded Gold Medal and Silver Medal.

THIS model was exhibited at Olympia, in September, 1925. It was not then in production, but we have now had ample time to satisfy ourselves in regard to the suitability of the machine for general road use. We may say at once that our expectations have been exceeded.

The Super Sports Model is remarkable for its combination of high speed with silkiness of running. When the engine has been run in, it reaches 55 m.p.h. without difficulty. This speed has been exceeded at Brooklands, with a high compression ratio.

To render the Super Sports Model suitable for ordinary road use, the compression has been slightly reduced, and a light Cast Iron Piston fitted. We have no hesitation in giving the machine our full recommendation to those who require a Sporting Mount of light weight and moderate cost, combined with brilliant performance.

The specification includes the 172 c.c. Villiers Super Sports Engine, with twin exhaust pipes and large expansion chambers; Semi-automatic Drip Feed lubrication, Dunlop Tyres and Terry Saddle.

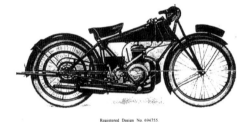

Registered Design No. 694755.

PRICE: Including Three-Speed, Clutch and Kick-Starter,
21/4in. Tyres and Terry Saddle -   -   -   -   **£37.10s**

Code Word: " ZARSUPER."

When Electric Lighting is required add AL to end of Code Word, thus : " Zarsuporal."
EXTRAS TO ORDER: Electric Head Light, 30/- ;   Electric Rear Light, 10/- ;   Acetylene Head Lamp and Generator, 17/-   10in. Bulb Horn, 6/6;   Leg Shields, 15/-
Carrier, 10/- ;   24" x 2 1/2" Dunlop Heavy Cord Tyres, 25/-
Carriage Paid to any Railway Station in Great Britain.
NB. Electric Lighting, if required, must be ordered with the machine as otherwise an alteration to the flywheel magneto is necessary

Manufactured by
FRANCIS & BARNETT, LTD., COVENTRY.
Works: LOWER FORD STREET

machines actually reached the production stage. However, the *Hints, Instructions and Spare Parts List Manual, Third Edition* covers 147cc and 172cc two-stroke machines and a 175cc four-stroke machine, but no 350cc machine.

The 1927 Season

By 1927 there was plenty of reason to believe that lightweight motorcycles had come to stay. Model No. 4 with its 147cc Villiers Mark VlllC engine was fast establishing a reputation for liking hard work, and it was amazingly reliable. Its 'pepper-box' silencer was giving it an exhaust note that identified it wherever it was to be heard – some criticized it, others admired it, but none could deny that whatever views were expressed as regards its line, it was truly functional. A short pipe from the cylinder leading into a round box-type silencer fastened to the bottom of the crankcase made it reasonably gas tight without any elaborate joints; in fact, the hole in the silencer was elongated, so by swivelling the silencer on the crankcase studs the hole was made to close on to the pipe – it was as simple as that. And the ease with which the system could be cleaned out needs no further explanation.

Machine Specifications

Model	175cc Four-Stroke No. 6	350cc Four-Stroke No. 7	1.75bhp Super-Sports No. 8
Manufacturing year	1926	1926	1926
Engine	JAP single-cylinder, air-cooled four-stroke	JAP single-cylinder, air-cooled four-stroke	Villiers Super-Sports single-cylinder, air-cooled two-stroke
Bore and stroke	60 × 62mm	70 × 90mm	57.15 × 67mm
Capacity	174cc	346cc	172cc
Lubrication	Sight drip feed	Hand pump	Semi-automatic with sight drip feed
Ignition	BTH magneto; variable	BTH magneto	Villiers flywheel magneto
Carburettor	Amac two-lever or Binks single-lever	Amac two-lever or Binks single-lever	Villiers
Primary drive	Renold chain 0.5 × 0.25in	Renold chain 0.5 × 0.31in	Renold chain 0.5 × 0.25in
Final drive	Renold chain 0.5 × 0.25in	Renold chain 0.5 × 0.31in	Renold chain 0.5 × 0.25in
Gearbox	Albion three-speed	Albion three-speed	Albion three-speed
Gearbox ratios		5.75; 8.5; 14.0:1	5.8; 8.5; 13.5:1
Frame	Fully triangulated, weldless steel tubing	Fully triangulated, weldless steel tubing	Fully triangulated, weldless steel tubing
Suspension front	Link action with 'C' spring	Link action with single compressed spring	Link action with 'C' spring
Suspension rear	Rigid	Rigid	Rigid
Wheels front and rear	24in knock-out spindle	27in knock-out spindle	24in knock-out spindle
Tyres front and rear	24 × 2.25in Dunlop cordless	27 × 2.75in Dunlop cord	24 × 2.25in Dunlop cord
Brake front	None	Internal expanding	None
Brake rear	Right foot and right hand, acting on rear wheel	Internal expanding	Right foot and right hand, acting on rear wheel

General Specifications

Fuel tank capacity	1.5gal (6.8ltr)	1.75gal petrol (8ltr)	1.5gal (6.8ltr)
Oil tank capacity	2.5 pints oil (1.4ltr)	3 pints oil (1.7ltr)	2.5 pints oil (1.4ltr)
Dry weight	150lb (68kg)	Not known	150lb (68kg)

Machine Specifications

Model	1.75bhp Super-Sports No. 9	1.75bhp Super-Sports No. 9	Pullman No. 10
Manufacturing year	1926–27	1928–30	1928–29
Engine	Villiers Super-Sports single-cylinder, air-cooled two-stroke	Villiers Super-Sports single-cylinder, air-cooled two-stroke	Villiers vertical twin in-line, air-cooled two-stroke
Number prefix	BZ	BZ	TW
Bore and stroke	57.15 × 67mm	57.15 × 67mm	57.15 × 67mm
Capacity	172cc	172cc	344cc
Lubrication	Automatic	Automatic	Villiers automatic system
Ignition	Villiers flywheel magneto	Villiers flywheel magneto	Villiers flywheel magneto
Carburettor	Villiers two-lever	Villiers two-lever with air filter	Villiers single-lever
Primary drive	Renold chain 0.5 × 0.25in	Renold chain 0.5 × 0.25in	Worm gear 2.5:1 reduction
Final drive	Renold chain 0.5 × 0.25in	Renold chain 0.5 × 0.25in	Renold chain 0.5 × 0.31in
Gearbox	Albion three-speed	Albion three-speed	Three-speed incorporated in one unit with engine
Gearbox ratios	6.2; 9.1; 14.5:1*	6.2; 9.1; 14.5:1	5.14, 7.7; 12.6:1
Gearbox ratios optional		6.2; 9.00; 14.5:1	
Frame	Fully triangulated, weldless steel tubing	Fully triangulated, weldless steel tubing	Fully triangulated, weldless steel tubing
Suspension front	Link action with 'C' spring	Link action with single compressed spring	Link action with single compressed spring; steering damper fitted
Suspension rear	Rigid	Rigid	Rigid
Wheels front and rear	24in knock-out spindle	25in well-base	25in knock-out spindles
Tyres front and rear	25 × 3in Dunlop balloon	25 × 3in Dunlop balloon	26 × 3.5in Dunlop balloon
Brake front	None	Internal expanding	7in internal expanding
Brake rear	Right foot and right hand acting on rear wheel	Internal expanding	7in internal expanding

General Specifications

	1929 specification		
Fuel tank capacity	1.75gal petrol (8ltr)	1.63gal (7.4ltr)	2.5gal (11ltr)
Oil tank capacity	2.5 pints oil (1.4ltr)	4 pints (2.3ltr)	Not known
Overall length	Not known	79.25in (2,013mm)	Not known
Overall width	Not known	31in (787mm)	Not known

Machine Specifications *continued*

❖

Wheelbase	Not known	49.63in (1,260mm)	Not known
Ground clearance	Not known	4.75in (120mm)	Not known
Seat height (min)	Not known	27in (686mm)	Not known
Dry weight	164lb (74kg)	187lb (85kg)	280lb (127kg)
	* Wide ratio gears to order		
	Spare parts list states 19 × 2.5in		
	wheel rims		

Looking back, one wonders (apart from appearances) why the motorcycle industry took so long to advance beyond such an efficient exhaust system. The four-stroke models were withdrawn in favour of yet a further edition of a Villiers engine, superior to the previous Super-Sports – in a struggle for superlatives, it was to be known as the T.T. Super-Sports, with the letters 'BZ' as the engine number prefix.

No belt-driven machines were marketed in 1927, and all models were fitted with electric lighting and rubber handgrips as standard. Other modifications included improved chain guards, which enclose the outer side at the front and the top run of the rear chain. The nose of the saddle was now attached to the twin top tubes by means of a hinge instead of using a curved leaf spring.

Francis-Barnett were adept at using events or exploits as advertisements to further the public interest in their products, be it trials, racing, round Britain rides or the ascent of mountains. Following on from the ascent of Mount Snowdon in 1926, a successful attempt was made in 1927 to ascend Ben Nevis by Mr Drew MacQueen.

If ever a machine captured the enthusiasm of the sporting rider it was Model No. 9. Many riders believed at the time, and some always averred, that the 172cc engine fitted to this machine was the most successful the Villiers Company had ever produced. The cast-iron piston now gave way to aluminium, thereby improving acceleration and removing a certain amount of engine vibration, which was inescapable with a cast-iron piston.

The Automatic Oil Lubrication System
The most outstanding feature this year, however, was the introduction of the automatic oil lubrication system.

Crankcase pressure was transferred along the centre of the crankshafts through drilled holes to correspond with grooves in the crankcase bushes. From there, channels led to plugs screwed into the front of the crankcase, into which copper pipes of short length were fitted, then a rubber tube, followed by a further length of copper pipe to the oil tank. On the Mark 1 automatic lubricator the pressure pipe extended to the top of the tank where the pressure was released. Since the tank itself was pressure tight, oil was then forced via a regulator and sight feed cup through a pipe leading to the front of the cylinder barrel. Here the lubricant divided, some being sucked directly on to the piston, the rest passing a channel in the cylinder down to the crankcase where it was again divided to feed the two crankcase bushes.

When the engine stopped, crankcase pressure dropped but some provision had to be made to release the pressure created at that time in the oil tank, otherwise the oil would continue to flow and so flood the engine. This was remedied by means of a vent hole in the sight feed cup. Oil-tank pressure is allowed to escape through the vent hole permitting a limited gravity feed through the oil pipe, causing the pump to stop working. There is a continuous passage of air through the vent hole even when the engine is running, which passes down to the engine with the oil, keeping the sight feed cup clear. The size of the vent hole should not be altered, but it was recommended that a small strand of Bowden cable, half an inch long and bent over at right angles at the top, was used to keep the hole clear.

The oil and pressure pipes were of a type employing the use of brass olives. The nipples were tightened into a union on one side by a nut, and on the other side each had corresponding tapers to mate with the olives. It will be seen that as the nut was tightened against the olive, it constricted on to the pipe. It is emphasized that the entire system could only operate on pressure, and so the importance of ensuring that there were no leaks in the pressure pipe, filler cap, oil pump body could not be ignored. Any suggestion of leakage at these points caused a surplus of oil at low speeds during which the system was working on gravity alone, and a restriction at high speeds, when there was no pressure at all. A fairly common fault was an apparent tightness in the oil-tank filler cap threads – the impression was given that the cap was right down when this was not so. Again, sometimes the leather washer in the cap would pucker and thereby prevent the cap from seating. It was fatal to use a filler cap with a vent hole.

The engine retained its previous features, such as a detachable cylinder head, but one new departure is worthy of mention: with the further increase of bhp (brake horse power) it became necessary to strengthen the big end bearing, and this was achieved by the specification of steel rollers and hollow bronze spacers. It was revealed that under certain conditions the all steel rollers, which had been common practice until then, were tending to skid, bringing about 'flats' and overheating on this account. The composite bearing was most effective, so much so that no further change was made in this direction until the introduction of the postwar 197cc engine unit.

Until the advent of the Super-Sports engine a single plate cork clutch was standard on all Albion gearboxes, two- or three-speed. However, the added surge gave rise to clutch slip, and despite increased spring pressure it became necessary to enlarge the effective clutch area. As a result the second plate was introduced, with outside pegs locating in the steel slot of the slotted drum riveted to the clutch springs. Incidentally, the sprocket ran on a bronze ring mounted on the back clutch plate, but this eventually gave trouble and was to be modified, as will be explained later.

A Change in the Exhaust System

There was one noticeable change in the exhaust system with the 'BZ' TT engine. Although the Oxford Bag expansion chambers had been the object of much favourable comment, it was becoming increasingly

difficult to silence them effectively, and the note they produced could scarcely be described as musical, resembling more of a staccato penetrating crack, which under certain conditions was undoubtedly objectionable. It was decided to use ordinary exhaust pipes, and to fit long tubular silencers with short tail pipes at the end. The silencers had three cone-shaped baffle plates evenly positioned at the forward end; at the rear was a baffle with a 0.5m hole. One disadvantage was the emulsifying effect these types of silencer produced. A brownish concoction of oil and water accumulated, which if not removed used to make the exhaust sound almost like a gurgle; this was remedied by drilling a 0.125m (3mm) hole at the forward end of the silencer on the bottom in its lowest position. This unfortunately attracted the attention of the law, so then the internal cones and baffle plates were slotted so that the emulsion could be exuded at the rear.

Model No. 9

Also in 1927 – this memorable year – a Model No. 9 was selected for the International Six Days Trophy Team, the first occasion in the history of the trial that England was represented by a machine under 200cc – which was some going in those days. Meanwhile abroad, this type of machine was constantly gaining laurels – Bulawayo, Port Elisabeth, Kimberley, Durban, all were the scenes of successful road racing. At home, this machine was also being put through its paces and was breaking records at Brooklands: 100 miles at 61.92mph (160km at 99.6km/h), two hours at 61.95mph (99.7km/h), 50km (31 miles) at 103.37km/h (64.2mph) and so on.

The 1928 Season

Improvements to Model No. 9

There seemed little need to make any serious modification to Model No. 9 for 1928. However, changes there were and plenty: to start with, 5in hub brakes made their first appearance on Francis-Barnett lightweights. From early manufacture the most noticeable feature were the extremely long torque arms front and rear; on both hubs these extended as far as 12in (30cm) or so, the idea being to provide a smooth and progressive application of each brake. The cones, however, were still

Trevor Wells' Model 9, seen at a FBOC AGM. (Courtesy FBOC)

mounted on hollow spindles with knock-out spindles passing through them to facilitate quick removal.

The 'C'-type fork spring arrangement gave way to a link action made up of steel stampings and a single compression spring. The Albion-type 'E' gearbox, used continuously since 1925, now went over to an improved edition known as the El type, its most obvious characteristic being the arrangement of the lay shaft at the side instead of being immediately underneath the main shaft. The gear-change mechanism was also improved, a long lever being mounted directly on the box where previously the gear change had operated through a quadrant attached to the box and a further short lever – the latter proved responsible for lost movement as soon as any wear was apparent.

Carburation was improved, although the two-lever Villiers instrument with variable jet control was an advantage over the previous single-lever pattern; a further improvement was made by increasing the size of the float chamber. The Villiers Brooklands 'Y'-type engine was also being fitted to certain 172cc machines to special order, although it was made especially for racing, and the number produced was quite negligible. Nevertheless, the specification of such an engine makes interesting reading. The cylinder barrel was cast iron with a heavily finned aluminium jacket shrunk on, the crankshafts were padded to increase compression ratio, and an outsize carburettor was employed, the power output 8.25bhp at 4,900rpm.

The Francis-Barnett Pullman

The year 1928 was a milestone in the history of the firm, because few motorcyclists at that time failed to doff a cap at the Francis-Barnett Pullman. As the catalogue of the day described it, it was a true luxury mount and constituted a complete breakaway once again from the groove of conventional motorcycle design. The guiding principles were not merely progressive, they were sound and unassailable. The perfect balance and even torque of a well designed, twin-cylinder two-stroke engine makes an immediate appeal to all enthusiasts; add to this the elimination of a high speed chain, the combining of the primary drive, clutch and gears in one unit with the engine to ensure perfect alignment and lubrication, and the specification would be as up to date today as it was then.

Oil was fed under pressure from the sump, the quantity being varied by the pressure in the crankcase, which in turn was controlled by the amount of the throttle opening. The supply of oil did not depend on engine speed but on the load applied to the engine.

Pullman Model 10, as found, at Bristol Show in 2006.

The primary drive was by worm gear, giving a 2.57 to 1 reduction running in oil, and ensured long life. The multi-plate clutch driven at engine speed provided finger-light control.

The gears were operated by an ingeniously simple movement of a lever mounted directly on the gearbox without the need for rods or any other connections. Top and bottom gears were selected by dogs, and the middle gear engaged by sliding pinions. The gear shaft running at a reduction of 2.5 times engine speed ensured easy gear changing, and an absolutely noiseless transmission. One could dwell on such an elegant design at great length.

Mention must be made of the uncanny silencing provided by this machine. The exhaust was just a pleasant purr, and far from being obtrusive in the slightest degree, was indeed very favourably commented upon even by non-motorists. The *Motor Cycling* road test of

the 1928 model stated: 'Comfort and silence impress themselves after an extended test.' It has been stated by some that the Pullman engine was designed and built by Villiers exclusively for Francis-Barnett; however, Jack Sizer was of the opinion that along with Francis-Barnett, SUN and Monet & Goyon of France took up this model. It was an in-line, two-stroke vertical twin with a 57.15mm bore and 67mm stroke producing 344cc capacity. As each cylinder had the identical bore and stroke of the 172cc Super Sports engine, there is a distinct possibility that it was a doubled-up version of that engine with some external alterations.

The pistons were aluminium, and the flywheel magneto was of typically conventional Villiers design, apart from a double pick-up on the ignition coil that was mounted forward of the engine and fitted to the crankshaft lengthways of the engine instead of across.

Immaculate Pullman now on display in the Sammy Miller Museum. (Courtesy FBOC)

Pullman in the process of being restored by owner D. Lonnergan, Bristol Show 2010.

The 1929 Empire Model No. 12.

It was priced at £68 5s, and suffered from cooling problems. Few were made, although use was later made of the surplus frames by fitting a Villiers IXA engine of 247cc and naming it the Empire.

The arrangement of the brakes on this machine is worthy of mention: 7in internal expanding front and rear brakes were coupled in such a manner that the pedal, adjoining the near-side footrest, applied them both almost simultaneously, the back one coming on just before the front. The pedal could literally be jumped on even on loose surfaces.

Pullman seen at the Bristol Show 2005. (Courtesy FBOC)

One more unique feature was the method of rear chain adjustment. The engine was attached to the frame at two points only: at the bottom was a heavy steel bar drilled right through eccentrically, and through which the footrest rod was passed. By loosening the outside footrest nuts, the engine assembly could be swivelled; an elongated hole was machined at the rear part of the aluminium engine casing to join up with the chain-stay frame tubes.

Lighting constituted a new departure, described by Villiers at the time as an 'accumulator charging type' – not to be confused with later types. Current generated from two coils on the armature plate was converted to direct current (DC) through a commutator, and conveyed to the battery and then on to the lamps.

The 1929 Season

For the 1929 season the company concentrated on appearance: the triangular petrol tank gave place to all steel welded saddle tanks, and Terry spring saddles were adopted, specially designed with extraordinary broad noses to fit flush and flat with the petrol tank. In addition Dunlop balloon tyres were introduced to all models. On Models No. 5 and No. 9, separate oil tanks

Machine Specifications

	Empire No. 12	'200' No. 14
Model	Empire No. 12	'200' No. 14
Manufacturing year	1929–30	1929–30
Engine	Villiers Mark XA single-cylinder, air-cooled two-stroke	Villiers Mark IE single-cylinder, air-cooled two-stroke
Number prefix	DZ, JZ	
Bore and stroke	67 × 70mm	61 × 67mm
Capacity	247cc	196cc
Lubrication	Automatic	Automatic
Ignition	Villiers flywheel magneto	Villiers flywheel magneto
Carburettor	Villiers two-lever with air filter	Villiers single-lever
Primary drive	Renold chain 0.5 × 0.25in	Renold chain 0.5 × 0.25in
Final drive	Renold chain 0.5 × 0.25in	Renold chain 0.5 × 0.25in
Gearbox	Albion three-speed	Albion three-speed
Gearbox ratios	5.25; 9.0; 16.0:1	5.8; 9.76; 17.6:1
Gearbox ratios optional	5.25; 7.6; 12.2:1	5.8; 8.5; 13.5:1
Frame	Fully triangulated, weldless tubing	Fully triangulated, weldless tubing
Suspension front	Link action with single compressed spring	Link action with single compressed spring
Suspension rear	Rigid	Rigid
Wheels front and rear	26in well-base	25in well-base
Tyres front and rear	26 × 3in Dunlop balloon	25 × 3in Dunlop balloon
Brake front	7in internal expanding	Internal expanding
Brake rear	7in internal expanding	Internal expanding

General Specifications

	1929 specification	1929 specification
Fuel tank capacity	1.63gal (7.4ltr)	1.63gal (7.4ltr)
Oil tank capacity	4 pints (2.3ltr)	Separate oil tank 4 pints (2.3ltr)
Overall length	81in (2,057mm)	79.25in (2,013mm)
Overall width	32in (813mm)	31in (787mm)
Wheel base	51.88in (1,318mm)	49.5in (1,257mm)
Ground clearance	5.38in (137mm)	4.75in (120mm)
Seat height (min.)	27.5in (698mm)	27in (686mm)
Dry weight	236lb (107kg)	181lb (82kg)

were fitted underneath the saddle, the Mark 2 Villiers automatic lubricator superseding the Mark 1. The principle was precisely the same, in that copper oil and pressure pipes throughout made the fitting of intermediate rubber connections unnecessary; at the same time the diameter of the pipes was increased from 0.25 to 0.313in (6 to 8mm).

The '200' Model No. 14

The range was supplemented that year by Model No. 14, known as the '200' Model and fitted with a 196cc engine, with a bore of 61mm and stroke of 67mm. Practically identical in design, apart from the capacity, to the 172cc 'Sports' engine, the 196cc was introduced essentially for use in a utility vehicle. With a low compression ratio it made for ridiculously easy starting and improved carburation, and extended the period between services to decarbonize the engine. The engine, identified by the prefix letters 'IE', was lubricated by the Villiers automatic lubricator so popular at the time, and was introduced largely with a view to increasing sales abroad: on certain parts of the Continent before the war, engines of less than 200cc were free of tax, and these were the markets it was intended to capture.

Empire Model No. 12

With the withdrawal of the Pullman, it became increasingly obvious that a demand had been created for a machine over and above 172cc. As a result of the demand, the Empire Model No. 12 came to be announced. Making very good use of the specification of the previous Pullman as regards frame, forks, hubs, handlebars and saddle, it only remained to complete the machine with the Villiers Mark IXA engine, which used the prefix letters 'DZ', having a bore and stroke of 67 × 70mm to give a capacity of 247cc.

Although speeds of 60mph (96km/h) were possible, the machine was most noted for its pulling power at low speeds, and contributing largely to this was the specification of an outside auxiliary flywheel fitted to the drive side of the crankshaft. It improved engine balance tremendously, providing something quite new in smooth running, particularly at low speeds. The long crankcase bushes undoubtedly helped, and much was made of a new idea in piston design: the Villiers inertia ring was a patented feature consisting of a special

The 1929 '200' Model 14 in the Sammy Miller Museum. (Courtesy E. J. Knoops)

steel ring placed above the compression ring in the top groove of the piston. The inertia ring was free to rotate and to move very slightly up and down in the groove. Obviously, as the inertia ring was free – being inert – it prevented the piston rings from gumming. If it is further explained that the ends of the inertia ring are made to butt, and that the section is such that the outer surface cannot touch the cylinder bore, perhaps its purpose will be even more obvious.

The gear change, previously mounted directly on to the gearbox, was moved up to the side of the petrol tank, where a small gate accommodated the short lever.

On this machine, 25 × 3in Dunlop balloon cord tyres were fitted as standard. The colour finish of all the 1929 range was black enamel: tank black cellulose with ivory white panels.

Prices and performance for the standard models were as follows: for No. 3, £26 and petrol consumption of 140mpg (2ltr/100km), with a maximum speed of 40mph (64km/h); for No. 4, £29, 140mpg (2ltr/100km) and 40mph (64km/h); for No. 5, £32 10s, 120mpg (2.4ltr/100km) and 48mph (77km/h); for No. 9, £36, 120mpg (2.4ltr/100km) and 55mph (88.5km/h); for No. 12, £39 10s, 90/100mpg (3/2.8ltr/100km) and 60mph (96km/h); and for No. 14, £33, 90/100mpg (3/2.8ltr/100km) and 50mph (80km/h). The petrol consumption and maximum speeds given were only approximate.

CHAPTER THREE

Manufacturing Seasons 1930–1940

The 1930 Season

The 1930 programme was virtually a consolidation of the previous year's. The cleaning-up process amounted to providing all internal expanding brake hubs with weather shields. Some trouble had been experienced through water finding its way into the hubs, and as a consequence brakes were fading in wet weather; the brake plates were therefore altered so they extended beyond the spoke flanges.

At the same time an opportunity was taken to strengthen the spokes of the wheels. All lightweight machines had previously been laced with twelve-gauge spokes, but as specifications grew, and engine power kept increasing, the added weight made it necessary to go up in gauge: thus ten-gauge were specified on the brake drum side of rear wheels. In addition, in order to relieve the heads of the spokes – some were breaking at this point – a modification was made by leading the spokes from the inside vertical face of the brake drum instead of from the outside flange. A much straighter pull was therefore provided, which effectively dealt with further trouble at this point.

The internal construction of the silencers remained the same. The length, however, was shortened, and the separate tail pipe gave way to an integral fish tail. The latter was a means of providing a subdued exhaust note, as long as the ends were not prised apart; they were welded so that the escape slot was only 0.063in, a measurement which caused practically every owner to think he could improve upon it. It is surprising how remarkably easy it is to mistake added (and objectionable) noise for increased engine power.

The only other thing that needs to be mentioned concerning the silencer was the manner in which the fixing strap was arranged. At first a butt weld was tried, followed by a strap welded part-way round the silencer. However, they both gave trouble insofar as they pulled a piece out of the silencer, and so it became necessary to specify a loose circlip, when there was no further trouble.

Gear-change controls were modified in detail only as regards the quadrant. Operation was simplified considerably, but the need for accurate adjustment of the linkage between the lever and the gearbox became a real necessity. Adjustment on the rod inbetween these two points was made by means of a yoke end, which was critical if accurate gear changing was to be enjoyed.

All 1930 models had electric lighting with large headlamps, adjustable footrests and spring-up rear stands. The colour finish was standardized for all machines as black enamel: tank black cellulose with ivory white panels and chromium-plated exhaust system.

Half of the models produced in 1929 were discontinued, namely Models 4 and 5, and the Pullman No. 10; Models 9, 12 and 14 continued in production. Model No. 4B was introduced in the place of Model 4, the differences between the two being in the transmission chain, the Terry spring seat and the internal expanding hub brakes. The 4B was priced at £30 for the standard model, the No. 9 at £36, the Empire No. 12 at £39, and No. 14 at £33 10s.

The Super-Sports '200' No. 15

The Super-Sports '200' Model No. 15 was next in line, using the Villiers 196cc Super-Sports engine,

1930 Model 9. (Courtesy FBOC)

Pre-war Cruiser and a Douglas machine owned by Tony Wright. (Courtesy FBOC)

A rare 1930 '200' Super-Sports Model 15. (Courtesy FBOC)

Machine Specifications

Model	1.5bhp No. 4B	Super-Sports '200' No. 15	Dominion No. 16
Manufacturing year	1930	1930	1930
Engine	Villiers Mark VIIIC single-cylinder, air-cooled two-stroke	Villiers Mark IE single-cylinder, air-cooled two-stroke	Villiers Mark IXB single-cylinder, air-cooled two-stroke
Number prefix	W	KZ, KZS	CZA
Bore and stroke	55 × 62mm	61 × 67mm	79 × 70mm
Capacity	147cc	196cc	342ccc
Lubrication	Petroil	Villiers autolube	Villiers autolube
Ignition	Villiers flywheel magneto	Variable	Variable
Carburettor	Villiers single-lever	Villiers two-lever	Villiers two-lever
Primary drive	Renold chain 10044	Renold chain 10044	Chain
Final drive	Renold chain 10044	Renold chain 10044	Chain
Gearbox	Albion two-speed	Albion three-speed	Albion three-speed
Gearbox ratios	6.75; 10.75:1	6.2; 10.5; 18.75:1	5.38; 8.0; 12.37:1
Gearbox ratios optional	Three-speed to order	6.2; 9.0; 14.5:1	5.38; 9.15; 16.36:1
Frame	Fully triangulated weldless tubes	Fully triangulated weldless tubes	Fully triangulated weldless tubes
Front suspension	Link-action type with single compression spring	Link-action type with single compression spring	Link-action type with single compression spring
Rear suspension	Rigid	Rigid	Rigid
Wheels front and rear	25in well-base	25in well-base	25in well-base
Brakes front	Internal expanding	Internal expanding	Internal expanding 7in
Brakes rear	Internal expanding	Internal expanding	Internal expanding 7in
Tyres front and rear	25 × 3in Dunlop cord	25 × 3in Dunlop cord	25 × 3in Dunlop cord

General Specifications

Fuel tank capacity	1.63gal (7.4ltr)	1.63gal (7.4ltr)	1.88gal (8.5ltr)
Wheelbase	49.75in (1,264mm)	49.63in (1,260mm)	51.88in (1,318mm)
Ground clearance	5.25in (133mm)	5.25in (133mm)	4.75in (120mm)
Overall width	29.25in (743mm)	28.5in (724mm)	28.5in (724mm)
Overall length	79.25in (2,013mm)	79.25in (2,013mm)	81.38in (2,067mm)
Seat height (min.)	27in (686mm)	27in (686mm)	27.5in (698mm)
Dry weight	168lb (76kg)	189lb (86kg)	222lb (101kg)

with prefix letters KZ and KZS. Bore and stroke were 61 × 67mm. Fitted with an aluminium piston and aluminium detachable cylinder head, its chief distinguishing feature was the extended finning on both the cylinder and head. In all other respects the design followed closely the same lines as the 172cc engine – certainly the big end, magneto and carburettor all interchanged. The price with electric lighting was £36 10s.

The Dominion No. 16

For the enthusiast who wanted something larger than the 250cc Empire, the Dominion Model No. 16 became available. Incorporated into the frame was the Villiers Mark IXB engine with a bore and stroke of 79 × 70mm, the capacity 342cc and the prefix CZA. The engine had a detachable aluminium cylinder head and aluminium piston, flywheel magneto and variable ignition. The Villiers two-lever type carburettor, complete with air filter, was fitted, and automatic lubrication with a separate oil tank was specified. The price with electric lighting was £40. In every respect all parts, except for the engine, interchanged with the Empire Model No. 12.

In retrospect the expected advantage of variable ignition was not in fact realized, as the system was being much abused. The armature plate was permitted a certain amount of movement on the crankcase bush, a steel lever extending from the plate providing the means by which the armature was moved round. With the lever half way between the extremes of the ratchet, timing was then 0.313in before top dead centre. However, over-enthusiastic owners would use too much advance, with the result that it became necessary to blank off the bottom half of the ratchet altogether.

Experience at the works was proving that more harm was done with the lever at full advance than at full retard, because the engine was then labouring and overheating. For this reason it was decided to remove the variable ignition lever, and it is interesting to note that such facilities were never considered again. Since then the ignition timing on all Villiers two-stroke engines was fixed.

Registered Design No. 694755.

Dominion Model No. 16.

342 c.c.

The 1930 Dominion Model No. 16.

Machine Specifications

Model	Black Hawk No. 17	Falcon No. 18	Merlin No. 19
Manufacturing year	1930	1930	1931
Engine	Villiers Mark IIE, single-cylinder, air-cooled two-stroke	Villiers IE Super-Sports, single-cylinder, air-cooled two-stroke *	Villiers Mark VIIIC, single-cylinder, air-cooled two-stroke
Number prefix	KZ, KZS	KZ, KZS; 172cc T, TL	W
Bore and stroke	61 × 67mm	61 × 67mm	55 × 62mm
Capacity	196cc	196cc	147cc
Lubrication	Petroil	Villiers autolube	Petroil
Ignition	Villiers flywheel magneto	Villiers flywheel magneto	Villiers flywheel magneto
Carburettor	Villiers single-lever	Villiers two-lever	Villiers two-lever
Primary drive	Renold chain 4193	Renold chain 4193	Chain
Final drive	Renold chain 10044	Renold chain 10044	Chain
Gearbox	Albion three-speed	Albion three-speed	Not known
Gearbox ratios	5.9; 10.0; 17.8:1	5.9; 10.0; 17.8:1	Not known
Frame	Fully triangulated weldless tubes	Fully triangulated weldless tubes	Fully triangulated weldless tubes
Front suspension	Link-action type with single compression spring	Link-action type with single compression spring: damper	Not known
Rear suspension	Rigid	Rigid	Not known
Wheels front and rear	25in well-base	25in well-base	Not known
Brakes front	5in diameter	5in diameter	5in diameter
Brakes rear	5in diameter	5in diameter	5in diameter
Tyres front and rear	25 × 3in Dunlop cord	25 × 3in Dunlop cord	Not known

General Specifications

Fuel tank capacity	1.63gal (7.4ltr)	1.63gal (7.4ltr)	Not known
Oil tank	Not known	Not known	Not known
Wheelbase	49.63in (1,260mm)	49.63in (1,260mm)	Not known
Ground clearance	5.25in (133mm)	5.25in (133mm)	Not known
Overall width	29.25in (743mm)	29.25in (743mm)	Not known
Overall length	80in (2,032mm)	80in (2,032mm)	Not known
Seat height (min.)	27in (686mm)	27in (686mm)	Not known
Dry weight	188lb (85kg)		Not known

* 172cc Super-Sports available with petroil or autolube

Probably identical to Merlin 23

Mrs Meeten's Five Day Journey

During the week 21–26 October 1929, Mrs Meeten, riding a 1930 model 172cc Francis-Barnett, completed a 1,000-mile (1,609km) economy test. Mrs Meeten, the wife of T. G. (Tommy) Meeten, in five days rode a distance of 1,007 miles (1,620km) at an average speed of 20mph (32km/h) and 196.5mpg (1.4ltr/100km). The first day's run was from the ACU Headquarters in London, to Wetherby. On the second day, Mrs Meeten's ride took her from Wetherby to Edinburgh, a distance in excess of 200 miles (322km). On the third day she had to contend with strong winds and rain as well as the mountain sections on her way to Carlisle via Shap Fell. The fourth day brought extremely adverse conditions, with continuous rain that flooded some stretches of road, but she took everything in her stride on her journey from the start of the stage at Warrington. The road section of the test on the fifth day finished with a long run in good weather conditions, from Bridgwater via Exeter and Salisbury to Dorking.

The machine was then taken to the Brooklands Circuit for speed and hill-climbing tests. Mrs Meeten did two laps of the track at 45mph (72km/h), followed by twenty hill-test climbs. Anyone trying to walk the distance would have needed to have had his boots soled and heeled twice, costing 15s (75p) even in those days, whereas by comparison the cost of petrol and oil amounted to almost 10s (50p); thus it was that Francis-Barnett maintained it was indeed cheaper to ride than walk.

There is an unconfirmed rumour that Mrs Meeten's machine is residing somewhere in Norfolk.

172 c.c. Super Sports Engine fitted to order.

HK demand for a Sporting Lightweight is constantly increasing. Our responsibility is to meet this demand with progressive improvement—to embody in each successive design features which experience dictates as necessary, or desirable. This we have done.

Study the detailed specification. It gives some impression of the completeness of the Falcon, and of the care devoted to its perfection.

Lighting is by Miller 6-volt set with 12 amp. battery, charged by separate dynamo. Diplite and Dimmer Switches and High Frequency Electric Horn form part of the equipment.

Years of competition experience are embodied in the Falcon. We offer it with high commendation.

ABOVE: The 1930 Black Hawk Model No. 17.

RIGHT: The 1930 Falcon Model No. 18.

The 1931 SEASON

After 1930, with its programme of six models, the company had to compete in a market that was proving difficult, and the challenge was met by producing only two models. In 1931 the bird series started, beginning with the Black Hawk Model No. 17.

The Black Hawk Model No. 17

Retaining the original frame layout, the diameter of the tubing increased from 0.625in to 0.75in, this providing increased lateral stability. Knock-out wheel spindles, which had been so characteristic of Francis-Barnetts for eight years, were then superseded by conventional solid axles.

The jockey sprocket arrangement for rear chain adjustment was dispensed with in favour of draw-back adjusters, the latter necessitating a brazed joint for the first time in the build-up of the triangular frame. The chain-stay frame tube was increased from 0.625in to 0.75in, and into the end was brazed a steel slotted pressing to take the wheel axle. After some early problems, second thoughts brought about an early modification of this particular pressing, after which no further trouble was experienced.

The long brake anchorage arms front and rear were shortened, and both were bolted to the frame by loose clips. A modification with the rear fixing clip was also necessary in order to withstand the load, and the introduction of a box clip to replace the original plain clip was all that was necessary to prevent further complaints arising from that source.

Of perhaps greater concern at that time was the need to deal with petrol tank failure. By increasing the strength of the frame it quickly became apparent that stresses not previously taken into account were breaking the petrol tank holding straps, and it was therefore a matter of urgency to improve matters in that department. Instead of a plain strap on the bottom of the tank, the edges were turned down at right angles, and once again further trouble was averted. Gear-change quadrants on the side of the petrol tank were altered slightly to make adjustment of the linkage less critical, and the notching for neutral position was removed entirely.

Model No. 17 had yet another version of a Villiers 196cc engine, this time inclined at an angle of 26 degrees; it was the Mark IIE, prefix letter XZ and XZA.

On this type of engine the bore and stroke were the same as the previous 196cc, also the cast-iron piston was retained. The Mark IIE had only one exhaust port compared with the Mark IE's two. The flange-fitting exhaust pipe, however, was replaced by a stub fixing.

A novel arrangement was also made to lubricate the front chain in this year's programme. The exhaust pipe was drilled, and a small tube mounted by a clip bypassed the oily residue from the exhaust gases on to the chain. The results were highly satisfactory; chain noise was reduced, on the one hand, by the specification of the 0.375in pitch-type chain – helped, of course, by the automatic lubricator from the exhaust.

Direct lighting was retained for Model 17, although a slight variation was made to the wiring: for the first time the bulbs were wired in parallel, and in addition a tubular dry battery was incorporated for stand-by purposes.

Specification included a single-lever Villiers carburettor with jet control, Albion three-speed gearbox and lubrication by petroil. The finish was black enamel, the tank black with white ivory panels. Exposed parts were chromium plated.

The Falcon No. 18

A companion model to the Black Hawk 17 was the Falcon Model No. 18. The distinguishing features of the machine were the 196cc Super-Sports engine as on the Model No. 15, but of greater importance was the provision, for the first time, of a Miller SUS dynamo and separate lighting set with a 6v wet battery. The dynamo, mounted on the engine plates at the rear, was chain driven. Two sprockets were attached by means of their left-hand threads to the engine sprocket adaptor, the inner sprocket driving the dynamo and the outer sprocket taking the front chain. The same dynamo was used on later machines – in fact until the beginning of World War II. The engine lubrication was automatic, with a separate 1gal capacity oil tank. The Albion gearbox was the same as was used for the Black Hawk, and the colour finish identical.

The year started off with all concentration on only two models, the frames, forks, wheels and controls all interchanging. Previously the machines had been assembled individually; however, it now became necessary to plan, not only in the specification and design stages, but also in the actual production of the

Machine Specifications

Model	Kestrel No. 20	Black Hawk Nos 21 and 21M	Falcon No. 22
Manufacturing year	1931	1932	1932
Engine	Villiers Mark VIIIC single-cylinder, air-cooled two-stroke	Villiers Mark VIIIC single-cylinder, air-cooled two-stroke	Villiers Mark IE Super-Sports single-cylinder, air-cooled two-stroke*
Number prefix	W	XZ, XZA	KZ, KZS
Bore and stroke	55 × 62mm	61 × 67mm	61 × 67mm
Capacity	147cc	196cc	196cc
Lubrication	Petroil	Petroil	Automatic, separate oil tank
Ignition	Villiers flywheel magneto	Villiers flywheel magneto	Villiers flywheel magneto
Carburettor	Not known	Villiers two-lever	Villiers two-lever
Primary drive	Not known	Renold chain 110036	Renold chain 110036
Final drive	Not known	Renold chain 110044	Renold chain 110044
Gearbox	Not known	Albion three-speed	Albion three-speed
Gearbox ratios	Not known	5.9; 10.0; 17.8:1	5.9; 10.0; 17.8:1
Frame	Fully triangulated weldless tubes	Fully triangulated weldless tubes	Fully triangulated weldless tubes
Front suspension	Not known	Link-action with single spring and shock absorbers	Link-action type with single compression spring, shock absorbers and steering damper
Rear suspension	Not known	Rigid	Rigid
Wheels front and rear	Not known	19 × 2.25in well-base	19 × 2.25in well-base
Brakes front	5in diameter	5in diameter	5in diameter
Brakes rear	5in diameter	5in diameter	5in diameter
Tyres front and rear	Not known	25 × 3in Dunlop cord	25 × 3in Dunlop cord

General Specifications

Fuel tank capacity	Not known	1.63gal (7.4ltr)	1.63gal (7.4ltr)
Oil tank	Not known	Not known	4 pints (2.3ltr)
Wheelbase	Not known	49.63in (1,260mm)	49.5in (1,257mm)
Ground clearance	Not known	5.25in (133mm)	5.25in (133mm)
Overall width	Not known	27.75in (705mm)	28in (711mm)
Overall length	Not known	80in (2,032mm)	80in (2,032mm)
Seat height (min.)	Not known	27in (686mm)	27in (686mm)
Dry weight	Not known	Model 21 186lb (84kg); 21M 198lb (90kg)	210lb (95kg)
	Probably identical to Kestrel 24		*Villiers 172cc Super-Sports engine as an alternative

machines. These were now assembled on a track system, and runners were laid down in the factory on which the assembly trolleys carried machines in the course of building. From end to end of the works huge piles of materials were laid out in various stages of assembly, some sub-assembled, others prefabricated, to use a modern hackneyed phrase, the objective being to speed up the building process while at the same time minimizing any unnecessary handling of material. The idea was successful, with more machines being built in 1931 than in any previous year.

The Merlin No. 19 and Kestrel No. 20

A mid-season machine was introduced following the budget concession of that year (1931), when machines with an engine capacity of less than 150cc were allowed a reduction in road tax. To take advantage of this concession, Models 19 and 20 – Merlin and Kestrel respectively – were brought out. Both machines employed the frame and fork layout of that year in common with the Black Hawk and Falcon; the specification of the Merlin was identical to the Kestrel, with the exception that electric lighting, leg-shields, carrier and horn were not included. In all other respects the specifications were identical.

With the Villiers Mark VIIIC reintroduced and fitted vertically in the frame, the machine was virtually a reversion to Model No. 4, which had been discontinued the previous year after an unbroken run of eight years, so strong was the following for this type

of machine. Lightweight 4in internal expanding brake hubs were fitted front and rear, and the mudguards were narrower than those fitted to other machines in the same programme. The gearbox was a two-speed Albion CJ pattern, the front chain being the heavy cycle type, as against the heavy motorcycle type fitted to the previous Model No. 4. The exhaust system reverted to a short pattern, very similar in outline and varying only in detail from the type current from 1923 to 1927 – a welcome return which was kind to the engine and a most efficient system.

In 1931 a new frame numbering system was started using a two-letter prefix, the first letter denoting the year, the second letter giving some indication of the model; 'I' and 'Q' were omitted, as were the years 1941 to 1946. 'A' was used for 1931 and the letter system ran to 1958, when 'Z' was used. 'A' was used again for 1959, and ended in 'I' for 1966, when the company ceased trading.

The 1932 Season

After such a good year in 1931 of vastly increased production, with fewer types of machines, one would have thought that the following year would have been better still. It was, however, becoming increasingly obvious that an extra good year was succeeded by only a fair year, and indeed, prosperity and mediocrity seemed to have alternated for a number of years. 1932 must be regarded as a year of mediocrity.

Four pre-war machines; one is a 1932 Falcon 22 (KJ 331), and another possibly a 'Zarelect' or Model 4 (RW 3579) at the end of the row. (Courtesy FBOC)

*1932 Falcon 22 on the FBOC stand,
Founders' Day 2009.*

The Black Hawk No. 21 and No. 21M

The Black Hawk and Falcon models were continued very largely as they were. The Black Hawk became Model No. 21 and No. 21M; the 21 had direct lighting from special coils in the flywheel, with parking lights operating from a dry battery, and the 21M was fitted with the Miller 6v 24w dynamo lighting set. A 7in diameter headlamp and rear light were standard. Colour finish was of black enamel, a black tank with ivory panels, and the bright parts chromium plated.

The Black Hawk 21 was priced at £25 15s, and the 21M at £28. The Falcon became Model No. 22. Harwil hubs gave place to British hubs, with solid spindles on all models except the Merlin and Kestrel, which now became the Merlin Model 23 and the Kestrel Model 24.

The characteristics of the fully triangulated frame and forks were retained, but with the forks being modified for several reasons: firstly, primarily to incorporate a friction damper; secondly, to eliminate the stampings from which the top and bottom links were made; and thirdly, to provide a more responsive action without increasing the cost of production. All three were served by a fork comprised chiefly of fabricated steel pressings. The subsidiary company, Clarendon Pressing & Welding Co. Ltd, was now beginning to assert itself, and was contributing in no small measure to design generally with its specialized presswork, steel and tubular components.

This was not to be wondered at when it is realized that Gordon Francis was the managing director of both companies. In formulating the design for the motorcycle, he was making increasingly good use of the facilities that the subsidiary company had available. The action of the fork was principally the same as before, except that in place of the bottom link there was now a pair of simple steel pressings. The top link comprised two banjo-shaped steel pressings brazed to a malleable centre casting. The banjo end of the links accommodated a bonded asbestos friction disc on each side.

The Lapwing No. 25 and No. 25M

Two new machines were to make their appearance in 1932, still keeping to the bird series. Within the frames of the Lapwing models 25 and 25M was the Villiers Mark XIIC engine, prefix letters GY and GYF respectively. With a bore and stroke of 53mm and 67mm, the engine was referred to as a 'long stroke 148cc'. Model 25 had direct lighting from special coils in the flywheel, with parking lights from a dry battery; Model 25M had a Miller 6v 24w dynamo lighting set.

Colour finish was of black enamel, a black tank with ivory panels, and the bright parts chromium-plated. Prices were £24 15s for Model 25, and £27 for Model 25M.

Villiers were breaking away from using the flanged exhaust ports, and now used two stubs facing forward to which the exhaust pipes were fixed by means of

Machine Specifications

Model	Merlin No. 23	Kestrel No. 24	Lapwing No. 25 and 25M
Manufacturing year	1932	1932	1932
Engine	Villiers Mark VIIIC single-cylinder, air-cooled two-stroke	Villiers Mark VIIIC single-cylinder, air-cooled two-stroke	Villiers Mark XIIC single-cylinder, air-cooled two-stroke
Number prefix	W	W	GY, GYF
Bore and stroke	55 × 62mm	55 × 62mm	53 × 67mm
Capacity	147cc	147cc	148cc
Lubrication	Petroil	Petroil	Petroil
Ignition	Villiers flywheel magneto	Villiers flywheel magneto	Villiers flywheel magneto
Carburettor	Villiers two-lever	Villiers two-lever	Villiers two-lever
Primary drive	Renold chain 170044	Renold chain 170044	Renold chain 110036
Final drive	Renold chain 110044	Renold chain 110044	Renold chain 110044
Gearbox	Albion two-speed	Albion two-speed	Albion three-speed
Gearbox ratios	7.0; 11.9:1	7.0; 11.9:1	6.9; 11.7; 20.9:1
Frame	Fully triangulated weldless tubes	Fully triangulated weldless tubes	Fully triangulated weldless tubes
Front suspension	Link-action type with single compression spring incorporating shock absorbers	Link-action type with single compression spring incorporating shock absorbers	Link-action type with single compression spring incorporating shock absorbers
Rear suspension	Rigid	Rigid	Rigid
Wheels front and rear	19 × 2.25in well-base	19 × 2.25in well-base	19 × 2.25in well-base
Brakes front	4in diameter	4in diameter	4in diameter
Brakes rear	4in diameter	4in diameter	4in diameter
Tyres front and rear	25 × 2.75in Dunlop cord	25 × 2.75in Dunlop cord	25 × 2.75in Dunlop cord

General Specifications

Fuel tank capacity	1.63gal (7.4ltr)	1.63gal (7.4ltr)	1.63gal (7.4ltr)
Ground clearance	49.62in (1,260mm)	49.63in (1,260mm)	49.63in (1,260mm)
Overall width	5.75in (146mm)	5.75in (146mm)	5.75in (146mm)
Overall length	27.75in (705mm)	27.75in (705mm)	27.75in (705mm)
Seat height (min.)	79.25in (2,013mm)	79.25in (2,013mm)	79.25in (2,013mm)
Dry weight	26.5in (673mm) 158 lb (72kg)	26.5in (673mm) 158lb (72kg)	26.5in (673mm) Model 25, 173lb (78.5kg); Model 25M, 187lb (85kg)
		Includes electric lighting, leg shields, carrier and horn	

The 1932 Merlin Model No. 23.

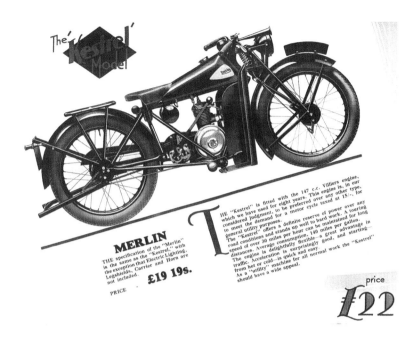

The 'Kestrel' Model

THE "Kestrel" is fitted with the 147 c.c. Villiers engine, which we have used for eight years. This engine is, in our considered judgment, to be preferred over any other type, to meet the demand for a motor cycle taxed at 15/-, for general utility purposes.

The "Kestrel" offers a definite reserve of power over any road conditions and stands up well to hard work. A touring speed of over 30 miles per hour can be maintained for long distances. Average consumption, 140 miles per gallon.

The engine is delightfully flexible—a great advantage in traffic. Acceleration is surprisingly good, and starting—from hot or cold—is quick and easy.

As a "utility" machine for all normal work the "Kestrel" should have a wide appeal.

price £22

MERLIN

THE specification of the "Merlin" is the same as the "Kestrel," with the exception that Electric Lighting, Legshields, Carrier and Horn are not included.

PRICE £19 19s.

loose clips. Engine performance was vastly superior to the previous 147cc short-stroke engine; it was capable of 40mph (64km/h) for long periods without fatigue, and petrol consumption was in the region of 110mpg (2.6ltr/100km). With such a good start it was inevitable that this was an engine type that had come to stay – and stay it did, until manufacture was discontinued in 1940.

Direct two-pole lighting was part of the specification, unless the Miller set was ordered as an extra. The Villiers middleweight carburettor with its two-lever control was continued, the only change being that regarding the combination of the jet and taper needle. All previous middleweight carburettors had used a No. 3 jet: now came the need to specify a No. 2.

While on the one hand complaints were occasionally made regarding the 'stodgy' design, on the other this

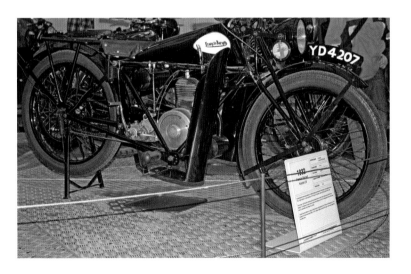

1932 Kestrel 24 owned by Sue Dorling, now in the CTM.

very conservative design – which at this time was large-ly a variation on the same theme (in that frame, forks, wheels, handlebars were the 'mixture as before') – was being applauded in many other quarters.

One of the most important features of buying a Francis-Barnett motorcycle was that it did not 'date' – the consequence of which was that abnormally high prices were always the rule whether buying or selling second-hand. Machines such as this – all fab-ricated of small components, many of which inter-changed on varying models – did simplify the firm's purchasing and storage, and the consequent saving was passed on to the purchaser. At this time, other makers were feeling the pinch of reduced personal income and consequential sales resistance; however, Francis & Barnett were pressing on regardless – and never were they more active than in the experimen-tal department.

The Condor No. 26

The other new machine to be introduced in 1932 was: the Condor Model No. 26. There was an insistent demand for a sprint machine with a 'sporty' appearance, and for those who wanted a dual-purpose machine for utility or sporting weekends, here was the machine. It used the 172cc Villiers 'Brooklands S' engine, a hotted-up version of the original T.T. Super-Sports with alu-minium detachable head; deep aluminium fins on the cylinder; aluminium piston with inertia ring; padded and polished crankshaft to give increased crankcase compression; and variable ignition.

A step forwards was made in engine design, and made available to the public for the first time. Up to this time, the Brooklands engine had been manufactured to order exclusively for named riders and works competi-tion machines. It was sometimes referred to as the 'Y'-type engine, because the engine number prefix was Y.

*Arthur Walls' prize-winning 1932
Condor Model 26. (Courtesy FBOC)*

*Another of Arthur Walls' rare
Condors. (Courtesy FBOC)*

Machine Specifications

Model	Condor No. 26	Lapwing No. 27	Lapwing No. 28
Manufacturing year	1932	1933	1933
Engine	Villiers 'Brooklands S', single-cylinder, air-cooled two-stroke	Villiers Mark XIIC, single-cylinder, air-cooled two-stroke	Villiers Mark XIIC, single-cylinder, air-cooled two-stroke
Number prefix	Not known	GY, GYF	GY, GYF
Bore and stroke	57.15 × 67mm	53 × 67mm	53 × 67mm
Capacity	172cc	148cc	148cc
Lubrication	Automatic, separate oil tank	Petroil	Petroil
Ignition	Villiers flywheel magneto	Villiers flywheel magneto	Miller coil
Carburettor	Villiers two-lever	Villiers two-lever	Villiers two-lever
Primary drive	Renold chain 110036	Appleby chain 10664	Appleby chain 10664
Final drive	Renold chain 110044	Appleby chain10844	Appleby chain10844
Gearbox	Albion three-speed	Albion three-speed	Albion three-speed
Gearbox ratios	6.9; 9.75; 15:1	6.8; 12.0; 19.5:1	6.8; 12.0; 19.5:1
Gearbox ratios optional	6.5; 11.0; 19.75:1	Not known	Not known
Frame	Fully triangulated weldless tubes	Fully triangulated weldless tubes	Fully triangulated weldless tubes
Front suspension	Link-action type with single compression spring, shock absorbers and steering damper	Triangulated; single compression spring	Triangulated; single compression spring
Rear suspension	Rigid	Rigid	Rigid
Wheels front and rear	19 × 2.25in well-base	19 × 2.25in well-base	19 × 2.25in well-base
Brakes front	5in diameter	4in diameter	4in diameter
Brakes rear	5in diameter	4in diameter	4in diameter
Tyres front and rear	25 × 3in Solo Sports	25 × 3in Dunlop cord	25 × 3in Dunlop cord

General Specifications

Fuel tank capacity	1.63gal (7.4ltr)	1.63gal (7.4ltr)	1.63gal (7.4ltr)
Oil tank	4 pints (2.3ltr)	N/A	N/A
Wheelbase	49.5in (1,257mm)	49.63in (1,260mm)	49.63in (1,260mm)
Ground clearance	6.75in (171mm)	5.75in (146mm)	5.75in (146mm)
Overall width	28in (711mm)	27.75in (705mm)	27.75in (705mm)
Overall length	80in (2,032mm)	79.25in (2,013mm)	79.25in (2,013mm)
Seat height (min.)	27in (686mm)	27in (686mm)	27in (686mm)
Dry weight	195lb (88kg)	187lb (85kg)	196lb (89kg)

1932 Lapwing Model 27 before restoration, owner Tony Woods. (Courtesy Tony Woods)

1932 Lapwing Model 27 after restoration, owner Tony Woods. (Courtesy Tony Woods)

1933 Lapwing Model 28, owner Jack Lloyd, seen at the Battlesbridge Show 2009.

Another notable feature of the Condor was the exhaust system. Reverting yet again to the earliest of exhaust systems, the two short exhaust pipes from the cylinder – of no more than 6in (15cm) in length – led into a cylindrical expansion chamber right up against the frame. It certainly was a high level system, for from the uppermost part of the expansion chamber a pipe led alongside the cylinder and on top of the magneto, and to this pipe was attached the exhaust silencer of the type standardized for other machines of the year. A torque stay was fitted between the cylinder head rear holding-down bolt and the frame. It was described as a highly tuned, Super-Sports job that would appeal to many riders in the 175cc class.

Dunlop Solo Sports tyres 25 × 3in, a chromium-plated tank, a twist-grip throttle control, direct lighting and a parking battery were included in the specification. The machine was advertised at a price of £35.

The 1933 Season

In 1933 the 147cc Villiers Mark VIIIC engine was deleted from the range of engines used. The XIIC of 148cc was so firmly entrenched that the short-stroke engine was rendered obsolete, and because of this, Merlin and Kestrel models went out of production.

Although there were few constructional changes in the 1933 range, those that were made were both practical and interesting. For instance, the clip fixing for the front of the engine was replaced by a lug to which the engine plates were bolted. The lug was attached to the main frame cross-member in an ingenious manner, in that the central portion of the main crossbar is straight-splined and pressed into the bore of the lug so that it cannot turn or move sideways. The system is simple and sound, and conforms to the Francis-Barnett practice of avoiding brazing as far as was possible.

Lapwings, Black Hawks and Falcons were continued, but with one major difference: although magneto ignition was still available to order, the accent was on the Miller coil ignition for the first time. In operation the Miller dynamo was fundamentally the same as the SUS system used in conjunction with the DMG3 dynamo of 1931–32. The current was 6v on all models – 24 watt on the Lapwing Model No. 28 and Black Hawk Model No. 30, and 36 watt on Falcon Model No. 31. The Lapwing models 27 and 28 used the Villiers Mark XIIC engine, prefix GY or GYF; the Black Hawk Models 29 and 30 the Villiers 196cc Mark IIE engine, prefix XZ or XZA; and the Falcon Model No. 31 the Villiers 196cc Mark IIE Super-Sports engine, prefix KS or KZS.

All five models used the Villiers two-lever carburettor and the Albion three-speed gearbox, and were equipped with knee grips, steering damper, 26 × 3in Dunlop tyres, twist-grip throttle control (with separate handlebar adjustment for the jet needle), front stand, chromium-plated silencers, and the system of exhaust-fed oiling for the primary chain developed by Francis-Barnett. The finish was the same in each case: black enamel cycle parts and a chromium-plated tank with black panels, or the option of red or blue panels.

1933 Falcon Model 31 with 196cc Villiers Mark IIE Super-Sports engine, owner Jack Lloyd, seen at the Battlesbridge Show 2009.

Machine Specifications

Model	Black Hawk No. 29	Black Hawk No. 30	Falcon No. 31
Manufacturing year	1933	1933	1933
Engine	Villiers IIE, single-cylinder, air-cooled two-stroke	Villiers IIE, single-cylinder, air-cooled two-stroke	Villiers IIE, single-cylinder, air-cooled two-stroke
Number prefix	XZ, XZA	XZ, XZA	KZ, KZS
Bore and stroke	61 × 67mm	61 × 67mm	61 × 67mm
Capacity	196cc	196cc	196cc
Lubrication	Petroil	Petroil	Villiers autolube
Ignition	Villiers flywheel magneto	Miller coil	Miller coil
Carburettor	Villiers two-lever	Villiers two-lever	Villiers two-lever
Primary drive	Appleby chain 10664	Appleby chain 10664	Appleby chain 10664
Final drive	Appleby chain 10344	Appleby chain 10344	Appleby chain 10344
Gearbox	Albion three-speed	Albion three-speed	Albion three-speed
Gearbox ratios	6.2; 11.0; 17.2:1	6.2; 11.0; 17.2:1	6.2; 11.0; 17.2:1
Frame	Fully triangulated weldless tubes	Fully triangulated weldless tubes	Fully triangulated weldless tubes
Front suspension	Triangulated; single compression spring	Triangulated; single compression spring	Triangulated; single compression spring
Rear suspension	Rigid	Rigid	Rigid
Wheels front and rear	19 × 2.25in well-base	19 × 2.25in well-base	19 × 2.25in well-base
Brakes front	5in diameter	5in diameter	5in diameter
Brakes rear	5in diameter	5in diameter	5in diameter
Tyres front and rear	25 × 3in Dunlop cord	25 × 3.00in Dunlop cord	25 × 3in Dunlop cord

General Specifications

Fuel tank capacity	1.63gal (7.4ltr)	1.63gal (7.4ltr)	1.63gal (7.4ltr)
Wheelbase	49.63in (1,260mm)	49.63in (1,260mm)	49.63in (1,260mm)
Ground clearance	5.75in (146mm)	5.75in (146mm)	5.75in (146mm)
Overall width	27.75in (705mm)	27.75in (705mm)	27.75in (705mm)
Overall length	79.25in (2,013mm)	79.25in (2,013mm)	79.25in (2,013mm)
Seat height (min.)	27in (686mm)	27in (686mm)	27in (686mm)
Dry weight	191lb (87kg)	198lb (90kg)	206lb (93kg)

The 1932 Cruiser Model No. 32.

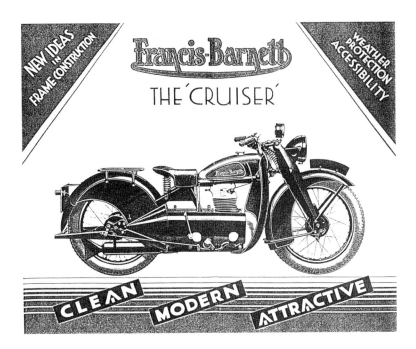

For those models that employed direct lighting, the Villiers Company had developed a new four-pole flywheel dynamo-magneto stated to give an increase of 50 per cent in the light output at high speeds, and an even greater percentage at low speeds; it essentially resembled the earlier two-pole flywheels, but by careful arrangement it had been possible to include four magnets and pole-pieces, thus increasing the output. This was to be incorporated on Lapwing Model No. 27 and Black Hawk Model No. 29; the four-pole direct lighting was specified on these machines, since it was a step forward. Previously, along with the two-pole magneto, two lighting coils wired in parallel were employed. Now came four poles in the flywheel equally spaced, the four magnets being held in position by top plates secured by the pole shoe-fixing screws. Along with this flywheel a single lighting coil was used, and the new design coincided with a change in the method of fixing the armature plate assembly.

At this time the steel split bush method was rendered obsolete in favour of a much more rigid attachment. A spigot was machined on the crankcase to correspond with a step in the armature plate, and this then fitted to the crankcase by means of two cheese-headed screws located inside the oil well and on either side of the mainshaft. A special lamp had been developed to suit this type of lighting, and the parking battery (a standard size of Ever-Ready battery, obtainable almost anywhere) was concealed within the body of the lamp itself. The parking-light bulbs were of the low consumption type, and both bulbs and battery were readily accessible and detachable.

The pre-war Cruiser was the machine that elicited the most correspondence to Francis & Barnett. In fact, from the number of letters that simply poured into the works practically every day, it is obvious that this type of machine created a great deal of interest in the motorcycling fraternity of the time.

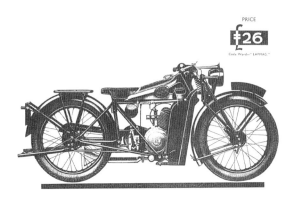

The 1934 Lapwing Model No. 33.

Machine Specifications

Model	Cruiser No. 32	Lapwing No. 33	Lapwing No. 34
Manufacturing year	1933	1934	1934
Engine	Villiers Mark XIVA, single-cylinder, air-cooled two-stroke	Villiers Mark XIIC, single-cylinder, air-cooled two-stroke	Villiers Mark XIIC, single-cylinder, air-cooled two-stroke
Number prefix	BYP	GY/GYF	GY/GYF
Bore and stroke	63 × 80mm	53 × 57mm	53 × 57mm
Capacity	249cc	148cc	148cc
Lubrication	Petroil	Petroil	Petroil
Ignition	Miller coil	Villiers flywheel magneto	Miller coil
Carburettor	Villiers two-lever	Villiers two-lever	Villiers two-lever
Primary drive	Appleby 0.375 × .230in	Renold chain 110036	Renold chain 110036
Final drive	Appleby 0.50 × .205in	Renold chain 110044	Renold chain 110044
Gearbox	Albion four-speed	Albion three-speed	Albion three-speed
Gearbox ratios	5.75; 7.75; 10.25; 16.75:1	6.8; 10.7; 18.9:1	6.8; 10.7; 18.9:1
Frame	Front member and head in one steel forging; side members in deep channel steel	Fully triangulated weldless tubes	Fully triangulated weldless tubes
Number prefix	CA	D	D
Front suspension	Box-section welded steel blades; single compression spring	Triangulated; single compression spring	Triangulated; single compression spring
Rear suspension	Rigid	Rigid	Rigid
Wheels front and rear	Not known	19 × 2.25in well-base	19 × 2.25in well-base
Brakes front	5in diameter	4in diameter	4in diameter
Brakes rear	5in diameter	4in diameter	4in diameter
Tyres front and rear	26 × 3.25in Dunlop cord	25 × 3in Dunlop cord	25 × 3in Dunlop cord

General Specifications

Fuel tank capacity	2gal (9ltr)	1.63gal (7.4ltr)	1.63gal (7.4ltr)
Wheel base	54in (1,372mm)	49.63in (1,260mm)	49.63in (1,260mm)
Ground clearance	6in (152.4mm)	5.75in (146mm)	5.75in (146mm)
Overall width	27.75in (705mm)	27.75in (705mm)	27.75in (705mm)
Overall length	82.5in (2,096mm)	79.25in (2,013mm)	79.25in (2,013mm)
Seat height (min.)	26.5in (673mm)	27in (686mm)	27in (686mm)
Dry weight	Not known	178lb (81kg)	198lb (90kg)

1933 Cruiser in immaculate condition, owner Trevor Wells; FBOC AGM, Hagley.

It must be mentioned, however, that although the Cruiser was the nearest to perfection in motorcycling once again as far as Francis & Barnett were concerned, sales never really boomed as might have been expected. That there was intense interest is not denied, and sales were also consistent and showed a progressive increase between 1933 and 1940, when production of all machines was discontinued. Notwithstanding the loyalty of dealers and Cruiser owners who were avid enthusiasts, the overall result was disappointing; this is perhaps why the Cruiser type was not immediately reintroduced post-war.

Just how did a machine of this specification come into being? It will be remembered that following the withdrawal of the Pullman came the Empire Model No. 12 of 247cc, and after that the Dominion Model No. 16 of 342cc. Successful as these two machines were, it became increasingly obvious that in the medium capacity field of 250cc, a completely new type of frame layout was required. Thereupon, with complete disregard for accepted practice, and in full knowledge of the fact that enclosure attempted by other makers had met with little success, a decision was made to attempt to do the job properly. There were to be no half measures, no conversions of any possible existing parts, and no incorporation of previous orthodox design.

The Cruiser No. 32

To start from absolute scratch several essentials were necessary, upon which the rest of the specification was to be built. It is not intended to list these essentials in order of their importance or seniority, since obviously such thoughts could only have been in the mind of the designer. It is, however, safe to say that by the very appearance of this machine, providing weather protection, and ensuring reasonable cleanliness of both machine and rider under all conditions, must have been priorities. After that the desire to ensure a combination of undoubted strength and simplicity, together with the great advantage of immediate accessibility, was also very apparent. In fact it would be well to outline twelve of the cardinal features of this famous machine:

- All mechanical parts, including the carburettor, were enclosed. The cylinder was exposed for cooling, the rider's clothing was protected from oil. Cleaning the machine was facilitated by the flowing, unbroken lines of the exterior.
- The engine shields were easily detachable, making all parts instantly accessible.
- The steering head and front frame member were in one steel stamping of immense strength ensuring perfect rigidity, eliminating the need for any brazed or welded joint. The remainder of the frame was of deep section channel steel.
- The aluminium expansion chamber for the exhaust was constructed on non-resonant principles, allowing the early expansion of gases. The silencer provided an unobtrusive exhaust note, quieter than any single-cylinder two-stroke of earlier design.

- The engine, gearbox and dynamo were held in one pair of plates, cradle fashion, rigidly attached to the frame at six points; the perfect alignment of the front chain and the dynamo chain were thus ensured.
- Weather protection for the rider was provided by the wide, valanced front and rear mudguards, supplemented and completed by made-to-measure leg-shields and undershield.
- Chain adjustment was accessible and easy, and the rear brake torque member was positively located, sliding along the channel section of the frame.
- The battery was carried under the engine shields, well protected in the dead centre of the gravity freed, completely free of vibration yet easily inspected when necessary. The toolbox was located beneath the saddle and so was protected from the weather.
- The rear mudguard was instantly detachable without tools.
- The petrol tank was of simple construction, positively secured to the frame at two points only.
- The front was of fabricated welded steel, with fork blades – box section with malleable iron links having long bearing areas.
- The saddle was of unique design with an extended forward hinge to ensure comfortable riding.

The Cruiser was first introduced as Model No. 32 in 1933, and advertised as 'Fully Equipped' at a price of £34 plus 30s tax. The only extras available were Fort Dunlop tyres at 10s each, and a Jaeger trip speedometer at £2 12s 6d. The engine was the Villiers 249cc Mark XIVA, with prefix letters BYP. The advertisement of the time stated:

> The introduction of this model marks another important stage in the evolution of the motorcycle. The cleaning of a Motorcycle has always been a tedious business, whereas with this model, a few minutes with a sponge and leather will dispose of the job.

It went on to say that the units employed – the 250cc Villiers engine, the gearbox and the dynamo – had stood the test of time and were the best quality available. On the one hand Francis-Barnett were implying that they had made a quantum leap forwards in motorcycle design, and on the other they were saying: 'Don't worry, these are all tried and tested parts.' All of the mechanical parts, including the carburettor, were enclosed, leaving only the cylinder exposed, for cooling purposes. Engine, gearbox and dynamo were held in one pair of cradle plates, which were rigidly attached to the frame at six points. The carburettor was the Villiers two-lever type with twist-grip throttle control, Albion four-speed gearbox and petroil lubrication.

The frame consisted of a front member and head in one steel forging, with side members of deep section channel steel. The fork was of special design, with box-section welded blades, single compression spring type. The brakes were 5in (13cm) internal expanding drums, and the mudguards were deeply valanced, 6in (15cm) at the front and 7in (18cm) at the rear.

An interesting pre-war Cruiser fitted with a 249cc Villiers Mark XIVA water-cooled engine. (Courtesy FBOC)

The finish was black enamel, and the tank chromium-plated with black, gold-lined panels.

Good use was made of the Clarendon Pressing & Welding Co.'s expertise in the manufacture of the Cruiser.

The 1934 Season

The year 1934 was one of refinement to existing models; of great significance was the provision of the Villiers Mark III automatic lubrication system. Working on the same principle as the Mark I and Mark II types, the main difference was the removal of the sight feed bowl. The oil tank was narrow, and the oil regulator was fitted in front of the flywheel and to the top of the tank; its standard setting was one and a half turns screwed anti-clockwise from the closed position. The optimum setting was obtained when a faint blue haze was emitted from the silencer.

The Cruiser No. 39

Midway through the season a decision was made to alter the specification of the gearbox, and the Albion HM was superseded by the Albion HJ. Exactly identical as regards operation, the HJ pattern was more robust in construction all round, and provided just that little extra margin of safety. In this respect the layout of the frame was very accommodating, it being only necessary to elongate the holes in the bottom frame members, moving the battery a little nearer to the fixed rear mudguard. The HJ gearbox needed no more clearance than this, yet the added strength gave a feeling of increased confidence. The modification was identified by an alteration to the coding of the frame number. Thus for 1934, Cruiser Model No. 32 now became Model No. 39 with automatic lubrication, the last Francis-Barnett to use this method of lubrication. The frame numbers of those with the HM gearbox were prefixed 'DA'; with the HJ gearbox the prefix letters were 'DB'.

The oil tank was concealed behind the off-side cover panel, with the filler cap projecting through the panel to enable the tank to be easily refilled. The rate of oil flow is set at the works, but an adjustment to the oil flow can be made if necessary. To facilitate the flow of oil to the crankcase when the engine is stationary, the oil tank is adjacent to the crankcase, which means

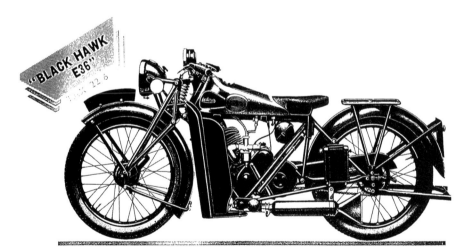

The "Black Hawk E36" is continued for 1935 without any modification of detail. Representative of our triangulated frame design, this model has enjoyed considerable popularity for several years, both in the Home and Overseas markets.

The "Black Hawk" has proved its sterling qualities in the British Dominions, often under very exacting conditions, and a fully satisfactory road performance may be relied upon. The tank is finished in chromium plating and an Electric Horn and Legshields are included in the standard equipment.

196 c.c. Villiers Engine. Miller 6 volt Dynamo Lighting Set. Miller Coil Ignition. 25″ × 3″ Dunlop Tyres. Electric Horn and Legshields. **£28·0·0**
With Flywheel Magneto, instead of coil - £29 . 1 . 0
Code Word : " Hawker."
Code Word with Flywheel Magneto : " Hawkermag."
(General Specification on page 11).

The 1935 Black Hawk Model No. E36.

Machine Specifications

Model	Lapwing No. 35	Black Hawk No. 36	Black Hawk No. 37
Manufacturing year	1934	1934–35	1934
Engine	Villiers Mark XIIC, single-cylinder, air-cooled two-stroke	Villiers IIE, single-cylinder, air-cooled two-stroke	Villiers IIE, single-cylinder, air-cooled two-stroke
Number prefix	GY/GYF	XZ, XZA	XZ, XZA
Bore and stroke	53 × 57mm	61 × 67mm	61 × 67mm
Capacity	148cc	196cc	196cc
Lubrication	Petroil	Petroil	Petroil
Ignition	Villiers flywheel magneto	Miller coil	Villiers flywheel magneto
Carburettor	Villiers two-lever	Villiers two-lever	Villiers two-lever
Primary drive	Renold chain 110036	Renold chain 110036	Renold chain 110036
Final drive	Renold chain 110044	Renold chain 110044	Renold chain 110044
Gearbox	Albion four-speed	Albion three-speed	Albion four-speed
Gearbox ratios	6.8; 9.18; 12.24; 19.8:1	6.2; 9.7; 17.24:1	6.2; 8.37; 11.16; 18.17:1
Frame	Fully triangulated weldless tubes	Fully triangulated weldless tubes	Fully triangulated weldless tubes
Number prefix	D	D, E	D
Front suspension	Triangulated; single compression spring	Triangulated; single compression spring	Triangulated; single compression spring
Rear suspension	Rigid	Rigid	Rigid
Wheels front and rear	19 × 2.25in well-base	19 × 2.25in well-base	19 × 2.25in well-base
Brakes front	4in diameter	5in diameter	5in diameter
Brakes rear	4in diameter	5in diameter	5in diameter
Tyres front and rear	25 × 3in Dunlop cord	25 × 3in Dunlop cord	25 × 3in Dunlop cord

General Specifications

Fuel tank capacity	1.63gal (7.4ltr)	1.63gal (7.4ltr)	1.63gal (7.4ltr)
Wheelbase	49.63in (1,260mm)	49.63in (1,260mm)	49.63in (1,260mm)
Ground clearance	5.75in (146mm)	5.75in (146mm)	5.75in (146mm)
Overall width	27.75in (705mm)	27.75in (705mm)	27.75in (705mm)
Overall length	79.25in (2,013mm)	79.25in (2,013mm)	79.25in (2,013mm)
Seat height (min.)	27in (686mm)	27in (686mm)	27in (686mm)
Dry weight	198lb (90kg)	201lb (91kg)	Not known

the pipework is short. The size of the rear brake hub was increased from 5in (13cm) to 6in (15cm); otherwise the specification and detail remained the same.

The Albion E1 pattern gearbox was superseded by the Albion EJ gearbox on all lightweight machines. Where coil ignition was specified, an auxiliary flywheel was fitted in place of the Villiers magneto.

The only other change was in connection with the front forks. Here the malleable castings were giving a little trouble as regards alignment – due to the need for toolroom machining limits – for which reason they were superseded by a simpler design. Four pressings, interchangeable for top or bottom, formed the links, and these were attached to spindles which swivelled in malleable lugs – no bushes were used in this or any other Francis-Barnett fork. Adjustment was simplicity itself: to take up lateral play it was necessary to place a box or similar object under the engine to clear the fork off the ground. Then loosen the nuts of the spindle one at a time, and with the squared end of the spindle, turn anti-clockwise until the excess play was taken out of the spindles, but leaving sufficient play to enable the spindle to work freely in its bearing. Finally tighten up the outside nuts.

For the rest of the 1934 models, there were only two changes of any significance, and one was in connection with the exhaust systems. Favourable comment had been made on the pleasing and unobtrusive exhaust note of the Cruiser, and so an attempt was made on other machines in the range to reduce exhaust noise. This was achieved by leading short pipes (one in the case of the Black Hawk) into a cylindrical expansion chamber in front of the crankcase. The outlet was via a pipe of the same diameter as the short pipes, and finally the standard silencer. This system had the virtues of being easily detachable for cleaning, it was extremely efficient in that it cooled the engine with no appreciable back pressure, and it provided an agreeable exhaust note. The whole of the exhaust system on all machines in this category were chromium-plated, as were the petrol tanks.

The other change applied only to the smaller models, and concerned improvement in a combined filler cap and oil measure designed to eliminate any leakage. An extra baffle was included, and the cap provided with a very large finger grip, by which it could be screwed firmly on to its leather seating. Also employed was a coarser screw thread. A battery of 13 amp hours replaced the 8ah batteries on the smaller models.

The Lapwing No. 33, No. 34 and No. 35

Three Lapwing models were now available with the Villiers Mark XIIC engine, Albion three-speed gearbox, the Villiers two-lever carburettor and twist-grip throttle control, and lubrication by petroil. The Lapwing Model No. 33 was fitted with Villiers' improved direct lighting from a four-pole flywheel dynamo magneto. The general specifications of models No. 34 and No. 35 were similar; where they differed from Model No. 33 was that the Lapwing 34 had a Miller 6v 24w dynamo lighting set with a 13ah battery and a Miller coil, and the Lapwing 35 had a 6v dynamo lighting set, flywheel magneto ignition and an Albion four-speed gearbox. The finish was the same in each case, the tank being chromium plated with black panels, or red or blue panels to order. The prices were £26, £27 and £29.

The Black Hawk No. 36 and No. 37

The other models available for 1934 were the Black Hawk No. 36 with the 196cc Mark IE Super-Sports engine, three-speed gearbox, Miller lighting and coil ignition, priced at £28. Its companion was the Black Hawk Model No. 37, with four-speed gearbox, flywheel magneto and separate Miller lighting system; it was priced at £30.

The Falcon No. 38

And finally there was the Falcon No. 38 with 196cc sports engine, automatic lubrication and three-speed gearbox, priced at £32 10s. The 172cc Super-Sports engine was available as an alternative to the Mark IE engine in the Falcon.

The 1935 Season

The year 1935 was noteworthy for an almost clean sweep of the previous year's machines, with only the Cruiser 39 and the Black Hawk 36 being retained; both these machines were continued exactly as before, with only a minor alteration. Plover and Seagull models made their debut. The frames and forks of the two machines were identical, except for the top back stays on the Seagull which were wider to accommodate a different rear wheel.

Machine Specifications

❖

Model	Falcon No.38	Cruiser No.39	Plover No.40
Manufacturing year	1934	1934–40	1935–40
Engine	Villiers IE, Super-Sports* single-cylinder, air-cooled two-stroke	Villiers Mark XIVA, single-cylinder, air-cooled two-stroke	Villiers Mark XIIC, single-cylinder, air-cooled two-stroke
Number prefix	KZ, KZS	BYP	GY/GYF
Bore and stroke	61 × 67mm	63 × 80mm	53 × 67mm
Capacity	196cc	249cc	148cc
Lubrication	Villiers automatic#	Villiers automatic#	Petroil
Ignition	Miller coil	Miller coil	Villiers flywheel magneto
Carburettor	Villiers two-lever	Villiers two-lever	Villiers
Primary drive	Renold chain 110036	Renold chain 0.375in	Renold chain 0.375in
Final drive	Renold chain 110044	Renold chain 0.5in	Renold chain 0.5in
Gearbox	Albion four-speed	Albion four-speed	Albion three-speed
Gearbox ratios	6.2; 6.37; 11.16; 18.17:1	5.7; 7.7; 10.26; 16.78:1	6.6; 10.4; 18.4:1
Frame	Fully triangulated weldless tubes	Front member and head in one steel forging; side members in deep channel steel	Two steel pressings as front frame members; a pressing from the head to the saddle, from there a tube down to the bottom chain stays
Number prefix	Not known	DA, DB, EB, FB, GB, HB, JB, KB,	EC, FC, GC, HC, JC, KC
Front suspension	Triangulated; single compression spring	Box-section welded steel blades; compression spring	Triangulated; single compression spring
Rear suspension	Rigid	Rigid	Rigid
Wheels front and rear	19 × 2.25in well-base	19 × 3.25in	19 × 3in
Brakes front	5in diameter	5in diameter, 1938 6in	4in diameter, 5in from 1939
Brakes rear	5in diameter	6in diameter	4in diameter; 5in from 1937
Tyres front and rear	25 × 3in Dunlop cord	26 × 3.25in Dunlop cord	25 × 3in Dunlop cord

General Specifications

Fuel tank capacity	1.63gal (7.4ltr)	2gal (9ltr)*	2gal (9ltr)*
Oil tank capacity	4 pints (2.3ltr) in separate tank	N/A	N/A

Machine Specifications *continued*

Wheelbase	49.63in (1,260mm)	54in (1,372mm)	51.25in (1,302mm)
Ground clearance	5.75in (146mm)	6in (152.4mm)	4.25in (108mm)
Overall width	27.75in (705mm)	28in (711mm)	28in (711mm)
Overall length	79.25in (2,013mm)	82.5in (2,096mm)	80.5in (2,045mm)
Seat height (min.)	27in (686mm)	26.5in (673mm)	26.5in (673mm)
Dry weight	205lb (93kg)	280lb (127kg)	182lb (83kg)
Power	Not known	9.4bhp @ 4,000rpm	Not known
	*Villiers 172cc Super-Sports engine as an alternative	# Petroil to order	*1938 3gal (13.6ltr)
		*1938 3gal (13.6ltr)	

The Cruiser No. 39

1934 saw the Cruiser further increasing its popularity, so the alterations for 1935 were confined to minor details. The specification for 1935 was as follows: Villiers 249cc Mark XIVA engine, Albion four-speed gearbox, Villiers automatic lubrication or petroil to order, Miller 6v 36w dynamo lighting, ammeter, dip switch and 13ah battery. The finish was black enamel and the tank chromium-plated with black panels gold lined.

In its new form the "Plover" is a worthy successor to the successful 150 c.c. models we have manufactured during the past ten years. The "Plover 40" has a wide range of utility. It appeals to all who require a machine which offers a good turn of speed, is an excellent hill climber, quiet and easily controlled, gives the minimum of trouble, and which is economical to buy and to maintain.

The "Plover" is the ideal machine for the cyclist. It will ease his labour, bring new pleasures and immensely widen the radius of his activities.

148 c.c. Villiers Long Stroke Engine. Direct Lighting from Flywheel Magneto. Flywheel Magneto Ignition. 25" × 3" Dunlop Tyres. Bulb Horn. - - - - - **£25·10·0**

Code Word : " Plough."   (General Specification on page 11).

The 1935 Plover Model No. E40.

*1935 Cruiser Model E39.
Another of Arthur Walls'
machines seen on the FBOC
stand, Kempton Park 2007.
(Courtesy FBOC)*

The "Plover 41" is identical in general design with the model described on the opposite page. It is, however, equipped with the Miller Dynamo Lighting, the ignition being by Flywheel Magneto. This attractive combination has increased in popularity during the past two or three years.

The frame of the "Plovers" affords great strength and rigidity, while the riding position is arranged to secure the greatest comfort. We confidently recommend the "Plovers" for service in all parts of the world. Their capabilities win the admiration of owners from the outset.

148 c.c. Villiers Long Stroke Engine. Miller 6 volt Dynamo Lighting Set. Flywheel Magneto Ignition. 25" × 3" Dunlop Tyres. Electric Horn.   -   -   -   -

£28·10·0

Code Word : " Ploughman."   (General Specification on page 11).

The 1935 Plover Model No. E41.

*The 1935 Seagull
Model No. E42.*

The present demand for a machine of the 250 c.c. class—a demand which is steadily increasing, has induced us to market the "Seagull." With this type of machine an eminently satisfactory performance, both as regards cruising speed and hill climbing, may be depended upon.

The "Seagull 42" is equipped with Flywheel Magneto and Direct Lighting. It offers an adequate touring performance,

simplicity of management, low cost price and great dependability.

249 c.c. Villiers Long Stroke Engine. Direct Lighting from Flywheel Magneto. Flywheel Magneto Ignition. 25″ × 3.25″ Dunlop Tyres. Bulb Horn. - - - - **£30·0·0**

Code Word : "Seaman."

The robust equipment of the "Seagulls" is evident at a glance. The instant impression is created of a sturdy, practical, well turned-out job—obviously the outcome of careful thought and long road experience. In the "Seagull 43" we include Chromium plated tank with Blue panels. Similar in build to the machine illustrated on the opposite page, it differs from it in having the Miller Dynamo Lighting Set and Electric Horn.

This model was the centre of lively interest at the Olympia

Show and we confidently predict for it a successful career.

249 c.c. Villiers Long-Stroke Engine. Miller 6-volt Dynamo Lighting Set. Flywheel Magneto Ignition. 25″ × 3.25″ Dunlop Tyres. Electric Horn. Tank Chromium plated, with blue panels, gold lined. **£32·10·0**

Code Word : "Sealark."   (General Specification on page 11).

*The 1935 Seagull
Model No. E43.*

Plovers and Seagulls

All Plovers had Villiers 148cc Mark XIIC engines – prefix letters GYF – fitted vertically, and Seagulls had the Villiers 249cc Mark XIVA engines – prefix letters BYP. The carburettors on both machines were identical, being Villiers middleweight two-lever pattern. Both the Plover 40 and Seagull 42 employed the Villiers four-pole direct lighting system. Albion EJ gearboxes of the pivot-fixing pattern were also specified on both machines.

The gearboxes themselves interchanged, apart from a variation in the shells which was necessitated by a difference in the chain line of the two types. Certainly the internals were the same, as were the clutches. Front chain adjustment was facilitated by merely loosening the two studs which passed through the top and bottom of the shell: there was a small pivot lever mounted on the top of the shell protruding to one side of the clamping plates, which when moved pivoted the gearbox on the bottom stud; the top hole in the shell was elongated in order to vary the front chain tension.

Plover 41 and Seagull 43 had Miller SUS dynamo lighting sets – DMG/3 24-watt dynamos. The latter were of exactly the same construction as fitted to the Cruiser model without the contact breaker. The finish on the Plovers and Seagulls was black enamel, with chromium plating for the cycle parts and gold-lined black tanks, except for the Seagull 43 which had its tank chromium plated with gold-lined blue panels.

1937 Plover Model H41, showing the rolling chassis. (Courtesy Raymond Holmen)

1937 Plover Model H41, showing the engine. (Courtesy Raymond Holmen)

Machine Specifications

Model	Plover No. 41	Seagull No. 42	Seagull No. 43
Manufacturing year	1935–40	1935	1935–40
Engine	Villiers Mark XIIC, single-cylinder, air-cooled two-stroke	Villiers Mark XIVA, single-cylinder, air-cooled two-stroke	Villiers Mark XIVA, single-cylinder, air-cooled two-stroke
Number prefix	GY/GYF	BYP	BYP
Bore and stroke	53 × 67mm	63 × 80mm	63 × 80mm
Capacity	148cc	249cc	249cc
Lubrication	Petroil	Petroil	Petroil
Ignition	Villiers flywheel magneto	Villiers flywheel magneto	Villiers flywheel magneto
Carburettor	Villiers	Villiers	Villiers
Primary drive	Renold chain 0.375in	Renold chain 0.375in	Renold chain 0.375in
Final drive	Renold chain 0.5in	Renold chain 0.5in	Renold chain 0.5in
Gearbox	Albion three-speed	Albion three-speed	Albion three-speed
Gearbox ratios	6.6; 10.4; 18.4:1	5.5; 8.6; 15.3:1	5.5; 8.6; 15.3:1
Gearbox ratios optional	N/A	N/A	1937: 5.2; 8.1; 14.4:1
Frame	Two steel pressings as front frame members; a pressing from the head to the saddle, from there a tube down to the bottom chain stays	Two steel pressings as front frame members; a pressing from the head to the saddle, from there a tube down to the bottom chain stays	Two steel pressings as front frame members; a pressing from the head to the saddle, from there a tube down to the bottom chain stays
Number prefix	EC, FC, GC, HC, JC, KC	EC	EC, FC, GC, HC, JC, KC
Front suspension	Triangulated; single compression spring	Triangulated; single compression spring	Triangulated; single compression spring
Rear suspension	Rigid	Rigid	Rigid
Wheels front and rear	19 × 3in	18 × 3.25in	18 × 3.25in
Brakes front	4in diameter, 5in from 1939	5in diameter	5in diameter
Brakes rear	4in diameter; 5in from 1937	5in diameter	5in diameter
Tyres front and rear	25 × 3in Dunlop cord	25 × 3.25in Dunlop	25 × 3.25in Dunlop

General Specifications

Fuel tank capacity	2gal (9ltr)*	2gal (9ltr)	2gal (9ltr)*
Wheelbase	51.25in (1,302mm)	51.25in (1,302mm)	51.25in (1,302mm)
Ground clearance	4.25in (108mm)	4.25in (108mm)	4.25in (108mm)
Overall width	28in (711mm)	28in (711mm)	28in (711mm)
Overall length	80.5in (2,045mm)	80.5in (2,045mm)	80.5in (2,045mm)
Seat height (min.)	26.5in (673mm)	26.5in (673mm)	26.5in (673mm)
Dry weight	199lb (90kg) *1938 3gal (13.6ltr)	215lb (98kg)	230lb (104kg) *1938 3gal (13.6ltr)

1937 Plover Model H41, showing the steering head. (Courtesy Raymond Holmen)

The Stag No. 44

The Stag Model No.44 marked a return to four-strokes after a period of nine years. It is believed that the engine was either designed by Francis-Barnett, which is doubtful, or they had it especially designed for them and built originally by Burney & Blackburne and later by Gillet & Stephens. It was an ohv engine with a bore and stroke of 68 × 68mm, giving a capacity of 248cc. In the layout of the engine the 'Z' type of overhead rockers were eliminated by the provision of straight rockers of simple design. Two cams were provided to operate each valve, and the whole of the valve was enclosed and lubricated under pressure.

The big-end bearing was of generous proportions in relation to the size of the engine. It had two rows of 0.25 × 0.25in rollers – seventeen in each row running on a crankpin 1.13in in diameter. Oil was positively fed to this bearing.

In the design of this engine we have aimed at mechanical silence combined with high efficiency. The push rods are enclosed throughout their entire length in tunnels cast in the cylinder. The large diameter rocker spindles are carried in detachable castings.

The oil sump below the crankcase has a capacity of 4¼ pints. A submerged pump of the roto-plunge type supplies oil through the centre of the timing side shaft to the big end bearing. An independent feed is arranged for the overhead valve gear. The filter is removable for cleaning without draining the sump.

The front frame member, with the head, is a steel forging. A machine of high performance and distinctive character, the "Stag" carries our strong recommendation.

248 c.c. Francis-Barnett O.H.V. Engine. Lighting and Ignition by Miller 6 volt 36 watt Dyno-Mag Set. Four-speed Gearbox. 26″ × 3.25″ Dunlop Tyres. Electric Horn. - - - - - **£48·0·0**

Code Word : "Stag."   (General Specification on page 2).

The 1935 Stag No. E44.

Machine Specifications

	Stag No. 44	Cruiser No. 45	Red Stag No. 46
Model	Stag No. 44	Cruiser No. 45	Red Stag No. 46
Manufacturing year	1935–1937	1936–1940	1937
Engine	Francis-Barnett ohv, single-port exhaust	Villiers Mark XVIIA single-cylinder, air-cooled	Francis-Barnett ohv, single-port exhaust two-stroke
Number prefix		BYX	
Bore and stroke	68 × 68mm	63 × 80mm	68 × 68mm
Capacity	248cc	249cc	248cc
Lubrication	Sump, 4.5 pints	Petroil	Sump, 4.5 pints
Ignition	Miller dynamo magneto	Villiers flywheel magneto	Miller dynamo magneto
Carburettor	Amal	Amal 6/125	Amal
Primary drive	Renold chain 0.5in	Renold chain 0.375in	Renold chain 0.5in
Final drive	Renold chain 0.5in	Renold chain 0.5in	Renold chain 0.5in
Gearbox	Albion four-speed	Albion four-speed	Not known
Gearbox ratios	5.65; 7.63; 10.2; 16.55:1	5.7; 7.7; 10.26; 16.78:1	Not known
Frame	Front member 'I' section steel forging	Front member and head in one steel forging; side members in deep channel steel	Front member 'I' section steel forging
Number prefix	ED, FD, GD	GB, HB, JB, KB	GD
Front suspension	Druid forks	Box-section welded steel blades; compression spring	Druid forks
Rear suspension	Rigid	Rigid	Rigid
Wheels front and rear	19 × 3.25in	19 × 3.25in	19 × 3.25in
Brakes front	6in diameter	5in diameter, 1938 6in	6in diameter
Brakes rear	7in diameter	6in diameter	7in diameter
Tyres front and rear	26 × 3.25in Dunlop	26 × 3.25in Dunlop	26 × 3.25in Dunlop

General specifications

	Stag No. 44	Cruiser No. 45	Red Stag No. 46
Fuel tank capacity	3.25gal (15ltr)	2gal (9ltr)*	3.25gal (15ltr)
Wheelbase	54.5in (1,384mm)	54in (1,372mm)	54.5in (1,384mm)
Ground clearance	4.25in (108mm)	6in (152.4mm)	4.25in (108mm)
Overall width	28in (711mm)	28in (711mm)	28in (711mm)
Overall length	83.5in (2,121mm)	82.5in (2,096mm)	83.5in (2,121)
Seat height (min.)	27in (686mm)	26.5in (673mm)	27in (686mm)
Dry weight	297lb (135kg)	283lb (128kg)	284lb (129kg)
Power	Not known	11bhp @ 4,500rpm *1938 3gal (13.6ltr)	Not known

The crankshaft was mounted on journal bearings, one on each side of the driving side of the shaft; there was a spiral groove to prevent oil leakage. On the timing side the inner race fitted tightly to the shaft, the crankcase being shrunk on to the outside. Cam wheel bearings were of plain phosphor bronze. The gudgeon pin was fully floating, fitted with end pads running in a plain small end bush. Valve rockers had plain bronze bushes lubricated under pressure. Cam rocker bearings were of large diameter, the rocker pin being a press fit in the crankcase and provided with a locknut at the inner end. The outer end of the rocker pin was supported in the timing cover.

The crankcase breather was located at the forward off-side corner of the cylinder base, being between the underside of the cylinder flange and the top of the crankcase base.

The oil pump was driven by worm drive from the timing side of the mainshaft, and the rotor – operating at one-eighth engine speed – extended into the sump immediately below the crankcase; the capacity of the sump was 4.5 pints (2.3ltr). The pump supplied two independent feeds of oil: one to the big-end bearing, and from there to the piston and other working parts; and the second passed through the cylinder and cylinder head through oil ways conveying the oil to the rocker bearings. Oil continually escaping from these bearings returned to the sump via the chamber in which the push rods were located, and provided additional lubrication for cam rockers, timing gear and so on. A tell-tale was provided to indicate that oil was being circulated, but unless it was in its extended position – approximately 0.19in outward movement – oil could not be passed through the bearings. A filter was provided in the sump below the oil filler spout, to be cleaned at regular intervals.

Primarily the aim was a quiet operation, and freedom from mechanical noise. The carburettor was Amal with a twist-grip throttle, the lighting and ignition was by Miller, a 6v 36 watt dyno-mag set, there were Druid forks with a rubber-insulated handlebar, with a hand-adjusted shock absorber and steering damper. Brakes were 7in rear and 6in front. The finish was black enamel and chromium plating, and the tank chromium plated with gold-lined black panels.

The Stag was intended to appeal to those who were especially interested in four-stroke ohv models in the 250cc class. In the 1935 ISDT, one Stag was entered and it was awarded a gold medal.

The 1936 Season

The Plover models 40 and 41, together with the Seagull Model No. 43 and the Stag Model No. 44, continued for 1936.

The Cruiser No. 39 and No. 45

The Cruiser Model No. 39 also continued in production, being joined by another Cruiser, Model No. 45. To look at them side by side there was not much difference in their outward appearance, probably the main one being the position of the electric horn: on the Cruiser 39 it was situated above the handlebar, and on the Cruiser 45 under and at the rear of the tank.

The obvious differences in the specifications were, firstly, the engines: in the Cruiser 45 it was the Villiers 249cc Mark XVIIA with a deflectorless piston, prefix BYX. The Cruiser 39 had the Villiers twist-grip throttle carburettor system, while the Cruiser 45 used the AMAL system. Both used the Albion four-speed gearbox and the Miller 6v 36w dynamo lighting set. Lubrication was automatic, with petroil lubrication to order on the Cruiser 39 and petroil on the Cruiser 45. The finish was identical for both models, black enamel on the cycle parts etc. and chromium plated tank with black gold-lined panels.

For 1936 the prices were as follows: for the Cruiser nos. 39 and 45, £37 5s and £39 10s; for the Plover model nos. 40 and 41, £25 10s and £28 10s; for the Seagull No. 43, £32 10s; and £45 for the Stag Model No. 44.

The 1937 Season

The year 1937 once again conformed to a policy of many years standing, in that the previous year's machines were continued, but with minor modifications.

The Red Stag No. 46

The Stag was joined by the Red Stag, Model No. 46; this was similar to the Stag but of a sportier nature. The specification of the two was similar, both having the 248cc Francis-Barnett ohv four-stroke engine with single port exhaust. The Red Stag had chromium-

1937 Red Stag Model G46, the off side, showing the 248cc ohv four-stroke engine. (Courtesy CTM)

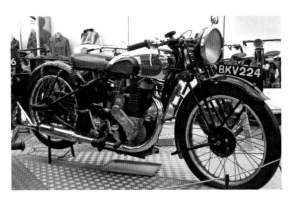

1937 Red Stag Model G46, the near side, showing the 248cc ohv four-stroke engine. (Courtesy CTM)

plated wheel rims with painted red centres lined gold. The finish was black enamel and chromium plating. The Stag had black wheel rims and a chromium-plated tank with black, gold-lined panels. The exhaust extension was tubular instead of a fish-tail. The price of the Red Stag was £48, and £46 for the Stag.

The performance of the high efficiency engine was indicated by comments in a road test report by *Motor Cycling*:

Very satisfactory average speeds could be registered over long distances, and that smoothness and silkiness of the engine already mentioned made fast going seem an unusually effortless business. The maximum speed in top gear was 65mph (105km/h). Acceleration was good, for a machine of this type, and the third ratio of the four-speed foot-operated gearbox proved of great use; the maximum in this gear was 53mph (85km/h). Second gear maximum was found to be 41mph (66km/h).

Braking power was of a very high standard on the 'Red Stag', and a figure of 32ft (9.75m) was registered as the stopping distance from 30mph (48km/h), using the rear brake alone. When both brakes were put into action the figure was cut down to 28ft (8.5m).

Despite this glowing report, the Stags did not survive another year.

The Plover No. G40 and No. G41
Plovers continued, with the Villiers Mark XIIC engines; two models were offered, one with direct four-pole lighting from the magneto, the other with

Miller separate dynamo lighting. These were known as the Plover G40 and Plover G41 respectively. On these machines the only change was in regard to the rear hubs, where the rear brake was increased from 4in to 5in, and British hubs were specified in the rear wheels in favour of the Harwil pattern. These were the only changes. The colour finish was black enamel and chromium plating. The G40 was priced at £26 10s, and the G41 at £29 10s. The Seagull G43 was continued exactly as before with no alterations.

The Cruiser No. 39 and No. 45
The Cruiser 39 with the Villiers Mark XIVA engine and the Cruiser 45 with the Villiers Mark XVIIA engine had one only alteration. In place of the .205in wide rear chain (Renold 110044) a 0.305in wide (Renold 110046) was used; this entailed fitting wider sprockets to the rear wheel and final drive of the gearbox, but did not interfere with the basic design; this upgrade could therefore be fitted retrospectively to older machines, if required, without difficulty.

The other change amounted to increasing the size of the rear wheel axle from 0.5in to 0.5625in, the former size having been regarded as obsolete for many years. As all replacement axles were supplied in the 0.5625in size, this necessitated changing the cones, nuts and distance pieces at the same time. Hub cups were a driving fit in the shell, and their removal was facilitated when the need arose by the simple method of tapping them out. A useful hint when fitting a replacement was to use the old cup upside down: it had to be hammered until the new cup was firmly and squarely in position, when the old cup could be levered away and the job finished by fitting the felt washer and metal dust washer. The cup extended just beyond the housing in the hub in order to facilitate its removal if the need arose. In such circumstances the outside dust washer and felt would first be removed, after which as large a steel punch as possible should be brought to bear on the cup inside the hub. A few well directed blows would invariably be effective – although be warned that if such force were not distributed over as large a portion of the cup as possible it might break, after which the difficulty of removal would be increased. The importance of using as large a drift or punch as possible was emphasized.

The Seagull No. G47

The Seagull Model No. G47 was introduced midway through the 1937 season; in outline this was similar to the Seagull G43, except that as there had been an insistent demand for a four-speed gearbox, some provision for this feature had to be made. A four-speed gearbox could not be conveniently fitted to the Seagull 43, therefore it was decided to rearrange the plates between the engine and the seat tube. The Villiers Mark XIVA engine was retained, but in place of the Albion EJ gearbox on the Seagull 43 the Albion HJ was used: the footchange-operating mechanism was enclosed as before, but this time at the side. The operating travel was reduced, and although the method of location was practically the same, the new arrangement eliminated all lost movement since there were no outside operating levers with squared ends or control rods to wear. Dismantling this gearbox required no special tools.

With the footchange lever now on the right-hand side, the rear brake pedal had to be carried over to the left-hand side. This was achieved by means of a cross-shaft passing through the bottom frame member. A square is milled to each end of this cross-shaft and a short operating lever having a square operated the brake rod, the pedal being machined to fit the square on the left-hand side.

The 1938 Season

1938 was virtually a continuation of the previous year's machines, with the exception of the four-stroke-engined Red Stag, which was discontinued. Petrol tanks on most models were of 3gal (13.6ltr) capacity, and attached to the top frame member by two brackets at the front and one at the rear.

Of considerable significance on all machines in the 1938 range was the exhaust system. With a conventional exhaust pipe, the silencer takes on the outline of a shell, inside which are welded three cones, or dividers, equally spaced. The internal tail pipe then extends the entire length of the silencer and is drilled criss-cross fashion to enable three baffle plates to be welded inside. The cones in the silencer are positioned equidistant from the baffles in the tail pipe, to make the exhaust gases percolate. This system has the virtue of simplicity in design, and it creates little back pressure; since 1938 all exhaust systems have been modelled on the same theory; the outside appearance may be slightly different, but the internal methods are the same.

Both the Cruiser 45 and the Seagull 47 had a change of engine towards the end of the year, from the Villiers Mark XVIIA to the Mark XVIIIA. The basic dimensions of bore, stroke and capacity, and the cylinder head, were the same in both engines. The Mark XVIIIA had a different design of piston; the gudgeon-pin bosses were lowered, and the connecting rod shortened to reduce piston 'rock'. The crankshafts were heavier, and double-row journal bearings were employed in place of the single-row type. Floating glands and spring seals replaced the original fixed glands. At the same time the Cruiser 45 hand-change gear mechanism was altered to foot-change, and it was reported that there was a certain amount of opposition to the change.

To effect the change, it was necessary to modify the front of the gearbox in order to accommodate the positive-stop gear-change. The Albion HJ gearbox internals remained unaltered, with only the front taking on a new shape. This modification imposed a further modification which entailed repositioning the foot-brake pedal from the right- to the left-hand side. This was achieved by drilling holes in the bottom frame members and the engine plates to take a cross-shaft, which was connected to the brake mechanism on the right and the brake pedal on the left.

The advertisements for the Cruiser and Seagull with the Mark XVIIIA engine did not appear until the following year, 1939, and it is assumed by many that

Machine Specifications

Model	Seagull No. 47	Snipe No. 48	Snipe No. 49
Manufacturing year	1937–1940	1939–1940	1939–1940
Engine	Villiers Mark XIVA, single-cylinder, air-cooled two-stroke	Villiers Mark 9D, single-cylinder, air-cooled two-stroke	Villiers Junior, single-cylinder, air-cooled two-stroke
Number prefix	BYX	AAA	BBA
Bore and stroke	63 × 80mm	50 × 62mm	50 × 50mm
Capacity	249cc	123cc	98cc
Lubrication	Petroil	Petroil	Petroil
Ignition	Villiers flywheel magneto	Villiers flywheel magneto	Villiers flywheel magneto
Carburettor	Villiers, 1938 AMAL	Villiers single-lever	Villiers single-lever
Primary drive	Renold chain 0.375in	Renold chain 0.375in	Renold chain 0.375in
Final drive	Renold chain 0.5in	Renold chain 110044	Renold chain 110044
Gearbox	Albion four-speed	Three-speed	Three-speed
Gearbox ratios	5.2; 7.0; 9.4; 15.2:1	7.8; 12.6; 22.7:1	7.8; 12.6; 22.7:1
Frame	As Seagull No 43	Semi-tubular	Semi-tubular
Number prefix	GC, HC, JC, KC	JE, KE	JE, KE
Front suspension	Triangulated; single compression spring	Druid ultra-lightweight pattern	Druid ultra-lightweight pattern
Rear suspension	Rigid	Rigid	Rigid
Wheels front and rear	18 × 3.25in	19 × 2.50in	19 × 2.50in
Brakes front	5in diameter	4in diameter	4in diameter
Brakes rear	5in diameter	4in diameter	4in diameter
Tyres front and rear	25 × 3.25in Dunlop	24 × 2.5in Dunlop	24 × 2.5in Dunlop
Hubs: front	Not known	Harwil 3.75in	Harwil 3.75in
rear	Not known	Harwil 4in	Harwil 4in

General Specifications

Fuel tank capacity	2gal (9ltr) *	2gal (9ltr)	2gal (9ltr)
Wheelbase	51.25in (1,302mm)	48.5in (1,232mm)	48.5in (1,232mm)
Ground clearance	4.25in (108mm)	5in (127mm)	5in (127mm)
Overall width	28in (711mm)	25.5in (648mm)	25.5in (648mm)
Overall length	80.5in (2,045mm)	77in (1,956mm)	77in (1,956mm)
Seat height (min.)	26.5in (673mm)	25.5in (648mm)	25.5in (648mm)
Dry weight	238lb (108kg)	127lb (58kg)	125lb (57kg)
	*1938 3gal (13.6ltr)	* 48T wheel with 24 × 2.5in tyre and 50T with 24 × 2.75in tyre	

that was when they became available. There are, however, more Cruiser 45s with the 1938 frame-number prefix of HB and the Mark XVIIIA engine-number prefix of UU, than there are with the Mark XVIIA engine prefix in the FBOC Register.

The 1939 Season

For 1939 there was a growing demand for economy in transport; this was due in part to the gathering popularity of the cheap and efficient lightweight staking a claim for itself, and partly to a forced economy as a result of the prospects of war with Germany, which for many seemed inevitable. Many industries' interests were being diverted to a war potential.

The preoccupation of Francis-Barnett continued to be in the production of cheap and reliable transport. In 1939 the range of machines available to the public rose to nine, equalled by the nine in 1926 and only exceeded by the ten in 1940. Six machines were continued from 1938: two Cruisers, J39 and J45; two Plovers, J40 and J41; and two Seagulls J43 and J47. These were joined by two versions of the Snipe lightweight motorcycle, Model No. J48 and Model No. J49, and the Powerbike Model No. J50. A new phase in pedal-assisted motoring was being experienced by the public, which paved the way for the Powerbike J50.

The Cruiser J39 was priced at £42 10s, or £42 with petroil lubrication and the J45 at £45. The Seagull J45 was £36, and the J47 £42. All were finished in black enamel, with a chromium-plated tank with black side panels.

In the Plover range the most noticeable change was the specification of 5in brakes front and rear. Other than this, the petrol tank mounting position on all 3gal tanks was redesigned: in the previous year's machines they were attached at three points on the bottom, some problems being remedied by moving the front fixings to the front vertical face, provision then being made by way of a lug integrated in the head casting to which the tank was bolted on either side.

The Plovers were priced at £28 19s for the J40, and £32 10s for the J41, and they had a similar finish to the Cruisers and Seagulls.

The Snipe No. 48 and No. 49

The two lightweight Snipe models, Nos. 48 and 49, were powered by Villiers 122cc Mark 9D and 98cc Junior engines respectively. The Villiers Mark 9D engine with a bore and stroke of 50 × 62mm had a capacity of 122cc, although Francis-Barnett advertised it as a 125cc engine. The three-speed gearbox, clutch and kick-starter were an integral unit with the engine.

Although the Snipe did not become available to the general public until late in 1938 (the start of the 1939 season), *Motor Cycle* printed a report in their 10 February issue on the Snipe, which stated that it had twin silencers with fishtails. The 'fishtail' at the end of the silencer were obviously dispensed with in the production models. Lubrication was by petroil, with a 2gal (9ltr) tank. Three different systems of Villiers direct lighting were fitted according to requirement.

The frame was semi-tubular in layout, the tubular part extending from the seat tube, under the engine

1939 Cruiser Model J39 in red, owner Ted Lloyd, at the Battlesbridge Show 2009.

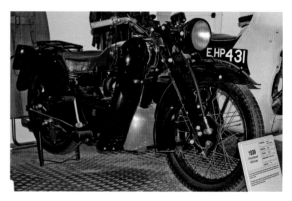

1938 Cruiser Model H45 with the 249cc Villiers XVIIIA engine. (Courtesy CTM)

The 1939 Snipe Models J48 and J49.

"SNIPE" J48 & J49

"SNIPE" J48

ENGINE. 125 c.c. Villiers, 50 mm. bore × 62 mm. stroke. Deflectorless Piston, Twin Exhaust Ports.
GEAR. Three-speed, clutch and kick-starter. Integral unit with engine. Ratios: 7·8, 12·6, 22·7.
TRANSMISSION. Rear, Renold motor cycle chain No. 110044, ⅜" P. Front ⅜" P. enclosed in aluminium oil bath case.
LUBRICATION. Petroil system. ½ pint oil to one gallon petrol.
LIGHTING. Villiers 6 pole 18w. Direct Lighting from flywheel dynamo magneto. Parking battery in headlamp. Dimmer switch.
IGNITION. Villiers Flywheel Magneto.

CARBURETTER. Villiers automatic, twist grip throttle control with strangler for easy starting.
TYRES. 2·50' × 19" (24" × 2¼") Dunlop.
TANK. Steel, welded. Capacity two gallons. Anti-splash filler cap. Two-level petrol tap fitted.
BRAKES. 4" diameter internal expanding hub brakes front and rear.
SADDLE. Dunlop "Drilastic."
EQUIPMENT. Bulb Horn, Licence Holder, Inflator, grease gun and tool kit.
FINISH. Best quality black enamel after bonderizing process, and chromium plating.

"SNIPE" J48   **£25.0.0**

Code word: "Snipeight."   *Speedometer extra—see back cover.*

"SNIPE" J49.   Specification as above, but fitted with 98 c.c. Villiers Unit.

"SNIPE" J49 . **£25.0.0**

Code word: "Snipnine."   *Speedometer extra—see back cover.*

"SNIPE" J48

right up to the bottom tank rails, the latter being angular steel strips. The aluminium steering head was attached to the frame by two steel pressings which fit and supplement the front frame tube down as far as a point just in front of the cylinder where they were bolted on on either side of the front tube.

The chain-stay loop was welded to the U-shape main frame so that, as a means of further description, they amount to U-shaped loops welded together, the attachment being facilitated by a steel pressing special-ly shaped. The top back stays were then bolted under the saddle and to the rear fork end. The engine was fixed at three points by lugs welded to the main frame tube, and to this at the bottom under the crankcase was a further welded pressing to accommodate the centre stand. The front fork was a Druid ultra-lightweight pattern, and the hubs were of Harwil manufacture, 3.75in at the front and 4in at the rear.

A feature of the rear hub was the beginning of some-thing new in wheel building. The sprocket was riveted to the brake drum to save weight on the one hand and

1940 Plover Model K41, as obtained before restoration. (Courtesy S. Penworth)

1940 Plover Model K41, after restoration. (Courtesy S. Penworth)

also for economy, but primarily as a means of arranging for brake and drive to operate on the left-hand side. The rear hub on the 1939 season model differed slightly from that employed the following year; the basic principles, with regard to design, nevertheless continued as before. Internal expanding hub brakes were fitted front and rear. The finish consisted of black enamel and chromium plating with the tank gold-lined.

The specification for the Snipe 49 was the same, but fitted with the 98cc engine. The price of both was £25. Colour finish was black enamel with chromium plating.

The Powerbike No. J50

For some time Villiers had been looking for a company or designer to exploit their Junior engine to its full potential. In the meantime, George Herbert Jones, the designer, was undertaking an exercise to develop a suitable model for the engine. Eventually he took out a design licence incorporating the new Villiers Junior 98cc engine. In 1938 the licence was taken up by Francis-Barnett, who announced its Powerbike J50 at the Earl's Court Motor Cycle Show for the 1939 season.

Front forks of the 1939 season model consisted of a steering-head stem brazed into a malleable casting, which accommodated two rubber buffers pressed tightly in position. To the fork-blade assembly was brazed a further malleable casting, machined with a platform and two outside lugs, through which passed a 0.5in diameter bolt to mate up with the head-stem lug. Fork action was limited to a slight back and forward movement cushioned by the two rubbers. For this specific reason,

adjustment of the steering-head bearing was critical: in practice it appeared that such adjustment was being neglected, which not only overloaded the head stem in certain circumstances, but transferred this load to the frame. This type of fork was superseded by an ultra-lightweight link-action fork, which was more or less standardized immediately after World War II.

As the rear brake was operated by back pedalling, it was therefore necessary to devise a system whereby the rear brake could be disengaged to allow the Powerbike to be wheeled backwards and an automatic system to re-engage the brake. To enable the machine to be wheeled backwards, the right-angle trip lever attached to the bottom bracket assembly on the left-hand side of the machine had to be moved to its fully extended clockwise position. To do this it may have been necessary to lift the clutch and move the pedals slightly forwards; occasionally, particularly if the adjuster nut has not been taken up far enough, the brake could give the impression of having jammed if the machine was wheeled back hard with the trip lever in the operative position. With the trip lever in the clockwise, inoperative position, as soon as the pedals were used either for starting the engine or pedalling the machine, the trip lever was automatically thrown forwards, and the brake mechanism was ready for use. Apart from the mechanics of the brake, the operative parts were the same as all other internal-expanding brakes fitted to autocycles.

Colour finish was black enamel for the frame and forks, with tank and side panels dull silver. The Powerbike was priced at £21.

"POWERBIKE" J.50

The "Powerbike" supplies the need for a motorised bicycle with all the luxuries generally associated only with larger machines.

A glance at the specification below will show that this model, in common with other Francis-Barnett machines, has been designed to give unfailing service and freedom from dirt. Many unique features are contained in the "Powerbike." A patented rear brake mechanism of remarkable smoothness, and rubber cushioned front forks are just two features which make the Francis-Barnett a leader of its class.

The renowned 98 c.c. Villiers Engine, with flywheel magneto is employed and the whole unit is neatly enclosed beneath light and quickly detachable shields.

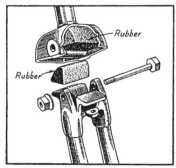

The simple rubber-sprung forks

SPECIFICATION

ENGINE. 98 *c.c.* Villiers Junior Unit. 50 m/m bore × 50 m/m stroke. Large expansion chamber and final silencer, providing exceptionally silent running.

CLUTCH. Running in oil, incorporated in engine unit. Rachet lever control on handlebar.

CARBURETTOR. Villiers automatic, controlled by single lever. Air strangler for starting.

TRANSMISSION. Renold chain, $\frac{1}{2}'' \times \frac{3}{16}''$. Independent adjustment provided for transmission and pedalling chains.

LUBRICATION. Petroil system. Oil measure fitted to tank filler cap. Proportion of oil to petrol—1 in 20.

LIGHTING. Villiers direct Lighting from Flywheel Dynamo. Parking battery in headlamp.

IGNITION. Villiers Flywheel Magneto.

FRAME. Cycle type, built with tandem strength fittings.

FORKS. Rubber cushioned (patented).

BRAKES. Internal expanding, 4" Rear and 3⅛" Front. **Rear brake, pedal operated by patent mechanism.** Front controlled by handlebar lever.

TANK. Steel, welded. Dull chromium plated finish, lined blue. Capacity 1¾ gallons. Two-level petrol tap fitted.

TYRES. 26" × 2" × 1¾" Dunlop.

SADDLE. Brooks Spring Top.

STAND. Rear. Clip up type.

CARRIER. Large tubular rear carrier fitted with neat metal tool box.

EQUIPMENT. Bulb Horn. Licence Holder. Inflator and Tools.

Annual Tax 12/-   PRICE ~~£12 12 0~~ **£21**   Third Party Insurance 15/-

MANUFACTURERS :

FRANCIS & BARNETT LTD., LOWER FORD STREET, COVENTRY

Telegrams : FRANBAR, COVENTRY   Telephone : 3054

The 1939 Powerbike Model No. J50.

The 1940 Season

For this season the model number was prefixed with the letter 'K', and in the motorcycle range there were two of each of the following models: Cruisers, the K39 and K45; Plovers, the K40 and K41; Seagulls, the K43 and K47; and finally Snipes, the K48 and K49. In addition two versions of the Powerbike were manufactured in 1940, both under Model No. K50. The Powerbike started off the year with the Villiers Junior engine prefix SH, and finished with the Villiers Junior de Luxe engine prefix XX or XXA.

The specification was the same as before, with the exception of the Cruiser Model No. K39, which did not specify a choice of lubrication by Villiers automatic or petroil for this year's model, and only one price is quoted. Prices for the Cruiser K39 and K45 were £46 5s and £49 10s; for the Plover K40 and K41, £31 5s and £35 15s; for the Seagull K41 and K43, £39 10s and £46 5s; and for the Snipe K48 and K49, both £27 10s.

Machine Specifications

Model	Powerbike No. 50	Powerbike DL No. 50
Manufacturing year	1939–40	1940
Engine	Villiers Junior, single-cylinder, air-cooled two-stroke	Villiers Junior de luxe, single-cylinder, air-cooled two-stroke
Number prefix	SH	XX, XXA
Bore and stroke	50 × 50mm	50 × 50mm
Capacity	98cc	98cc
Lubrication	Petroil	Petroil
Ignition	Villiers flywheel magneto	Villiers flywheel magneto
Carburettor	Villiers single lever	Villiers single lever
Transmission	Renold chain 0.5 × 0.19in	Renold chain 0.5 × 0.19in
Gearbox	Single speed	Single speed
Frame	Cycle type, built with tandem strength fittings	Cycle type, built with tandem strength fittings
Number prefix	JG, KG	KG
Front suspension	Cycle type, rubber cushioned	Cycle type, rubber cushioned
Rear suspension	Rigid	Rigid
Wheels front and rear	26in	26in
Brakes front	3.63in internal expanding, hand-operated	3.63in internal expanding, hand-operated
Brakes rear	4in internal expanding, pedal-operated	4in internal expanding, pedal-operated
Tyres front and rear	26 × 2 × 1.75in Dunlop	26 × 2 × 1.75in Dunlop

General Specifications

Fuel tank capacity	1.75gal (8ltr)	1.75gal (8ltr)

CHAPTER FOUR

Manufacturing Seasons 1946–1956

The manufacture of motorcycles at Lower Ford Street did not recommence immediately after the cessation of hostilities in 1945, but in the following year with one pre-war and one new model in the line-up. One of the post-war era conundrums was the non-appearance of either of the Cruiser models nos 39 and 45. Mr Eric Barnett's message to the many riders who had hoped to see the famous 249cc enclosed Cruiser returning to production was:

> Much as we would like to satisfy the growing and insistent demand for the reintroduction of the 'Cruiser', we must bow to force of circumstances and just say how sorry we are in not being able to produce it again *just yet*.

At the end of his sentence I have emphasized the words 'just yet', as his statement leads me to believe that it was the intention of the company to reintroduce the pre-war Cruiser at the appropriate moment. There was, however, a shortage of raw materials for some time after the war had ended, and as the Cruiser required an abnormal amount compared to other machines, in terms of materials it would not have been a viable proposition to manufacture. By the time there *were* sufficient supplies of materials available, designs and the requirements of the motorcycling public had moved on, and the all-enclosed pre-war Cruiser was consigned to history.

The 1946 Season

The manufacturing of motorcycles was recommenced in 1946 with two models, one based on the pre-war era, the Powerbike, which retained its name, and the Merlin, which appeared, at first glance, similar to the earlier Snipe model but had only the Villiers Mark 9D engine in common. The frame numbering system carried on from where it had left off in 1940 when the letter K was prefix for that year; thus for 1946 the letter L was the prefix.

The Merlin No. L51

The Merlin Model No. L51 was fitted with the Villiers Mark 9D engine, prefix 597. In essence it was rather antiquated in design, with girder-type forks fitted with a central spring and a hand-change gear lever placed awkwardly by the rider's right leg. The machine was small and light and could easily be lifted on and off the stand. The equipment was Spartan, with a rear carrier, a bulb horn and direct lighting, and a speedometer as an optional extra. The frame number prefix was LK.

The 122cc Mark 9D engine was coming to the end of its useful life when fitted to the Merlin, a pre-war design that incorporated DKW-inspired 1930s technology based upon the Schnurle loop scavenging system. This system allowed engine manufacturers to dispense with the use of a deflector piston and to improve the efficiency of the combustion chamber. DKW also developed a highly efficient arrangement of transfer ports. The engine, of unit construction, was attached to the frame at three points.

The gearbox was integral with the crankcase, and the front chain was fully lubricated, running in an enclosed chaincase. The handlebars were held in fully adjustable clips and could be set for height and angle.

The footrests also had a wide range of adjustment. Unfortunately the saddle was not adjustable, and was set for a rider of average height. The brakes were 5in in diameter front and rear. A separate oil tank of 3 pints (1.7ltr) capacity, identical in size and shape to the toolbox, was mounted between the rear frame stays on the near side. The oil measure was an integral part of the petrol tank filler cap.

The original exhaust pipes, silencers and extension pipes were made in one piece, making it impossible to remove the build-up of carbon in the silencer to any large extent. When this happened it became necessary to cut off the silencers and replace them with detach-able silencers available from the company or other suppliers. The finish was black enamel, with gold-lined tank; exhaust pipes, silencers and so on were chromium-plated.

The maximum speed was about 40mph (64km/h), with a cruising speed of slightly less, at 35mph (56km/h); fuel consumption was in excess of 100mpg (2.8ltr/100km) at 30mph (48km/h). The price was £60 plus a whopping 27 per cent purchase tax of £16 4s. A speedometer was available at £3 3s 6d plus purchase tax.

Bulletin No. 12 regarding the clogging up of the silencers is shown [*below*]. It affected models of other

1946 Merlin Model L51, seen at the FBOC AGM 2009. (Courtesy FBOC)

Bulletin No. 12

Exhaust System with Non-detachable Silencer

1949/50 'Merlin' and 'Falcon'

Isolated complaints have reached us regarding the falling off of power on the above machines, and in some cases it would seem that congested exhaust systems are responsible. It is realised how difficult it is to remove the carbon from the silencer but in any event quite a number of enthusiasts have asked whether we can provide an exhaust silencer of the detachable type.

We are now in a position to offer a 'Burgess' silencer complete with clip and circlip, which has been made up to our requirements and we can supply this at a cost of 35/- (£1.75p) retail. To fit this, the non-detachable silencer will now have to be sawn off the present system and the 'Burgess' silencer can then be clipped to the pipe in an orthodox manner.

We are most anxious to keep in touch with the wishes of the private owner and we are quite sure that this 'Burgess' silencer, which we know to be popular with many riders, will give satisfaction.

ISSUED 26 JULY 1951

Machine Specifications

❖

Model	Powerbike 50	Merlin 51	Merlin 52
Manufacturing year	1946–49	1946–48	1949–53
Engine	Villiers Junior de Luxe, single-cylinder, air-cooled two-stroke	Villiers Mark 9D, single-cylinder, air-cooled two-stroke	Villiers Mark 10D, single-cylinder, air-cooled two-stroke
Number prefix	XXA, 434	597	823, 935, 206A
Bore and stroke	50 × 50mm	50 × 62mm	50 × 62mm
Capacity	98cc	122cc	122cc
Compression ratio	Not known	6.5:1	8:1
Lubrication	Petroil	Petroil	Petroil
Carburettor	Not known	Lightweight single lever	Lightweight single lever
Ignition	Flywheel magneto	Flywheel magneto	Flywheel magneto
Primary drive	Chain	Renold chain 110038	Renold chain 110038
Final drive	Renold chain 111044	Renold chain 110044	Renold chain 110044
Gearbox	Single speed	Three-speed; hand change	Three-speed
Gearbox ratios - standard	Not known	8.00; 13.4; 23.60:1	7.18; 10.00; 19.1:1
Frame	Tubular loop-welded	Tubular, welded and brazed	Tubular, welded and brazed
Number prefix	LH, MH, NH, OH	LK, NK, OK	OL, PPL, RL, SL, TL, TTL
Suspension front	Girder; from 1948 link-action fork with rubber suspension	Girder; link type with compression spring	Telescopic fork with 20in three-rate springs
Suspension rear	Rigid	Rigid	Rigid
Tyres: front	26 × 2 × 1.75in	3 × 19in Dunlop ribbed	3 × 19in Dunlop ribbed
rear	26 × 2 × 1.75in	3 × 19in Dunlop	3 × 19in Dunlop universal
Hubs: front	3.63in; cup and cone bearings	Cup and cone bearings	Cup and cone bearings
rear	4in; cup and cone bearings	Cup and cone bearings	Cup and cone bearings
Brakes front	3.63in handlebar lever	5in diameter drum	5in dia. internal expanding
Brakes rear	4in back pedal	5in diameter drum	5in dia. internal expanding

General Specifications

	Powerbike 50	Merlin 51	Merlin 52
Fuel tank capacity	1.75gal (8ltr)	2.25gal (10ltr)	2.25gal (10ltr)
Overall length	Not known	Not known	78.5in (1,994mm)
Overall width	Not known	26in (660mm)	26.5in (673mm)
Overall height	Not known	Not known	37in (940mm)
Wheelbase	Not known	50.5in (1,282mm)	49in (1,245mm)
Ground clearance	Not known	5in (127mm)	5in (127mm)
Seat height (min.)	Not known	26in (660mm)	27.75in (705mm)
Dry weight	Not known	178lb (81kg)	181lb (82kg)
Power	Not known	3.2bhp @ 4,000rpm	4.9bhp @ 4,400rpm

years besides those of 1949/50; my 1948 Merlin L51, for example, suffered from carbon build-up, and a previous owner had overcome this by knocking large holes in the bottom of the silencers. There must have been more than isolated instances of complaints over this problem. The current cost of replacing the whole exhaust system is around £250, slightly more than it was in 1951at the equivalent £1 75p.

The Powerbike No. L50

The other 1946 machine was the Powerbike L50, which was a continuation of the pre-war machine under the same name and model number. It employed the 98cc Villiers JDL engine with the identifying prefix of XXA. For 1946, Webb ultra-lightweight forks were specified, having a link action and a central steel spring. Top and bottom links were identical, the spindles fitting in plain bearings with no bushes, and the action controlled by the links with no adjustable damper fitted. There were thirty-eight ball bearings of 0.188in in diameter in the head bearing, with nineteen in each race. There were two slightly different hubs used in the wheels: 'British Hubs' and 'Harwil' hubs; where the latter were used, a letter 'H' was added as a suffix to the frame number. The wheels were completely interchangeable, and in both instances ten 0.25in diameter ball bearings were fitted in each of

the cup and cone bearings. The tank and engine shields were black enamel, gold-lined; the handlebar, wheel rims and other bright parts chromium-plated. The frame number prefix was LH.

The 1947 Season

Both the Merlin and Powerbike models were continued into 1947, and basically the only changes that were made were to prices, and the Villiers engine numbering system. The Mark 9D engine now had the prefix 597, and the JDL 434; the frame prefixes were LK (unchanged from 1946) for the Merlin, and MH for the Powerbike. The Merlin was priced at £66 plus £17 16s 5d purchase tax, and the Powerbike £44 plus £11 17s 7d purchase tax. The tax remained at 27 per cent for 1947.

The 1948 Season

Manufacture of the Merlin L51 and Powerbike 50 models continued into 1948 almost unchanged. The Powerbike did, however, have an alteration to its front suspension, with rubber-suspended front forks being introduced. The suspension was by means of four rubber bands mounted in two pairs. Single-strut-type blades were used, a lug taking the cross spindle for the

1948 Merlin Model L51 owned by T.J. Crockett. (Courtesy FBOC)

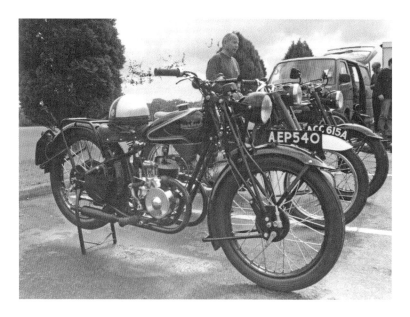

1948 Merlin Model L51 seen at the FBOC AGM, Hagley, 2009. (Courtesy FBOC)

links being brazed to the blades. It was subsequently found necessary to weld an additional tube in front of the single blade, making it similar to a girder fork; in the spares list for the 1950 Powerbike 56 it refers to the 'fork girder RH' and 'fork girder LH'.

There seems to be some doubt as to when the fork with the rubber suspension was first introduced. Goddard states: 'The 1947 Powerbike saw the introduction of rubber-suspended front forks. Midway through the year it was found necessary to go over to welding an additional tube in front of the single blade.' The *Hints and Spares Manual* for the Powerbike models LH and MH makes reference to the 'front fork – 1946 – compression spring type' and the 'front fork – 1947 – rubber suspension type', and an undated sales brochure allegedly from 1947 describes the forks as 'tubular, link action, with rubber suspension'; the image of the machine does not have the additional tubes to the forks. However, a report in *Motor Cycle* of 16 October 1947 on the machines available for 1948 refers to the 'new front forks', and the image shows the original fork without the additional tubes to the front of the blades.

There is no doubt that the new forks were introduced at some time in 1947, but whether it was in the 1947 season or early in the 1948 season – that is, in the last three months of the 1947 calendar year – is open to debate. In this instance the alteration to the

forks is included in the 1948 season. The engine and frame number prefixes for the Powerbike were 434 and NH; for the Merlin, 597 and NK. The prices remained unchanged for 1948.

The 1949 Season

The Powerbike remained virtually unaltered for 1949; the frame number prefix was OH. The Merlin L51, the last production model fitted with girder-type forks, was discontinued for the 1949 season. It was replaced by not one, but four new models: the Merlin models O52 and O53, and the Falcon models O54 and O55.

The Merlin No. O52 and No. O53; and Falcon No. O54 and No. O55

These four models used the same cycle parts but different engines and electrical systems. Thus the Merlins used the successor to the Villiers Mark 9D engine, the Mark 10D. It had the same bore and stroke of 50 × 62mm and a capacity of 122cc; the prefix was 823. The Falcons used the Villiers Mark 6E engine, prefix 824.

The lighting system for the Merlin O.52 and the Falcon O.54 was direct lighting from the flywheel dynamo magneto with parking battery and bulb horn. The Merlin O53 and the Falcon O55 had a battery lighting set and an electric horn; 7in (18cm) headlamps were standard.

Machine Specifications

Model	Merlin 53	Falcon 54	Falcon 55
Manufacturing year	1949–53	1949–53	1949–52
Engine	Villiers Mark 10D, single-cylinder, air-cooled two-stroke	Villiers Mark 6E, single-cylinder, air-cooled two-stroke 1953: Mark 8E	Villiers Mark 6E, single-cylinder, air-cooled two-stroke
Number prefix	823, 935, 206A	824, 946, 207A, 387A	824, 946, 207A
Bore and stroke	50 × 62mm	59 × 72mm	59 × 72mm
Capacity	122cc	197cc	197cc
Compression ratio	8:1	7.56:1	7.56:1
Lubrication	Petroil	Petroil	Petroil
Carburettor	Lightweight single-lever	Middleweight two-lever	Middleweight two-lever
Ignition	Flywheel magneto	Flywheel magneto	Flywheel magneto
Primary drive	Renold chain 110038	Renold chain 110044	Renold chain 110044
Final drive	Renold chain 110044	Renold chain 110044	Renold chain 110044
Gearbox	Three-speed	Three-speed	Three-speed
Gearbox ratios – standard	7.18; 10.00; 19.1:1	5.87; 8.20; 15.6:1	5.87; 8.20; 15.6:1
Frame	Tubular, welded and brazed	Tubular, welded and brazed	Tubular, welded and brazed
Number prefix	OL, PPL, RL, SL, TL, TTL	OM, PPM, RM, SM, TM, TTM	OM, PPM, RM, SM
Suspension front	Telescopic fork with 20in three-rate springs	Telescopic fork with 20in three-rate springs	Telescopic fork with 20in three-rate springs
Suspension rear	Rigid	Rigid	Rigid
Tyres front	3 × 19in Dunlop ribbed	3 × 19in Dunlop ribbed	3 × 19in Dunlop ribbed
rear	3 × 19in Dunlop universal	3 × 19in Dunlop universal	3 × 19in Dunlop universal
Hubs front	Cup and cone bearings	Cup and cone bearings	Cup and cone bearings
rear	Cup and cone bearings	Cup and cone bearings	Cup and cone bearings
Brakes front	5in diameter internal expanding	5in diameter internal expanding	5in diameter internal expanding
rear	5in diameter internal expanding	5in diameter internal expanding	5in diameter internal expanding

General Specifications

Fuel tank capacity	2.25gal (10ltr)	2.25gal (10ltr)	2.25gal (10ltr)
Overall length	78.5in (1,994mm)	78in (1,981mm)	78in (1,981mm)
Overall width	26.5in (673mm)	26.5in (673mm)	26.5in (673mm)
Overall height	37in (940mm)	37in (940mm)	37in (940mm)
Wheelbase	49in (1,245mm)	49in (1,245mm)	49in (1,245mm)
Ground clearance	5in (127mm)	5in (127mm)	5in (127mm)

Machine Specifications *continued*

Seat height (min.)	27.75in (705mm)	28in (711mm)	28in (711mm)
Dry weight	193lb (87.5kg)	187lb (85kg)	199lb (90kg)
Power	4.9bhp @ 4,400rpm	8.4bhp @ 4,000rpm	8.4bhp @ 4,000rpm

All models had telescopic front suspension, three-speed gearboxes with foot change, 5in internal expanding front and rear brakes, a 'spring-up' rear stand, 5in (13cm) wide mudguards, and the matching toolbox and oil tank as fitted to the Merlin L51. The telescopic front suspension consisted of a single tri-pressure coil spring fitted inside the slider tube in each leg, held in position by rotating the spring from one and a half to two complete turns clockwise, which secured it at the bottom of the slider tube. A threaded spring anchor was fitted inside the top of the spring, which was in turn attached to a spring support cup by the anchorage screw, which passed through the cup and screwed into the spring anchor. This had the effect of compressing the spring inside the fork-tube assembly. The three-rate loading of the spring was designed to work by compressing the coils closest together first, and then compressing the coils further apart should the road surface dictate that this was required. Four Tufnol bushes, two in each leg, were pressed into the fork H-section. Initially the bushes were fitted by selective assembly with a maximum tolerance of 0.003in.

The frame prefix for the Merlin 52 and 53 was OL; for the Falcon 54 and 55 it was OM. Colour finish was black enamel, and the tank was gold-lined; the handlebar, exhaust system and other bright parts were chromium-plated. Models were priced as follows: the Merlin O52 £67, the Merlin O53 £71, the Falcon O54 £73, and the Falcon O55 £77; in addition purchase tax at the rate of 27 per cent was also payable.

ABOVE RIGHT: 1949 Merlin Model O53. (Courtesy FBOC)

RIGHT: 1949 Merlin Model O52. (Courtesy FBOC)

1952 Falcon Model 55. (Courtesy FBOC)

The 1950 Season

The two Merlin models nos 52 and 53, plus the two Falcon models nos 54 and 55, continued for 1950. Special provision was made for the adjustment of the saddle height and tilt, three positions being provided at the nose support, and adjustable spring posts at the rear. The year letter was dropped from the model numbers. The engine and frame prefixes for the Merlins were 935 and PPL, and for the Falcons 946 and PPM. Included in the 1950 advertisement for these four machines was the fact that they were equipped with a foot-operated gear change. Inclusive in the price was a Smiths lightweight speedometer for the Merlins, and a Smiths trip speedometer for the Falcons. The

Merlin 52 retailed at £70 3s 6d and the 53 at £74 3s 6d, and the Falcon 54 at £77 and the 55 at £81; in addition purchase tax was charged at 27 per cent.

The Powerbike No. 56

The new Powerbike Model No. 56 superseded the No. 50, and the 98cc Villiers Mark 2F engine; prefix 801 replaced the Villiers JDL engine. The main feature of this unit was the increased lifespan compared with its predecessor. The new design provided a built-up crankshaft using a parallel crankpin with the crankshaft supported by a 6205 bearing fitted on either side. The big end of the connecting rod was ground and hardened to take steel and bronze rollers fitted alternately.

1953 Merlin Model 53. (Courtesy FBOC)

1950 Powerbike Model 56.

The brakes on the Powerbike 56 were basically identical to the previous Powerbike models, but with an alteration to the operating lever on which the actuating cam was fitted. The function of the trip lever in the inoperative position was to allow the machine to be wheeled backwards. As soon as the pedals were rotated forwards, the effect was to move the trip lever anti-clockwise to enable the brake to be activated. The brake rod had to be adjusted so that the wheel spun freely and only a small backward pressure applied the brake.

The rear wheel was constructed in the same manner as a normal bicycle wheel. It had an 18T freewheel with a left-hand thread fitted. Ten 0.25in ball bearings were used each side in the cup and cone bearings. Care had to be taken if rebuilding a wheel to ensure that everything was absolutely concentric with the hub. Improvements were made to the rider's comfort by changing from 2in section tyres to 2.25in, and providing a large spring top saddle. The frame prefix was PN.

The 1951 Season

The five models continued for 1951: these were the Merlin 52 and 53, the Falcon 54 and 55, and the Powerbike 56. The oil tank on the near side of the Merlins and Falcons was discontinued. The one-piece pattern exhaust system was replaced by detachable silencers on all models, with the Powerbike's being a scaled-down version. A screwed rod was welded to the exhaust downpipe and threaded through the silencer; it then protruded through a recess at the end of the silencer where it was held in place by two 0.25in nuts. An oil-resistant rubber seal was fitted at the front of the silencer, and as the nuts were tightened on the threaded rod, the silencer was pushed against the seal, making it gas tight.

The colour finish was now black or Azure Blue enamel to order; the tank was gold-lined, and the handlebar, exhaust system and other bright parts were chromium-plated. The engine and frame prefixes for the Merlins were 935 or 206A and RL; for the Falcons 916 or 207A and RM; and for the Powerbike 801 or 189A and RN. The second engine number prefix shown reflects the new system that used a combination of numbers and letters to denote the engine type, and the firm or firms to which it had been supplied. The previous all-number system had become too cumbersome to continue with.

The prices of the Merlins and Falcons remained the same as 1950.

The 1952 Season

After two fairly quiet manufacturing years, the 1952 season heralded the start of what might be called the Francis-Barnett golden age. 1952 was the last year in production of the Powerbike No. 56; the engine and frame prefixes were 189A and SN. The Merlins 52 and

LEFT: 1951 Merlin Model 53 in azure blue, owner Moira J.Woods.

BELOW LEFT: 1952 Powerbike Model 56, one of the last made, owner Mike Jackson. (Courtesy FBOC)

53 and the Falcons 54 and 55 were joined by the Merlin Model No. 57 and the Falcon Model No. 58. The engine and frame prefixes for the Merlins 52 and 53 were 206A and SL, and for the Falcons 54 and 55 207A and SM. The Villiers Mark 10D engine of the Merlin 57 had a prefix of 208A, and the Villiers Mark 6E of the Falcon 58 had a prefix of 209A.

The Merlin No. 57 and Falcon No. 58

The Merlin Model No. 57 and the Falcon Model No. 58 were the first two machines to be fitted with the swinging arm-type rear suspension. The rear wheel axle slots into the rear spring arm attached to the main frame assembly by a hinge just above the rear engine fixing plate. The hinge allowed the spring arm to pivot up when the spring in the rear suspension was compressed, and down when it was decompressed. The rear suspension units were semi-oil damped, and the action was mainly by oil cushioning with a spring support. Each unit had approximately 30cc or 1fl oz of SAE 30 oil situated in the bottom of the unit. There were two tubes inside the unit which could telescope, with the inner one being fitted with an absorber bush. This bush regulated the flow of oil that could pass from one tube to the other under pressure as the spring unit was compressed.

Alternative springs were available with different loading values. The factory standard was a lightweight spring, a medium-weight spring for heavier riders, and a heavyweight spring for use when carrying a pillion passenger. The maximum travel allowed for was approximately 4in (10cm).

Not long after these two models came into production in 1952, a modification was made to the hinge. The original hinge was referred to as the 'series one hinge' and the modified one as the 'series two hinge'. It is comparatively easy to identify the machines fitted with the series one hinge, as the frame number prefix is SLS for the Merlin and SMS for the Falcon. The machines with the series two hinge were SSLS for the Merlin and SSMS for the Falcon.

The construction of the hinges is easily explained. In the series one hinge, a Harrisflex rubber bush was press-fitted into a lug on each side of the frame, through which a pivot shaft passed; the hinge stud went through the shaft. The flanges of the rubber bushes were held in torsion as they were compressed by pivot pressure plates bolted in position. The alteration in the hinge to produce the series two hinge was to simplify construction of the hinge by using Silentbloc bearings which did not require the use of pressure plates.

The following is an extract from Bulletin No. 19, issued 11 July 1952, regarding the frame and also the then current position on the supply of wheels:

> **Frame**: In order to simplify dismantling and reassembly of the front hinge of the swinging arm, the design has been slightly modified. We have dispensed with the Harrisflex bearings in favour of Silentbloc bearings, and machines with this modification bear an additional 'S' to the prefix letters of the frame number. This change is not taken care of by our current Spares List, and frame numbers and prefix letters should always be quoted whenever spares for the rear suspension are needed.
>
> **Wheels**: Because of the difficulty of maintaining continuity of one type of hub, our supply is being supplemented from various sources. We are taking care that wheels complete will interchange, but we fear that there may be some little variation in components and we may not be able to identify any particular type of wheel by its frame number, but we shall avoid this non-interchange as much as we possibly can.

The frame, forks and rear suspension were identical in both the Merlin 57 and the Falcon 58; the advertisement for these machines stated that: 'The swinging rear fork gave 4in movement: oil damping prevented clashing: a rubber buffer controlled the rebound, and all pivots were rubber bushed to cut maintenance to a minimum.' The telescopic front fork had three-rate springs, 20in (50cm) long. Francis-Barnett really pushed the suspension in their advert, under the banner 'Satin-Smooth Suspension'.

The rigid frame machines were fitted with a 15T final drive sprocket, but because of the proximity of the swinging arm hinge it was changed to a 17T final drive sprocket for the 'springers'; to compensate for this the rear wheel sprocket was increased to 44T for the Merlin and 50T for the Falcon. A further alteration was made in 1952, this time to the rear wheels of the springers. The front wheels retained the cup and cone system, and the rear wheels had 6202 journal bearings fitted. The tubular carrier was omitted from the specification of the Falcons 57 and 58, and now became available at extra cost.

After almost a quarter of a century, Francis-Barnett officially supported and sponsored reliability trials – although in the 1949/50 winter season, what was obviously a works-prepared 197cc prototype appeared in a popular trial. It was not long before this 197cc trial prototype was again in action, with Jack Botting putting up the best class performance in the 1950 'British Experts'. In the 1951 Victory, Kickham and Mitchell Open Trials, Brian Martin secured the 125cc class awards on a smaller machine.

The Merlin No. 59 and Falcon No. 60

In 1952, Francis-Barnett introduced two competition models, the Merlin Competition Model No. 59 and the Falcon Trials Model No. 60. Both of these were loosely based on their rigid frame counterparts, but used competition versions of the Villiers engines. The Mark 6E installed in the Falcon had a compression ratio of 8.25:1 and developed 9.5bhp at 4,500rpm. The M2306 ignition coil was fitted to the magneto for higher efficiency. The unit construction, three-speed gearbox with positive stop foot-change mechanism had standard ratios of 6.8, 11.55 and 22:1. The Amal carburettor No. 6/125 was used, rather than a Villiers type, and because of this the manifold was not a Villiers design but a 'special' to allow the Amal to be used. The air cleaner was readily detachable to allow the cartridge and felt washers to be cleaned or replaced quickly, and was of Vokes design.

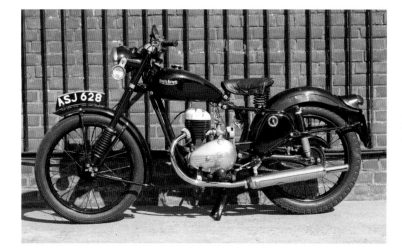

1953 Falcon Model 54 with Villiers 8E engine, seen at an East of England section meeting of the FBOC.

1953 Merlin Model 57, seen at the FBOC AGM Gaydon, owner Sue Dorling. (Courtesy FBOC)

A 1953 Merlin Model 57, later stolen from Villiers Services. (Courtesy FBOC)

ABOVE: 1953 Falcon Model 58 (left), 1957 Falcon Model 74 (right). (Courtesy FBOC)

1953 Falcon Model 58. (Courtesy FBOC)

1953 Falcon Model 58, owner S. Elkes. (Courtesy FBOC)

1953 Falcon Model 58 in azure blue, restored by Des Heckle. (Courtesy Des Heckle)

Machine Specifications

	Powerbike 56	Merlin 57	Falcon 58
Model	Powerbike 56	Merlin 57	Falcon 58
Manufacturing year	1950–52	1952–53	1952–53
Engine	Villiers Mark 2F, single-cylinder, air-cooled two-stroke	Villiers Mark 10D, single-cylinder, air-cooled two-stroke 1953: Mark 12D	Villiers Mark 6E, single-cylinder, air-cooled two-stroke 1953: Mark 8E
Number prefix	801, 189A	208A, 405A	209A, 387A
Bore and stroke	47 × 57mm	50 × 62mm	59 × 72mm
Capacity	98cc	122cc	197cc
Compression ratio	8:1	8:1	7.56:1
Lubrication	Petroil	Petroil	Petroil
Carburettor	Villiers 'Junior'	Lightweight single-lever*	Middle weight two-lever
Ignition	Flywheel magneto	Flywheel magneto	Flywheel magneto
Primary drive	Renold chain 0.5in pitch	Renold chain 110038	Renold chain 110044*
Final drive	Renold chain 0.5in pitch	Renold chain 110044	Renold chain 110044
Gearbox	Single-speed	Three-speed	Three-speed
Gearbox ratios – standard	10.76:1	7.18; 10.00; 19.10:1	5.87; 8.20; 15.60:1
Frame	Tubular loop; brazed and welded	Tubular cradle type, brazed and welded	Tubular cradle type, brazed and welded
Number prefix	PN, RN, SN	SLS, SSLS, TLS, TTLS	SMS, SSMS, TMS, TTMS
Suspension: front	Girder	Telescopic fork with 20in three-rate springs	Telescopic fork with 20in three-rate springs
rear	Rigid	Swinging fork arm two-rate springs†	Swinging fork arm two-rate springs†
Tyres: front	2.25 × 21in Dunlop	3 × 19in Dunlop ribbed	3 × 19in Dunlop ribbed
rear	2.25 × 21in Dunlop	3 × 19in Dunlop universal	3 × 19in Dunlop universal
Hubs: front	Cup and cone bearings	Cup and cone bearings	Cup and cone bearings
rear	Cup and cone bearings	Journal bearing 6202	Journal bearing 6202
Brakes: front	4in handlebar lever	5in diameter drum	5in diameter drum
rear	4in back pedal	5in diameter drum	5in diameter drum

General Specifications

	Powerbike 56	Merlin 57	Falcon 58
Fuel tank capacity	1.5gal (6.8ltr)	2.25gal (10ltr)	2.25gal (10ltr)
Overall length	77.75in (1,975mm)	78.5in (1,994mm)	78in (1,981mm)
Overall width	23in (584mm)	26.5in (673mm)	26.5in (673mm)
Overall height	40in (1,016mm)	37in (940mm)	37in (940mm)
Wheelbase	Not known	49in (1,245mm)	49.5in (1,257mm)
Ground clearance	Not known	5in (127mm)	5in (127mm)
Seat height (min.)	Not known	27.75in (705mm)	28in (711mm)

Machine Specifications *continued*

Dry weight	125lb (57 kg)	210lb (95kg)	218lb (99kg)
Power	2bhp @ 3,750rpm	4.9bhp @ 4,400rpm *Villiers S.19 carburettor with Mark 12D engine † Silentbloc fitted later	8.4bhp @ 4000rpm ‡Silentbloc fitted later *1953 110038 for 8E

Machine Specifications

Model	Competition Merlin 59	Competition Falcon 60	Trials Merlin 61
Manufacturing year	1952	1952	1953
Engine	Villiers Mark 10D, single-cylinder, air-cooled two-stroke	Villiers Mark 6E or 7E, single-cylinder, air-cooled two-stroke	Villiers Mark 12D, single-cylinder, air-cooled two-stroke
Number prefix	166A	158A	402A
Bore and stroke	50 × 62mm	59 × 72mm	50 × 62mm
Capacity	122cc	197cc	122cc
Compression ratio	Not known	8.4:1	Not known
Lubrication	Petroil	Petroil	Petroil
Carburettor	Not known	Amal 6/125	Not known
Ignition	Flywheel magneto	Flywheel magneto	Flywheel magneto
Primary drive	Chain	Chain	Chain
Final drive	Chain	Chain	Chain
Gearbox	Three speed	Three-speed	Four-speed
Gearbox ratios - standard	9.06; 15.41; 29.45:1	6.8; 11.51; 22:1	Not known
Frame	Tubular loop frame brazed and welded	Tubular reinforced with widened rear stays	Tubular loop frame brazed and welded
Rim size: front rear	WM1-21 WM2-19	WM1-21 WM2-19	WM1-21 WM2-19
Number prefix	SLC	SMC	TTLC
Suspension front	Telescopic fork	Telescopic fork with stiffened three-rate springs	Telescopic fork
Suspension rear	Rigid	Rigid	Rigid
Tyres: front rear	2.75 × 21in 3.25 × 19in	2.75 × 21in 3.50 × 19in	2.75 × 21in 3.25 × 19in

continued overleaf

Machine Specifications *continued*

Hubs: front	Cup and cone bearings	Cup and cone bearings	Cup and cone bearings
rear	Cup and cone bearings	Cup and cone bearings	Cup and cone bearings
Brakes: front	5in diameter drum	5in diameter drum	5in diameter drum
rear	5in diameter drum	5in diameter drum	5in diameter drum

General Specifications

Fuel tank capacity	2.25gal (10ltr)	2.25gal (10ltr)	2.25gal (10ltr)
Wheelbase	49in (1,245mm)	49in (1,245mm)	49.5in (1,257mm)
Ground clearance	7in (178mm)	7in (178mm)	7.50in (190mm)
Seat height (min.)	32.25in (819mm)	32.25in (819mm)	30.5in (775mm)
Dry weight	Not known	178lb (81kg)	Not known
Power	Not known	9.4bhp @ 4,250rpm	Not known

The frame was of specially reinforced tubular design with widened rear stays to permit a 4in rear tyre to be used by the works team. The telescopic front forks contained stiffened three-rate springs giving extra front wheel clearance; a Tufnol bush was fitted at the top end of the forks, making three in all. Journal bearings were fitted to the front and rear wheel hubs. Short, lightweight mudguards were fitted, giving ample clearance.

The colour finish was black enamel with chromium-plated handlebars.

The Falcon was priced at £97 plus £26 18s 11d, a total of £123 18s 11d. A direct lighting set was available at a total cost of £6 7s 10d.

Goddard states that the Merlin was fitted with the Villiers Mark 11D engine, prefix 166A, and Bacon states it was the Villiers Mark 10D engine, also with prefix 166A: this appears to be confirmed in the book *Classic British Two-Stroke Trials Bikes*. They both disagree on the Falcon, with Goddard stating that it had a Villiers Mark 7E engine, prefix 158A, and Bacon that it had the Villiers Mark 6E engine, prefix 158A. Again Bacon appears to be correct, as a press report indicates that it was fitted with the Mark 6E engine, although another source states that both engines were fitted and both used the same engine number prefix of 158A.

There is very little surviving regarding these two machines, the Merlin 59 and Falcon 60; the information on the Merlin is very sparse indeed and at times contradictory. Some information on the Falcon exists, and a photograph of one appears in Roy Bacon's book *Villiers Singles and Twins*. The Merlin is identified by the frame number prefix SLC, and the Falcon by the prefix SMC, and both were only produced during the 1952 season.

The 1953 Season

During 1953, ten different models were produced, and of those ten, at least five of them had a Series I and Series II versions so it is possible to say that fifteen models were produced that year. The Merlin models 52, 53 and 57 were continued from 1952, as were the Falcon models, 54, 55 and 58. Because of the changes that took place during the year, those machines with the original specification were referred to as Series One (or Series I) and those with the enhanced specification as Series Two (or Series II). Each one can be identified without difficulty by reference to the prefix of the frame number. For the Series I rigid frame models, the year prefix letter T for 1953 was followed by L for Merlins and M for Falcons; for the spring-frame models, the year letter T was followed by LS for Merlins and MS for Falcons. For the Series II models, each prefix commenced with two Ts followed by L, M, LS or MS as appropriate.

The main changes were replacing the Mark 10D engine in the Merlin 57 with the Mark 12D engine, prefix 405A, and the Mark 6E engine in the Falcon 58 with the Mark 8E engine, prefix 387A. At the same time a minor change was made in the dimensions of the front forks and a variation in the hubs and handlebars.

Machine Specifications

❖

Model	Trials Falcon 62	Scrambler Merlin 63	Scrambler Falcon 64
Manufacturing year	1953–55	1953	1954
Engine	Villiers Mark 7E, single-cylinder, air-cooled two-stroke	Villiers Mark 12D, single-cylinder, air-cooled two-stroke	Villiers Mark 7E, single-cylinder, air-cooled two-stroke
Number prefix	375A	403A	374A
Bore and stroke	59 × 72mm	50 × 62mm	59 × 72mm
Capacity	197cc	122cc	197cc
Lubrication	Petroil	Petroil	Petroil
Carburettor	Amal 276; Vokes air filter	Not known	Amal 276; Vokes air filter
Ignition	Flywheel magneto waterproofed	Flywheel magneto	Flywheel magneto
Primary drive	Chain	Chain	Chain
Final drive	Chain	Chain	Chain
Gearbox	Four-speed	Four-speed	Four-speed
Gearbox ratios – standard	6.25; 8.45; 14.40; 21.70:1	Not known	6.25; 8.45; 11.25; 18.10:1
Frame	Brazed and welded loop type with bolt-on rear stays	Not known	Brazed and welded loop type with bolt-on rear stays
Number prefix	TTMC, UTM, VTM	TTLS	TTMS, UTMS
Suspension front	Telescopic fork with stiffened 20in three-rate springs	Telescopic fork	Telescopic fork with stiffened 20in three-rate springs
Suspension rear	Rigid	Swinging fork arm	Swinging fork arm with hydraulically damped spring units
Rim size: front	WM1-21	Not known	WM1-21
rear	WM2-19	Not known	WM2-19
Tyres: front	2.75 × 21in Dunlop	2.75 × 21in	2.75 × 21in Dunlop
rear	3.50 × 19in Dunlop*	3.50 × 19in	3.50 × 19in Dunlop
Hubs: front	5in full width – journal bearings	5in full width – journal bearings	5in full width – journal bearings
rear	5in full width – journal bearings	5in full width – journal bearings	5in full width – journal bearings
Brakes: front	5in diameter drum	5in diameter drum	5in diameter drum
rear	5in diameter drum	5in diameter drum	5in diameter drum

General Specifications

Fuel tank capacity	2.25gal (10ltr)	2.25gal (10ltr)	2.25gal (10ltr)
Overall length	77in (1,955mm)	Not known	77.75in (1,975mm)

continued overleaf

Overall width	26.5in (673mm)	Not known	26.5in (673mm)
Overall height	41in (1,041mm)	Not known	41in (1,041mm)
Wheelbase	49.5in (1,257mm)	50.25in (1,276mm)	50.25in (1,276mm)
Ground clearance	7.5in (190mm)	7.5in (190mm)	7.5in (190mm)
Seat height (min.)	30.5in (775mm)	31in (787mm)	31in (787mm)
Dry weight	200lb (90kg)	Not known	212lb (96kg)
Power	9.5bhp @ 4,200rpm	Not known	9.5bhp @ 4,200rpm
	*1955; 4 × 19in Dunlop		

Outwardly there was very little difference in appearance between the Mark 10D and Mark 12D engines, but very few of the engine parts were interchangeable. The Villiers S.19 carburettor was fitted to the Mark 12D. The cylinder on the standard Mark 8E had an integral carburettor induction stub, but because of the lack of space in the frame, the actual cylinder used was similar to that on the Mark 6E, with a separate induction stub and a Villiers S.24 carburettor fitted.

The Merlin No. 61 and Scrambler No. 63; Falcon No. 62 and Scrambler No. 64

The competition models Merlin 59 and Falcon 60 were discontinued for 1953; in their place came the Merlin Trials No. 61 and the Scrambler No. 63, both with telescopic forks, and a rigid frame for the Merlin 61 and swinging arm for the Merlin 63; and the Falcon Trials No. 62 and the Scrambler No. 64, again both with telescopic forks and a rigid frame for the

Falcon 62 and swinging arm for the Falcon 64. The Merlin 61, frame number prefix TTLC, was fitted with the Villiers Mark 12D with a four-speed gearbox, usually shown as 12D/4, engine prefix 402A. The Merlin 63, frame number prefix TTLS, was also fitted with the Villiers 12D/4 engine, engine prefix 403A. The '4' indicates a four-speed gearbox, fitted with wide ratios for the 402A and standard for the 403A.

The following statement is from a Francis-Barnett booklet, *Hints and Tips for Trials Scrambler Models*:

It is particularly pointed out that the number of these machines available for production is severely limited and does not justify the issue of an elaborate instruction booklet or spares list. Spares prices of any particular parts are available upon application.

It therefore seems appropriate to reproduce here the majority of the information contained in the booklet.

1955 Falcon Scrambles No. 72 which replaced the Falcon Scrambles No. 64.

Both the Falcons had the high compression Villiers Mark7E/4 fitted with a special waterproofed magneto, with the engine number prefix 375A and frame number prefix TTMC for the Falcon 62, and 374A and TTMS for the Falcon 64. Competition-type handlebars were standard on both machines, as was the upswept exhaust system.

The forty-eight-tooth rear wheel sprocket was standardized on both machines. The overall ratios could be altered by fitting alternative rear wheel sprockets that were available in even numbers, from forty-eight to fifty-four teeth inclusive. The internal ratios of the gearbox could also be altered from close to wide by fitting a different mainshaft slider and the corresponding low gear, and the layshaft second gear slider and the corresponding low gear. It was therefore possible to change the gearbox ratios from wide to close or vice versa by exchanging the four gearbox internals. An optional extra low bottom gear for trials could be provided by replacing the mainshaft and layshaft bottom low gears to provide a 3.9 reduction.

It was recommended that a mixture of light oil and grease in equal proportions be used in the gearbox, as there was a tendency for oil to leak if this was added alone.

On the Scrambler the oil-damped rear spring units were assembled with precision, and would not call for any attention whatever for many thousands of miles, the outer plated and enamelled tubes being merely dust covers. The damper unit consisted of two concentric tubes; the outer one, which was an integral part of the bottom anchorage, was in fact the reservoir for the SAE.20 oil (1fl oz, or approximately 30cc). The inner tube was detachable, having a ball-seated valve at the lower end and a metering hole 1in (2.5cm) from the bottom. The plunger rod was screwed and locked into the aluminium top anchorage. On the bottom of the rod was a cut-away brass piston which formed the seating for a valve, the latter having a certain amount of free movement on the rod for a purpose described later.

As the spring unit was compressed, the plunger rod descended, and since the bottom ball was then seated, the oil had to pass through a metering hole supplemented by the amount that could pass between the valve and seat (on the downward stroke the valve moved away from the seat). Conversely when the unit

was depressed, the spring action caused a rebound, so that as the piston ascended the ball valve was opened to take in oil supplemented by the intake through the metering hole. On the upward stroke, however, the valve would be seated against the piston and would then not permit such a free escape of oil as on the downward stroke. It was on the rebound that the advantage of the hydraulic action was most effective.

The telescopic fork inner tubes were guided in the outer tubes by widely spaced bearings pressed into the outer tubes; the fork end stampings were brazed into the lower ends of the inner tubes to carry the wheel spindle. Inside the inner tube at its lower end was fixed a smaller diameter tube, which was concentric and extended approximately half way up the inner leg. This damper tube was sealed at the bottom, and screwed into the top was a bush, which served as a guide for the damper rod and also retained the lower end of the main load spring. In the wall of the damper tube were drilled holes of varying diameter, to act as inflow port and metering holes.

Inside the top of the outer tube an adaptor carried the upper end of the main coil spring and also served to fix the upper end of a rod that was central and concentric with the fork tubes, and extended down the centre of the leg inside the coil spring, through the bush in the top end of the damper tube and into the damping cylinder. At its lower end was fixed a small piston, which was a sliding fit in the damper tube. Light lubricating oil (2fl oz – 55cc – SAE. 30) filled the bottom of each leg to a level which completely submerged the damping chamber. The oil would also filter into the chamber on both sides of the piston so that in the normal riding position the system was completely filled with oil. As the wheel rose over a bump, or the head dropped on braking, the inner tube together with the damper tube would lift relative to the outer tube, and the piston would drop in the chamber with little resistance from oil until the port in the tube wall was blocked by the piston. Further movement of the piston tended to compress the oil, and force it out of metering holes in the chamber with an ensuing retarding effect on the fork stroke.

Continuing downwards, the piston closed the first metering hole so that oil had to pass either through a minute metering hole or past the piston, thus causing increased drag on fork movement. When the piston closed all the jets, further fork stroke had to force oil only past the piston, with consequent high pressure and resistance to movement. Upon returning to normal due to spring pressure, suction would be caused in the cylinder beneath the piston, with a slight retarding effect on the return stroke; the suction reduced as oil was sucked past the piston and entered metering holes until the piston passed the inflow port and all drag ceased. On the recoil stroke, oil on top of the piston came under pressure and escaped through the top jet until the piston closed it; subsequently the oil had to escape past the piston or along the piston rod bearing, with consequent drag on fork recoil.

Finally, on returning to riding level due to the weight of the machine, the cylinder above the piston became a semi-vacuum until oil returned by the way it was forced out, with reducing drag until it was back to a normal position, when no pressure existed. Thus for normal riding on good roads no damping took place for small deflections, and as fork deflection increased in either direction due to bad road surface, hydraulic damping increased proportionately. Journal bearings were specified for the front and rear wheels.

The Falcon No. 65 (Overseas)
The last new machine to leave the works in 1953 was the Falcon 65 (Overseas), which was nothing less than a road-going trials machine. Today it would be termed a trail bike, and in 1953 not many would have known what that was. It used the Falcon 58 frame with special stiffened 20in three-rate springs for heavy duty loading, giving extra front wheel clearance. The swinging rear arm was lengthened for added clearance, and two-rate springs with a hydraulic damper were housed in the rear spring units. The 2.25gal (10ltr) petrol tank was recessed to give maximum lock, which to the uninitiated appeared to be accident dents.

The Villiers Mark 8E engine, prefix 668A, with a three-speed gearbox was fitted in the frame, prefix TMSO; a four-speed was an optional extra. The carburettor was the AMAL 276. Electrics were 6-volt AC rectified with a 6in sealed beam headlamp. The colour scheme for 1953 was black enamel with gold-lined tank, and chromium and cadmium plating as appropriate:

This model is provided specifically to cater for the requirements of those markets where a machine of moderate weight yet rugged construction is needed for operation mainly under cross-country conditions. It is a sturdy, practical machine built for hard work – and has proved its worth in many countries.

The 1954 Season
Only four models were carried forward to 1954: Falcons 58, 62, 64 and 65 – and only one of those was a road-going machine. The Overseas Falcon 65 was fitted with the 2.75gal (12.5ltr) petrol tank for 1954. The finish was black enamel with the tank and rims lined gold; bright parts were chromium- or cadmium-plated. The frame number prefix for 1954 was UMSO.

The two competition machines, the Falcon 62 and 64, remained unchanged for 1954; the Mark 7E/4 engine continued to be used with the engine number prefix of 375A and 374A as before. The frame number prefixes for 1954 were UTM and UTMS.

The Kestrel No. 66
The first new model on the scene was one with a new bird name, the Kestrel, Model No. 66, aimed at the mass market with low initial cost and economical running. The Kestrel frame was of orthodox tubular type, brazed and welded with prefix U. It was fitted with the Villiers Mark 13D engine with a three-speed gearbox, engine prefix 618A. The engine was a combination of the Mark 10D cylinder and head, and the Mark 12D crankcase assembly, with a bore and stroke of 50 × 62mm, giving a capacity of 122cc. The model had direct lighting from the flywheel magneto with a parking battery fitted in the toolbox, a 6in sealed beam headlamp, a rear light and a Smith's speedometer. Cup and cone bearings were used in the hubs. The front brake was a 4in drum and the rear a 5in drum. The telescopic fork action was by single-pressure coil springs secured at each end by screw-type adaptors. The sliders operated in Tufnol bushes that were pressed into the outer tubes and line reamered after being fitted. The plunger rear suspension action was through load and rebound coil springs, with lubrication by grease gun every 1,000 miles (1,609km). The finish was Azure Blue enamel, with gold-lined tank and chromium and cadmium plating. The Kestrel was priced at £74.15, plus £14 19s

purchase tax. Several items of additional equipment were available, including leg-shields, pillion seat, wind-shield and pannier equipment, at extra cost.

The Falcon No. 67

The Falcon Model No. 67 also made its debut in 1954, replacing Falcons 54, 55 and eventually 58. Although the Falcon 58 continued to be produced early on in the 1954 season, it did not appear in any of the sales literature for that year. It remained unchanged, with the Villiers Mark 8E engine and a prefix of 387A, and the frame number prefix for 1954 of UTTMS. The same engine unit with the identical prefix of 387A was fitted to the Falcon 67, together with a flywheel mag-neto and the Villiers S.24 carburettor. An alteration was made in 1954 to the steering head angle: where-as previously it was 28 degrees, it was altered to 26.5 degrees, and this meant that the frame top tube had a pronounced bend in it. The bend was normally con-cealed beneath the petrol tank, and when this was removed it appeared to the uninitiated that the machine had been in an accident and as a result the top frame tube had been bent; the frame number prefix was UM. The capacity of the petrol tank was increased from 2.25 to 2.75gal (10.2 to 12.5ltr).

The suspension consisted of a swinging rear fork with fully damped hydraulic spring units, with a movement of 4in (10cm); the telescopic front forks had 20in (50cm) three-rate springs with a movement of 5in (13cm). Wheel rims were 19in with journal bearings in the hubs and 5in drum brakes. In the first production models the front hub was fitted with cup

1955 Kestrel Model 66 in azure blue, owner Ryan Swindells; seen at the FBOC AGM. (Courtesy FBOC)

1954 Falcon Model 67. (Courtesy R. & R. Baxter)

1954 Overseas Falcon 65, restored by Des Heckle. (Courtesy Des Heckle)

1954 Cruiser Model 68. (Courtesy D. Lloyd)

Machine Specifications

	Falcon 65 (Overseas)	Kestrel 66	Falcon 67
Model	Falcon 65 (Overseas)	Kestrel 66	Falcon 67
Manufacturing year	1953–54	1954	1954
Engine	Villiers Mark 8E, single-cylinder, air-cooled two-stroke	Villiers mark 13D, single-cylinder, air-cooled two-stroke	Villiers Mark 8E, single-cylinder, air-cooled two-stroke
Number prefix	668A	618A	387A
Bore and stroke	59 × 72mm	50 × 62mm	59 × 72mm
Capacity	197cc	122cc	197cc
Compression ratio	7.25:1	8:1	7.56:1
Lubrication	Petroil	Petroil	Petroil
Carburettor	Amal 276, Vokes air filter	Villiers 3/4 single lever	Villiers S.24
Ignition	Flywheel magneto	Flywheel magneto	Flywheel magneto
Primary drive	Chain	Renold 110038	Renold 110038
Final drive	Chain	Renold 110044	Renold 110044
Gearbox	Three or four-speed	Three-speed	Three or four-speed
Gearbox ratios standard	8.25; 8.75; 16.6:1	7.4; 10.5; 19.5:1	5.75; 8.0; 15.3:1
Gearbox ratios alternative	6.15; 8.45; 11.25; 18.10:1		5.75; 7.75; 10.32; 16.65:1
Gearbox ratios alternative			5.75; 7.75; 13.2; 22.58:1
Frame	Tubular cradle type using 1.25in 14-gauge tube	Orthodox tubular brazed and welded	Tubular cradle brazed and welded
Number prefix	TMSO, UMSO	U	UM, UUM
Suspension front	Telescopic fork with stiffened 20in three-rate springs	Telescopic fork	Telescopic fork with 20in three-rate springs
Suspension rear	Swinging fork arm, lengthened for extra clearance	Plunger type with coil springs	Swinging fork arm with hydraulically damped spring unit
Rim size: front	WM1-21	WM0-19	WM1-19
rear	WM2-19	WM0-19	WM1-19
Tyres: front	2.75 × 21in Dunlop trials	2.75 × 19in Dunlop	3 × 19in Dunlop
rear	3.25 × 19in Dunlop trials	2.75 × 19in Dunlop	3 × 19in Dunlop
Hubs: front	5in journal bearings	4in drum cup and cone bearings	5in drum journal bearings
rear	5in journal bearings	5in drum cup and cone bearings	5in drum cup and cone bearings*
Brakes: front	5in dia. internal drum	4in dia. internal drum	5in dia. internal drum
rear	5in dia. internal drum	5in dia. internal drum	5in dia. internal drum

General Specifications

	1954 specification	1954 specification	1954 specification
Fuel tank capacity	2.75gal (12.5ltr)	2.25gal (10ltr)	2.75gal (12.5ltr)

Machine Specifications *continued*

Overall length	77.75in (1,975mm)	78in (1,981mm)	78in (1,981mm)
Overall width	26.5in (673mm)	25.5in (650mm)	26.5in (673mm)
Overall height	41in (1,041mm)	???	37in (940mm)
Wheelbase	50.25in (1,276mm)	49in (1,245mm)	49.5in (1,257mm)
Ground clearance	5.75in (146mm)	5in (127mm)	5in (127mm)
Seat height (min.)	31in (787mm)	28in (711mm)	28in (711mm)
Dry weight	227lb (103kg)	164lb (74kg)	218lb (99kg)
Power	8.4bhp @ 4,000rpm	4.9bhp @ 4,400rpm	8.4bhp @ 4,000rpm * Series II journal bearings

and cone bearings, and these machines were known as Series I; when journal bearings were fitted to all wheels, these machines were known as Series II. The finish was black enamel or Azure Blue to order, with gold-lined tank and chromium and cadmium plating.

The Cruiser No. 68

The Cruiser name was resurrected for another new model for 1954: Model No. 68. The frame for the Cruiser was a completely new design, and was used by several versions of Cruiser from 1954 until 1966; also a variation of it was used for the Norton Jubilee. The basic frame consisted of four parts: an oval front frame member formed by two pressings welded together and to the steering head at the top end, and at the bottom another pressing with the front engine mount and a

fixing point for the left and right frame tubes, which were also bolted to the front frame member at a point just below the steering head. The fourth part of the basic frame was the hollow frame centre section which sat to the rear and in between the two side tubes; the frame number had the prefix UB. Fitted inside the centre section were the rectifier, coil and battery, and the dual seat covered the top. The centre stand was connected to the bottom of the centre section.

The front forks and rear suspension were exactly the same as the Falcon 67. The engine unit, new for 1954, was the 225cc Villiers Mark 1H with a bore and stroke of 63 × 72mm, having a capacity of 224cc; a 7:1 compression ratio gave 10bhp at 4,500rpm. The four-speed gearbox with indicator and a fully enclosed Villiers S.25 carburettor had the prefix 842A. Lighting and ignition

1955 Falcon Model 70. (Courtesy J. Biggin)

1955 Falcon Model 70. (Courtesy N. Thomson)

1955 Falcon Model 70 with optional chrome tank. (Courtesy J. Baker)

were by an AC generator unit with an AC/DC switch on the headlamp. The petrol tank was 3.5gal (16ltr) capacity, with two level petrol taps. The wheel rims were 19in with 6in brake drums.

The finish was green, with a gold-lined tank, and a dual seat in matching green; the rims were chromium-plated and lined green and gold, and the bright parts were chromium- or cadmium-plated.

The 1955 Season

Almost a clean sweep was made of the 1954 machines, with only the Falcon 62 carried forward into 1955.

The Kestrel No. 69

The Kestrel now became Model No. 69, with several new features. The engine unit used was the 147cc

Villiers Mark 30C with three-speed gearbox, flywheel magneto, and Villiers lightweight carburettor, prefix 958A. The front forks were modified at the bottom end to take the full-width hub now fitted, and at the top end for the adjustable handlebar position. The handlebar was now bolted to the top fork plate through two slotted concave recesses. To adjust the handlebar, the two bolts should be slackened, the handlebar moved to the desired position, and the bolts retightened. The wheel rims were 19in, and full width hubs with 4in brakes on the front and 5in on the rear. The petrol tank capacity remained at 2.25gal (10ltr). The finish was black enamel, the tank gold-lined, and it had chromium and cadmium plating.

The Falcon No. 70

The Falcon Model No. 70 was unlike the Falcon models that preceded it, only the Villiers Mark 8E engine being retained. The engine unit contained a three-speed gearbox indicated by the prefix 070B, or a four-speed, as an optional extra, when the prefix was 071B. The basic frame consisted of four parts: the main part of the frame, comprising the top tube and front down-tube, welded to the steering head and the rear down-tube; a left and right rear stay assembly; and a toolbox sitting astride the top frame tube at the rear and fitted with a lid on either side. The 12ah battery, rectifier and electric horn were accommodated in the toolbox unit. The front forks were similar to those described for the Cruiser 71, with only slight differences in the steering stem assembly.

ABOVE RIGHT: 1955 Cruiser Model 71 (and yes, it does say Cruiser 75 on the notice!). (Courtesy FBOC)

1955 Cruiser Model 71. (Courtesy R. Adams)

Machine Specifications

Model	Cruiser 68	Kestrel 69	Falcon 70
Manufacturing year	1954	1955	1955
Engine	Villiers Mark 1H, single-cylinder, air-cooled two-stroke	Villiers Mark 30C, single-cylinder, air-cooled two-stroke	Villiers Mark 8E, single-cylinder, air-cooled two-stroke
Number prefix	842A	958A	070B, 071B four-speed
Bore and stroke	63 × 72mm	62 × 55mm	59 × 72mm
Capacity	225cc	147cc	197cc
Compression ratio	7:1	8.25:1	7.25:1
Lubrication	Petroil	Petroil	Petroil
Carburettor	Villiers S.25	Villiers S.19	Villiers S.24 or S.25
Ignition	Flywheel magneto	Flywheel magneto	Flywheel magneto
Primary drive	Renold chain 110038	Renold chain 110038	Renold chain 110038
Final drive	Renold chain 110046	Renold chain 110044	Chain
Gearbox	Four-speed	Three-speed	Three- or four-speed
Gearbox ratios standard	6.23; 8.25; 11.84; 19.05:1	6.5; 8.7; 16.45:1	5.75; 8.00; 15.30:1
Gearbox ratios alternative	n/a	n/a	5.75; 7.75; 10.38; 16.65:1
Frame	Oval forward section with duplex loop tubes	Orthodox tubular brazed and welded	Tubular main frame with bolt-on duplex loop tubes
Number prefix	UB	V	VM
Suspension front	Telescopic fork with 20in three-rate springs	Telescopic fork	Telescopic fork
Suspension rear	Swinging fork arm with hydraulically damped spring units	Plunger type with coil springs	Swinging fork arm with hydraulically damped spring units
Rim size: front	WM1-19	WM0-19	WM1-19
rear	WM2-19	WM0-19	WM1-19
Tyres: front	3.00 × 19in Dunlop	2.75 × 19in Dunlop	3 × 19in
rear	3.25 × 19in Dunlop	2.75 × 19in Dunlop	3 × 19in
Hubs: front	6in – journal bearings	4in full width – cup and cone bearings	5in full width – journal bearings
rear	6in – journal bearings	5in full width – journal bearings	5in full width – journal bearings
Brakes: front	6in diameter drum	4in diameter drum	5in diameter drum
rear	6in diameter drum	5in diameter drum	5in diameter drum

General Specifications

		1955 specification	
Fuel tank capacity	3.5gal (16ltr)	2.25gal (10ltr)	2.75gal (12.5ltr)
Overall length	80in (2,032mm)	78in (1,980mm)	78in (1,980mm)

Machine Specifications *continued*

◈

Overall width	26in (660mm)	28.25in (720mm)	28.25in (720mm)
Overall height		36.75in (935mm)	38.25in (970mm)
Wheelbase	51in (1,295mm)	49in (1,245mm)	49.75in (1,265mm)
Ground clearance	6.5in (165mm)	5in (127mm)	6in (152.4mm)
Seat height (min.)	31.5in (800mm)	28in (711mm)	31in (787mm)
Dry weight	280lb (127kg)	170lb (77kg)	243lb (110kg)
Power	10bhp @ 4,500rpm	5.5bhp @ 4,250rpm	8.4bhp @ 4,000rpm

The rear suspension units were also identical to those fitted to the Cruiser 71. The wheel rims were 19in, with 5in diameter brakes accommodated in full width hubs with journal bearings front and rear. The dual seat sat over the toolbox unit, giving it a neat appearance.

The colour finish was black enamel, the tank gold-lined, the rims chromium-plated and lined in gold and black, and with chromium and cadmium plating. Maximum speed was in the region of 55–60mph (88–97km/h), and fuel consumption 70–75mpg (4–3.8ltr/100km) at 50mph (80km/h). The Falcon was priced at £106 plus £21 4s purchase tax.

The Cruiser No. 71

The Cruiser 68 now became the Cruiser Model No. 71, keeping the Villiers Mark 1H engine, prefix 842A. A new type of front fork was fitted, and the basic design of this fork continued to be used on many machines right up to the demise of the company, and can be referred to as the James Mark 1 fork. This latter changed to the James Mark 2 to accommodate the QD wheel spindle. The forks consisted of two main tubes with fixed external bearings and welded crown and top pressings. Long coil springs were attached at the bottom to a damper post, which in turn was held in position by a retaining screw at the lower end of the fork sliding tube. A screw adapter was fitted in the top of the coil spring to enable it to be attached to the top pressing by a screw that also serves as an oil filler plug. As the fork slider and damper tube moved against the resistance of the spring, oil was forced up through the annular clearance between the damper tube and slider leg. As the damper tube was tapered, the clearance was reduced progressively, in effect increasing hydraulic resistance to the upward movement of the fork slider. When the maximum diameter of the damper post entered the end of the tube, clearance was restricted, consequently providing a hydraulic limit stop. Oil drag provided rebound damping.

The wheel rim size remained at 19in, with 6in brakes now accommodated in full width hubs and journal bearings. The model was finished in deep green enamel, with a gold-lined tank, chromium-plated rims, lined green and gold, and with chromium and cadmium plating.

The competition model, Falcon No. 62, continued for 1955 with only slight changes. The engine unit was still the Mark 7E/4 with a wide ratio gearbox, and the engine prefix was 375A. The frame number prefix for 1955 was VTM.

The Falcon No. 72

A new competition model was available for 1955: the Falcon Scrambler Model No. 72 replaced the Falcon 64. The Falcon 72 was also available in Trials trim under the same model number. The main difference between the Falcon 64 and the Falcon 72 was in the rear frame, which now consisted of detachable triangulated rear stays for added strength. The Villiers Mark 7E/4 engine unit with the prefix 374A continued to be used. Frame number prefix for 1955 was VMS. The finish for both competition models was black enamel, chromium-plated rims, gold-lined tank and chromium and cadmium plating.

The 1956 Season

No models were carried forwards from 1955 to 1956.

The Plover No. 73

The first all-new model for 1956 was the Plover Model No. 73, which was unlike anything that had preceded it. Primarily designed as a solo machine for the to-and-from work run, it was strongly constructed. The frame was built around the frame dorsal tube of 2in (5cm) diameter, with the steering head at one end and bolted to the pressed-steel centre section at the other.

The centre section held the battery, main cables and toolbox, and provided rear engine and footrest mountings. The engine loop tube, bolted at the top to the dorsal frame tube and to the centre section at the bottom, carried the front and bottom engine mounting plates. A pressed steel fork pivoted within the centre section on Silentbloc bushes, in which the rear wheel was mounted. The fork was attached to the centre section by two 5in (13cm) bolts passing through the reinforced pressing into the tapped ends of the pivot tube. Two barrel coil springs in compression formed the suspension medium. Lugs welded to the top of the fork arms provided lower attachment points for the concealed coil springs. The springs passed through rubber grommets in the centre section, and were bolted to fixed lugs on the rear transverse member of the dorsal tube. Angularity of movement was taken up in the springs. Standard springs were suitable for carrying a total load up to a maximum of 300lb (136kg). If the total load habitually exceeded this, it was recommended that heavy duty springs were fitted.

Externally the lightweight telescopic forks were similar in appearance to those fitted to the Cruiser and Falcon. They consisted of steering head and fork crown pressings, to which were welded two stanchion tubes with fixed external phosphor bronze bushes, providing bearing surfaces for the sliding members. The movement of each slider was controlled by a short tension spring encircling a 0.375in diameter rod positioned in the centre of the slider. The lower end of the rod located in a hole in the centre of the fork end, where it was secured by a transverse anchor bolt engaging in a slot in the rod. The top end of the spring was tapered and retained on the rod shoulder by a washer and locknut. The lower coils of the spring were opened out to accept a slotted washer bearing against a shoulder in the stanchion tube and held in position

by a washer and circlip. When the wheel and slider moved upwards, the spring was extended in tension.

Oil carried in the slider tube provided hydraulic damping on the compression stroke, and also lubricated the sliding parts. As the fork was compressed, the slider moved up and oil could not pass beyond the lower bushes. It was forced through the gap between the spring-retaining washer and the rod, into the stanchion tube. Rebound damping was obtained as a result of the partial vacuum occurring as the fork returned to its static position. The capacity of each fork leg was 82.5cc or 1½ tank filler cap measures of SAE 20 lubricant. Grub screws at the mudguard bridge brackets enabled the oil level to be checked.

The adoption of the 18in-diameter wheel as the standard size for non-competition machines commenced with the Plover 73. From 1956 all machines were fitted with 18in-diameter wheels, with two exceptions: the Cruiser 75 and the Cruiser Twin 91. The full-width hubs held 4in front and 5in rear brakes.

Like the Kestrel that preceded it, the Plover 73 was fitted with the 147cc Villiers Mark 30C engine unit, prefix 295B, with a three-speed gearbox, flywheel magneto ignition and Villiers carburettor S19. The exhaust pipe led into an alloy silencer casting fitted transversely, and exhausting through twin pipes. A direct lighting system was fitted as standard, with a rectified lighting system, battery and electric horn available as an optional extra.

From 1956 the green finish was for the first time described as 'Arden Green', having previously been described as a rich green. The tank was lined gold, and the bright parts chromium- and cadmium-plated. With speeds up to 50mph (80km/h) and fuel consumption of 120mpg (2.4ltr/100km) at 30mph (48km/h), Francis-Barnett emphasized the exceptional value for money the standard machine was at £82 plus £19 13s 7d purchase tax (approximately 22 per cent).

The Cruiser No. 75

The Cruiser 71 now became the Cruiser Model No. 75, with very slight differences between the two. The alteration to the forks was identical to that made to those of the Falcon 74. The front wheel rim was now a WM2-18, whilst the rear remained a WM2-19.

1956 Cruiser Model 75, prize winner Bristol Show 2010, owner G. Pugsley.

1956 Cruiser Model 75. (Courtesy D. Carr)

ABOVE: 1956 Cruiser 75, displayed at an FBOC East of England section meeting.

BELOW: 1956 Trials Falcon 76. (Courtesy FBOC)

ABOVE: 1956 Trials Falcon 76, owner J. Salvidge, Bristol Show 2010.

RIGHT: 1956 Ex-works Trials Falcon 76. (Courtesy FBOC)

1957 Falcon Model 74 with the owner Des Heckle. (Courtesy FBOC)

The old-style centre stand was replaced with a double action, high and low lift centre stand: on the 'low' lift the wheels were on the ground, and on the 'high' lift the rear wheel was lifted off the ground to facilitate the removal of the rear wheel. The engine unit remained the Villiers Mark 1H with four-speed gearbox, prefix 842A and the frame number prefix WB. The 3.75gal (17ltr) fuel tank was made using an underpan, two sides and a top. The top was stitch welded to the two side panels, and the underpan acetylene-welded into position. Although two welds ran the whole length of the upper surface, they were impossible to spot.

The finish was Arden Green, the tank gold-lined, the rims chromium-plated and lined with green and gold, and with chromium and cadmium plating. The price was £136, plus £32 12s 10d purchase tax.

The Falcon No. 74

The replacement Falcon for 1956 was the Falcon Model No. 74, and there was very little to distinguish between the two. The Villiers 8E engine unit with three-speed gearbox and Villiers S.25 continued to be used, with the prefix 070B and 071B if fitted with the optional four-speed gearbox. The method of connecting the forks to the steering head was altered.

Machine Specifications

Model	Cruiser 71	Scrambles Falcon 72*	Plover 73
Manufacturing year	1955	1955	1956
Engine	Villiers Mark 1H, single-cylinder, air-cooled two-stroke	Villiers Mark 7E, single-cylinder, air-cooled two-stroke	Villiers Mark 30C, single-cylinder, air-cooled two-stroke
Number prefix	842A	374A	295B
Bore and stroke	63 × 72mm	59 × 72mm	55 × 62mm
Capacity	225cc	197cc	147cc
Compression ratio	7:1	8.25:1	8.25:1
Lubrication	Petroil	Petroil	Petroil
Carburettor	Villiers S.25	Amal 276	Villiers S.19
Ignition	Flywheel magneto	Flywheel magneto waterproofed	Flywheel magneto
Primary drive	Renold chain 110038	Renold chain 110038	Renold chain 110038
Final drive	Renold chain 110046	Chain	Perry chain
Gearbox	Four-speed	Four-speed	Three-speed
Gearbox ratios: standard	6.23; 8.25; 11.84; 19.05:1	6.25; 8.45; 11.25;18.10:1	6.24; 8.36;15.90:1
Frame	Oval forward section and duplex loop tubes	Reinforced loop tube brazed and welded	2in main tube and pressed-steel centre section
Number prefix	VB	VMS	W
Suspension front	Telescopic fork	Telescopic fork with stiffened 20in three-rate springs	Telescopic fork
Suspension rear	Swinging fork arm with hydraulically damped spring units	Swinging fork arm with hydraulically damped spring units	Swinging fork arm with coil springs
Rim size: front	WM1-19	WM1-21	WM1-18
rear	WM2-19	WM2-19	WM1-18
Tyres: front	3 × 19in Dunlop	2.75 × 21in Dunlop Sports	3 × 18im
rear	3.25 × 19in Dunlop	3.50 × 19in Dunlop Sports	3 × 18in
Hubs: front	6in full width – journal bearings	5in full width – journal bearings	4in full width – cup and cone bearings
rear	6in full width – journal bearings	5in full width – journal bearings	5in full width – journal bearings
Brakes: front	6in diameter drum	5in diameter drum	4in diameter drum
rear	6in diameter drum	5in diameter drum	5in diameter drum

General Specifications

			Instruction Manual Specifications
Fuel tank capacity	3.5gal (16ltr)	2.25gal (10ltr)	2.25gal (10ltr)

continued overleaf

Machine Specifications *continued*

Overall length	80in (2,032mm)	77.75in (1,975mm)	76.5in (1,945mm)
Overall width	28.25in (720mm)	26.5in (673mm)	26.5in (673mm)
Overall height	38.25in (970mm)	41in (1,041mm)	37.5in (955mm)
Wheelbase	51in (1,295mm)	50.25in (1,276mm)	49.5in (1,257mm)
Ground clearance	6.5in (165mm)	7.5in (190mm)	6in (152.4mm)
Seat height (min.)	31.5in (800mm)	31in (787mm)	29.5in (750mm)
Dry weight	282lb (128kg)	212lb (96kg)	190lb (86kg)
Power	10bhp @ 4,500rpm	9.5bhp @ 4,200rpm *Also available in Trials trim	5.45bhp @ 4,250rpm

Machine Specifications

Model	Falcon 74	Cruiser 75	Trials Falcon 76
Manufacturing year	1956–57	1956–57	1956–57
Engine	Villiers Mark 8E, single-cylinder, air-cooled two-stroke	Villiers Mark 1H, single-cylinder, air-cooled two-stroke	Villiers Mark 7E, single-cylinder, air-cooled two-stroke
Number prefix	070B, 071B four-speed	842A	375A
Bore and stroke	59 × 72mm	63 × 72mm	59 × 72mm
Capacity	197cc	225cc	197cc
Compression Ratio	7.56:1	7:1	
Lubrication	Petroil	Petroil	Petroil
Carburettor	Villiers S.25	Villiers S.25	Amal 276
Ignition	Flywheel magneto	Flywheel magneto	Competition Flywheel magneto
Primary drive	Renold chain 110038	Renold chain 110038	Renold chain 110038
Final drive	Renold chain 110044	Renold chain 110046	Chain
Gearbox	Three- or four-speed	Four-speed	Four-speed

Machine Specifications *continued*

Gearbox ratios: standard	6.28; 8.41; 16:1	6.21; 8.20; 11.80; 19.05:1	6.52; 8.75; 15.00; 22.50:1
Gearbox ratios: alternative	6.28; 8.45; 11.32; 18.16:1	n/a	n/a
Gearbox ratios: alternative	6.28; 8.45; 14.45; 21.85:1	n/a	n/a
Frame	Tubular main frame with bolt-on duplex loop tubes	Oval forward section and duplex loop tubes	Heavy-gauge loop; bolt on top and bottom stays
Number prefix	WM,YM	WB,YB	WTM
Suspension front	Telescopic fork	Telescopic fork	Telescopic fork
Suspension rear	Swinging fork arm with hydraulically damped spring units	Swinging fork arm with hydraulically damped spring units	Swinging fork arm with Girling spring units
Rim size: front	WM2-18	WM2-18	WM1-21
rear	WM2-18	WM2-19	WM2-18
Tyres: front	3.25 × 18in Dunlop	3.25 × 18in	2.75 × 21in Dunlop
rear	3.25 × 18in Dunlop	3.25 × 19in	4.00 × 18in Dunlop
Hubs: front	5in full width – journal bearings	6in full width – journal bearings	5in full width – journal bearings
rear	5in full width – journal bearings	6in full width – journal bearings	5in full width – journal bearings
Brakes: front	5in diameter drum	6in diameter drum	5in diameter drum
rear	5in diameter drum	6in diameter drum	5in diameter drum

General specifications

	Instruction Manual specifications		
Fuel tank capacity	2.75gal (12.5ltr)	3.5gal (16ltr)	2gal (10ltr)
Overall length	78in (1,981mm)	80in (2,032mm)	78.75 (2,000mm)
Overall width	28in (711mm)	28in (711mm)	28.5in (725mm)
Overall height	38.25in (970mm)	38.25in (970mm)	44in (1,118mm)
Wheelbase	49.75in (1,265mm)	51in (1,295mm)	51.75in (1,314mm)
Ground clearance	6in (152mm)	6.5in (165mm)	8.25in (210mm)
Seat height (min.)	30.5in (775mm)	31in (787mm)	31in (787mm)
Dry weight	243lb (110kg)	282 lb (128kg)	230lb (104kg)
Power	8.4bhp @ 4,000rpm	10 @ 4,500rpm	9.5bhp @ 4,200rpm

Machine Specifications

Model	Scrambler Falcon 77
Manufacturing year	1956–1957
Engine	Villiers Mark 7E, single-cylinder, air-cooled two-stroke
Number prefix	374A
Bore and stroke	59 × 72mm
Capacity	197cc
Lubrication	Petroil
Carburettor	Amal 276
Ignition	Competition flywheel magneto
Primary drive	Renold chain 110038
Final drive	Chain
Gearbox	Four-speed
Gearbox ratios: standard	6.52; 8.75; 11.73; 18.90:1
Frame	Heavy-gauge loop; bolt-on top and bottom stays
Number prefix	WSM
Suspension: front	Telescopic fork
rear	Swinging fork arm with Girling spring units
Rim size: front	WM1-21
rear	WM2-19
Tyres: front	2.75 × 21in Dunlop Sports
rear	3.50 × 19in Dunlop Sports
Hubs: front	5in full width – journal bearings
rear	5in full width – journal bearings
Brakes: front	5in diameter drum
rear	5in diameter drum

General Specifications

Fuel tank capacity	2gal (10ltr)
Overall length	78.75 (2,000mm)
Overall width	28.5in (725mm)
Overall height	44in (1,118mm)
Wheelbase	51.75in (1,314mm)
Ground clearance	8.25in (210mm)
Seat height (min.)	31.5in (800mm)
Dry weight	233lb (106 kg)
Power	9.5bhp @ 4,200rpm

Previously a steering stem bolt was inserted through the top plate of the forks, then through the steering head and finally through the bottom plate. The new method was to use a steering stem, threaded at both ends, and inserted from the bottom; a domed nut was fitted to the top of the stem, which protruded through the top plate; an adjusting nut and a lock-nut fitted to the bottom of the stem. This method made adjusting the steering much simpler and easier. The frame number prefix for 1956 was WM. In keeping with the change to 18in-diameter wheels, the rims were now WM2-18, full-width hubs and 5in brakes front and rear. The finish was Arden Green, the tank lined gold, rims chromium-plated and lined gold and green; with chromium and cadmium plating. The price was £111 plus £26 12s 10d purchase tax.

The Falcon No. 76 and Falcon No. 77

Two new competition models appeared in 1956: the Falcon Trials Model No. 76 and the Falcon Scrambles Model No. 77, which shared many details. The 197cc Villiers competition high compression Mark 7E engine continued to be used. Ignition was competition flywheel magneto with lighting coils for direct lighting if required. The exhaust system consisted of a crossover pipe leading into a detachable upswept silencer. The use of the crossover pipe was ostensibly to prevent damage and provide easy access to primary and secondary drives. The fuel tank held 2gal

(9ltr), with a reserve of 1 pint (approximately 0.5ltr). The AMAL 276 carburettor with Vokes air filter was specified.

The main frame was heavy gauge loop, brazed and welded, with bolt-on top and bottom rear stays, the top stay extending forwards to reinforce the main frame; there were chain guards on the upper and lower chain runs with a chain guide. The full-width hubs ran on journals, and contained 5in brakes front and rear. The suspension consisted of the two-way hydraulically damped front telescopic fork with wide-angle steering lock and stiffened three-rate springs for heavy duty loading; also a swinging rear fork with fully damped hydraulic spring units.

The Falcon 76 gearbox was four-speed with wide ratios, and a 50T rear wheel sprocket as standard. Two tyre security bolts were fitted to each wheel. The seat was a Dunlop rubber trials saddle. The engine prefix was 375A and frame prefix WTM. The price was £124 10s plus £29 17s 7d purchase tax.

The Falcon 77 was also four-speed, but with close-ratio gears, and a 50T rear wheel sprocket as standard. Two tyre security bolts were fitted to each wheel. The seat was a foam rubber twin seat. The engine prefix was 374A, and the frame YSM. It was priced at £126 10s plus £30 7s 2d purchase tax. The finish for both machines was Arden Green enamel, the tank dull chrome-lined green, the rims and bright parts plated, and with polished alloy mudguards.

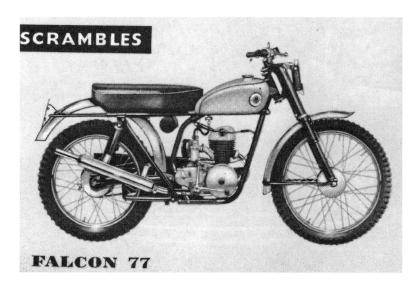

1956 Scrambles Falcon Model No. 77.

CHAPTER FIVE

Manufacturing Seasons 1957–1966

The 1957 Season

The year 1957 began the last decade of the manufacture of motorcycles by Francis-Barnett; it was also the year that AMC introduced their own brand of engines for use by Francis-Barnett and James. Francis-Barnett rear suspension units gave way to Girling adjustable spring units with hydraulic damping in 1957. The Falcon 74 changed to the Girling spring unit mid-season, commencing with frame number YM83083.

The sales catalogue also had a makeover in 1957; as George Denton, sales manager, observed – out went the traditional choice of 'olde worlde' Cotswold village backgrounds, and in came the new contemporary atmosphere of Tile Hill. Pictured on the front cover with the Francis-Barnett Cruiser 80 were Jacqueline Denton, the sales manager's daughter, and Bob Haines of the competition department.

The Plover No. 78

Of the five machines manufactured in 1956, the Plover 73 was discontinued and replaced by the Plover Model No. 78. Perhaps the word 'discontinued' is inappropriate here, as the Plover, introduced in 1956 with the

1957 sales brochure.

Plover 78 at Strumpshaw Steam Engine Rally 2010.

Villiers 147cc Mark 30C engine and the S.19 carburettor, continued in production with the same specification and only slight modifications until 1960. It used the same engine prefix of 295B and a frame prefix of Y.

The frame consisted of a 2in (5cm) diameter main tube of pressed steel cantilevered from the top; the centre section contained the battery, main cables and toolbox, and provided the mounting for the rear engine and footrests; the auxiliary tube carried the front and bottom engine plates.

Experience with the original exhaust system showed that a build-up of carbon in the exhaust system could create back pressure and a subsequent loss of power. From 1957, a new exhaust system was designed for the Plover 78 using a sheet steel expansion chamber instead of the original aluminium one, plus a barrel silencer. The new design allowed the carbon build-up to be easily removed.

With a new dual seat and an electric horn that was fitted at the front of the centre enclosure, the Plover was priced at £87 plus £20 17s 8d purchase tax.

The remainder of the machines – the Falcon 74, Cruiser 75 and the Falcons 76 and 77 – continued in production, though in the case of the Cruiser 75, only for a short period of time. Cruiser Model No. 80 superseded Cruiser 75 with the Villiers Mark 1H engine.

The Cruiser No. 80

The new Cruiser used the same cycle parts as the previous Cruiser; the frame prefix was now YC, but it had

the AMC Piatti-designed 249cc two-stroke engine designated the 25T, incorporating a four-speed gearbox bolted to the rear of the engine, bore and stroke of 65.99 × 72.8mm and a compression ratio of 8.1:1; the carburettor was the AMAL monobloc 389/17. The rpm at 30mph (48km/h) in top gear was 2,430.

1957 Falcon Model 74; now AAS 881. (Courtesy FBOC)

Machine Specifications

❖

Model	Plover 78	Light Cruiser 79	Cruiser 80
Manufacturing year	1957–59	1958–60	1957–62
Engine	Villiers Mark 30C, single-cylinder, air-cooled two-stroke	AMC 17/T, single-cylinder, single-cylinder, air-cooled air-cooled two-stroke	AMC 25T, two-stroke
Number prefix	295B	17T	25T, 25T80
Bore and stroke	55 × 62mm	59 × 62.68mm	66 × 73mm
Capacity	147cc	172cc	249cc
Compression ratio	8.25:1	8.25:1	8.1:1
Lubrication	Petroil	Petroil	Petroil
Carburettor	Villiers S.19	AMAL monobloc 370/1	AMAL monobloc 389
Ignition	Flywheel magneto	Lucas alternator and coil	Wipac alternator with coil
Primary drive	Renold chain 110038	Renold chain 110038	Renold chain 110038
Final drive	Perry chain	Renold chain 110044	Renold chain 110046
Gearbox	Three-speed	Four-speed	Four-speed
Gearbox ratios	6.64; 8.91; 16.94:1	6.9; 8.96; 12.77; 20.15:1	5.9; 7.7; 10.9; 17.4:1
Frame	2in (5cm) main tube cantilevered from top of pressed steel centre section	Welded box section forward member with bolt-on duplex loop tubes	Oval section forward member and bolt-on duplex loop tubes; pressed steel centre section
Number prefix	Y, Z, A	ZD, AD, AAD, BD, BBD	YC, ZC, AC, BC, BBC, CC, DC
Rim size: front	WM0-18	WM1-18	WM2-18
rear	WM0-18	WM1-18	WM2-18
Front suspension	Telescopic fork	Telescopic fork	Telescopic fork
Rear suspension	Swinging arm with spring units	Swinging arm fork with adjustable spring units	Swinging arm fork with adjustable spring units
Tyres: front	3 × 18in	3 × 18in	3.25 × 18in
rear	3 × 18in	3 × 18in	3.25 × 18in
Hubs: front	Full width 4in, cup and cone	Full width 5in	Full width 6in
rear	Full width 5in, journal bearings	Full width 5in	Full width 6in
Brakes: front	4in drum	5in drum	6in drum
rear	5in drum	5in drum	6in drum

General Specifications

Fuel tank capacity	2.25gal (10ltr)	3.75gal (17ltr)	3.75gal (17ltr)
Overall length	76.5in (1,943mm)	78in (1,981mm)	80in (2,032mm)
Overall width	26.5in (673mm)	26in (660mm)	27.5 (698mm)

Overall height	37.5in (953mm)	39in (990mm)	39in (990mm)
Wheelbase	49.5in (1,257)	51in (1,295mm)	51.5in (1,308mm)
Ground clearance	6in (152.4mm)	5.5in (140mm)	5.5in (140mm)
Seat height	29.5in (750mm)	29.5in (750mm)	30in (762mm)
Dry weight	190lb (86kg)	247lb (112kg)	290lb (131kg)
Power	5.45bhp @ 4,250rpm	Not known	Not known

1957 Cruiser Model 75. The late Bob Gingell on his Fanny Barnett. (Courtesy Mrs R. Gingell)

1957 Cruiser Model 80, owner Rod Buckenham; FBOC East of England section meeting, Leiston.

The electrics, although mainly of WIPAC manufacture, could be substituted by a LUCAS alternative as original equipment, and consisted of coil ignition with fixed timing, a permanent magnet alternator charging the 6-volt 12-amp hour battery via a full-wave rectifier, and 5in (13cm) diameter headlamp with pre-focus light unit. Both wheels now had 18in rims fitted with 18 × 3.25in tyres. The finish was Arden Green with the tank lined in gold; the rims were chromium-plated and lined in green and gold. Francis-Barnett advertised the Cruiser 80 as having five new features:

- New engine with a relatively flat torque curve
- Close-ratio four-speed gearbox
- An extra large expansion chamber with minimum back pressure, which reduces exhaust clamour and is quickly detachable for cleaning
- New Wico-Pacy AC generator, which gives full amperage at low engine speeds: special ignition circuit ensures a fat spark whether battery condition is up or flat
- A 3.75gal (17ltr) fuel tank, which breaks with traditional line and has a flush-fitting splash-proof cap.

Top speed was approximately 70mph (113km/h), cruising speed 50–60mph (80–96km/h), and petrol consumption about 100mpg (2.8ltr/100km) at 50mph (80km/h). It was priced at £140 plus £33.12s purchase tax.

The Falcons 76 and 77 both used the 197cc Villiers competition high compression Mark 7E engine. The frame number prefix for the Falcon 76 was YTM, and YSM for the Falcon 77. In all other respects they were identical to the 1956 models described in Chapter 4.

Prices for the 1957 basic models were £129 plus £30 19s 3d purchase tax for the Falcon 76, and £131 plus £31 8s 10d for the Falcon 77.

The 1958 Season

Only two models were continued from 1957 into 1958: the Plover 78 with its 147cc Villiers Mark 30C engine, with the same number prefix and a frame number prefix of Z; and the Cruiser 80, which had little alteration except for a change to the petrol filler cap, which reverted to the standard form of a raised push-in type. Later during the year, a slight change

was made to the wiring harness: where previously the speedometer light lead was black and connected to the same terminal as the rear lamp, in the revised wiring the lead was dark green and connected to the ignition switch. The frame number prefix for this year was ZC.

The Light Cruiser No. 79

A new model introduced in 1958, and the second model to have an AMC engine fitted, was the Light Cruiser Model No. 79. This engine was a scaled-down version of the 25T engine which it resembled, having a capacity of 171cc, a bore and stroke of 59 × 62.7mm, a compression ratio of 8.25:1 and designated the 17T. A four-speed gearbox was bolted to the rear of the engine.

The Light Cruiser 79 frame consisted of composite pressed steel and was of tubular construction, partly welded and partly bolted. The frame was built up from four separate parts; the front frame member, similar to that of the Cruiser 80, had the steering head, a substantial malleable iron casting, welded to the top. The left and right frame tubes were bolted top and bottom to the front frame member, a centre assembly covered by side panels held in place by Oddie fasteners. The carburettor, rectifier, battery and toolkit were all hidden from sight behind the covers, giving a clean and neat appearance. The frame number prefix was ZD. The AMAL carburettor 370/1 was used in conjunction with the 17T engine.

The front forks were the same type as fitted to the Cruiser 80, and the rear swinging-arm movement was controlled by special lightweight Girling units. WM-1 rims front and rear with full width hubs accommodated 5in brakes.

Electrics were provided by the LUCAS RM13 AC lighting-ignition unit, a six-pole alternator consisting of a permanent magnet rotor rotating within a laminated wound stator. The rotor was driven by an extension of the engine crankshaft; a full-wave rectifier was included in the circuit for converting the alternating current of the alternator to uni-directional current, essential for battery charging.

The finish was Arden Green; the tank and side covers were lined white, and the wheel rims green and gold. The Light Cruiser was listed at £132 plus £32 13s 5d, making a total of £164 13s 5d.

1958 Light Cruiser Model 79. (Courtesy FBOC)

The author's 1958 Cruiser Model 80 during restoration.

1958 Falcon Model 81 and 1961 Falcon 87. (Courtesy FBOC)

The Falcon No. 81

An additional new model for 1958 was Falcon Model No. 81, a replacement for Falcon 74. The new Falcon was similar in looks to the previous Falcon models, with side panels held on by Oddie fasteners, but had many different components. The Villiers Mark 10E, in unit with a three-speed gearbox, was built into the frame; the prefix was 662B. A smaller, lighter flywheel magneto was enclosed in the right-hand engine casing instead of being on the outside; this reduction in weight allowed the crankshafts to be increased in size, giving smoother running. The carburettor was the Villiers type S.25/3, which was similar in operation to the type S.19.

The frame consisted of a brazed and welded tubular main frame with bolt-on duplex cradle-type loop tubes forming rear stays. The frame prefix number was ZN. Now-standard telescopic front forks were fitted; the swinging rear fork employed Girling adjustable spring units with hydraulic damping. The lighting was AC/DC. A 6in (15cm) diameter headlamp with pre-focused bulb and a large wide-angle tail lamp with provision for a stop light were standard equipment. The rectifier, electric horn, battery and tools were carried in compartments under the dual seat and covered by side panels. Maximum speed was just under 60mph (97km/h), and petrol consumption about 70mpg (4ltr/100km) at 50mph (80km/h). The finish was Arden Green, and the tank was gold-lined; the rims were chromium-plated and lined gold and green.

The new Falcon was priced at £128 plus £31 13s 7d purchase tax, giving a total of £159 13s 7d.

Allegedly, two new competition models became available in 1958: the Scrambles Model No. 82 and the Trials Model No. 83. Records appear to show that the Scrambles model was available in 1958, but the Trials model did not come on to the market until 1959. The former will be dealt with under the 1958 season, and the latter under the 1959 season.

The Scrambler No. 82

Although not on general sale until 1958, the works riders first competed on the Scrambler 82 in 1957. This machine used a tuned version of the 249cc AMC 25T, engine prefix 25S, with a close-ratio gearbox and a short racing exhaust pipe without a silencer. A special racing-type alternator with a matched HT ignition coil was included in the specification. The main frame was heavy-gauge loop, brazed and welded, with a 1.5in (4cm) section down tube; bolt-on top and bottom rear stays, with the top one extended forwards to give reinforcement to the main frame; and polished alloy mudguards. The frame number prefix was ZCS.

The suspension consisted of a special heavy duty, two-way hydraulically damped front fork, basically Norton pattern, having polished alloy sliders and a quickly detachable front spindle with Girling rear spring units. The full width hubs enclosed 6in brakes

1959 Trials Model 83. (Courtesy J. Baker)

1958 Scrambler Model 82 with what looks like a Mark 32A transplant. (Courtesy FBOC)

in the front and 5in in the rear; there were two tyre security bolts per wheel, and a 56T rear wheel sprocket as standard (54T, 58T and 60T sprockets were available as extras). A foam rubber seat was provided, and ball-ended clutch and brake levers for safety. The finish was Arden Green enamel; the tank was dull chromed to resist special fuels, and lined green. Rims and bright parts were chromium-plated.

As the model was specifically designed for cross-country speed events, no equipment was available to enable it to be used on the road. It was priced at £155, plus £38 7s 3d purchase tax.

The 1959 Season

Eight models were available for 1959: the Plover 78, Light Cruiser 79, Cruiser 80, Falcon 81, Scrambler 82 and Trials 83, Cruiser 84 and Plover 86.

The Plover No. 78
The Plover 78 continued from 1958 with its 147cc Villiers Mark 30C engine, which used the same number prefix. A frame number prefix of 'A' signified the standard colour finish of Arden Green, and 'AR' for the optional colour finish of Burma Red, although in some instances the 'R' was shown as a suffix to the number.

The price for the basic 1959 model was £98 10s plus £24 7s 7d purchase tax.

The Light Cruiser No. 79
The Light Cruiser 79 continued in production, but two important alterations were soon made to the engine. At first the flywheels were circular in design, but to increase crankshaft turbulence and help in crankcase lubrication, flats were machined on the circumference of the flywheels.

The second alteration was a major modification to the piston, which in turn entailed modification to the cylinder to adjust the height of the induction port. Up to engines numbered 17T/3033 the piston skirt had a slight cutaway, which limited the effective length of the skirt, and it was critical to match the piston and cylinder to reduce the level of piston noise. To overcome this problem, a full-skirted piston was used. The models incorporating this modification were referred to as Series II, and the unmodified ones as Series I. A Series I engine could be modified by using the same type of piston and cylinder together. It was impractical to use a Series II piston in a Series I cylinder or vice versa. The Series I frame number prefix was AD, and the Series II, AAD.

For 1959 two finishes were available: Arden Green throughout, or Arden Green frame, forks and so on, and Dover White mudguards and tank and the two side covers. This alternative colour finish was denoted by the addition of 'W' as a suffix to the frame number. The rims and bright parts were chromium plated and finished off with a two-tone twin seat.

Machine Specifications

	Falcon 81	Scrambler 82	Trials 83
Model	Falcon 81	Scrambler 82	Trials 83
Manufacturing year	1958–1959	1959–1962	1959
Engine	Villiers Mark 10E, single-cylinder, air-cooled two-stroke	AMC 25T, single-cylinder, air-cooled two-stroke	AMC 25T, single-cylinder, air-cooled two-stroke
Number prefix	662B	25S	25C
Bore and stroke	59 × 72mm	66 × 73mm	66 × 73mm
Capacity	197cc	249cc	249cc
Compression ratio	7.25:1	10.5:1	9.25:1
Lubrication	Petroil	Petroil	Petroil
Carburettor	Villiers S.25	AMAL monobloc 389/28	AMAL monobloc 376/138
Ignition	Flywheel magneto	WICO special alternator	WICO special alternator
Primary drive	Renold chain 110038	Renold chain 110038	Renold chain 110038
Final drive	Perry chain	Renold chain 110046	Renold chain 110046
Gearbox	Three-speed	Four-speed	Four-speed
Gearbox ratios	6.1; 8.2; 15.6:1	8.0; 10.4; 14.9; 23.4:1	8.0; 11.5; 19.4; 28.6:1
Frame	Brazed and welded main frame with bolt-on duplex cradle-type loop tubes forming rear stays	Heavy-gauge loop brazed and welded. 1.5in section down tube with bolt-on top and bottom stays	Heavy-gauge loop brazed and welded. 1.5in section down tube with bolt-on top and bottom stays
Number prefix	ZN; AN	ECT, F92, H92, I92	ACT
Rim size: front	WM2-18	WM1-21	WM1-21
rear	WM2-18	WM2-19	WM2-19
Front suspension	Telescopic fork	Norton Road Holder-type telescopic fork	Norton Road Holder-type telescopic fork
Rear suspension	Swinging-arm fork with adjustable spring units	Swinging-arm fork with Girling spring units	Swinging-arm fork with Girling spring units
Tyres: front	3.25 × 18in	2.75 × 21in Sports	2.75 × 21in Trials
rear	3.25 × 18in	3.50 × 19in Sports	4 × 19in Trials
Hubs: front	Full width 5in	Full width 6in	Full width 6in
rear	Full width 5in	Full width 5in	Full width 5in
Brakes: front	5in drum	6in drum	6in drum
rear	5in drum	5in drum	5in drum

General Specifications

Fuel tank capacity	2.75gal (12ltr)	2.25gal (10ltr)	2.25gal (10ltr)
Overall length	78in (1,981mm)	80.5in (2,045mm)	80.5in (2,045mm)
Overall width	28in (711mm)	29.5in (750mm)	29.5in (750mm)

Overall height	38.25in (972mm)	43in (1,092mm)	Not known
Wheelbase	49.75in (1,264mm)	52.75in (1,340mm)	52.75in (1,340mm)
Ground clearance	6in (152.4mm)	8.5in (216mm)	8.5in (216mm)
Seat height	30.5in (775mm)	31in (787mm)	32.75in (832mm)
Dry weight	244lb (111kg)	263lb (119kg)	273lb (124kg)
Power	8.4bhp @ 4,000rpm	Not known	Not known

The Light Cruiser 79 was priced at £132 plus £32 13s 5d purchase tax. A chromium-plated tank was also available at £4 1s 1d.

The Cruiser No. 80

The Cruiser 80 also continued in production, with only cosmetic changes. The AMC 249cc engine number prefix was now 24T-80, and the frame number AC. An alternative to the Arden Green finish became available, consisting of Arden Green frame, forks, toolbox, and Dover White mudguards, tank and centre section. The rims and bright parts were chromium-plated. A suffix of 'W' to the frame number indicated the use of the alternative colour finish.

The Cruiser had a list price of £148 10s plus £36 15s purchase tax. A chromium-plated tank was available at £4 1s 1d.

The Falcon No. 81

Another machine with the option of two colour finishes was the Falcon 81. The 197cc Villiers Mark 10E engine, prefix 662B, was retained for 1959; the frame number prefix was AN, and as with the Cruiser and Light Cruiser, a suffix of 'W' indicated the use of the alternative colour finish. The option was similar to that available for the other machines: Arden Green frame, forks, toolbox, and Dover White mudguards, tank and side panels; the rims and bright parts were chromium-plated. Interestingly, a Falcon 81 appears on the *FBOC Register* with a frame suffix of 'R' and annotation of the colour finish being green and red.

ABOVE: *1959 Falcon Model 81. (Courtesy FBOC)*

LEFT: *1959 Falcon Model 81. (Courtesy FBOC)*

1961 Cruiser Model 84 on the FBOC stand at the Bristol Show. (Courtesy FBOC)

Cruiser 84 with an incorrect front mudguard. (Courtesy FBOC)

The Falcon 81 was listed at £128 plus £31 13s 7d purchase tax. A chromium-plated tank was also available at £4 1s 1d.

The Cruiser No. 84

A new Cruiser appeared on the scene in 1959: Cruiser Model No. 84. It was evocative of the pre-war Cruiser as it was designed to provide maximum weather protection, although on its debut the fairing and windshield were still in the design stage. The front down member carried leg-shields and a chromium-plated safety bar. The rear of the machine from behind the engine was enclosed in light but tough side panels moulded in fibreglass, into which the passenger footrests folded flush when not in use. These panels swept back to a combined stop and rear light. As with most machines, the rear number plate was easily detached to facilitate the changing of the rear wheel.

The identical engine to that fitted in the Cruiser 80 frame was used, with a prefix of 25T-84 to the number; this was also the case with the AMAL monobloc carburettor type 389.

Only a few items were interchangeable between the Cruiser 80 and 84, and these were mainly the front frame member, top and bottom chain guards, tank and wheels; the frame number prefix was AE. The finish was Arden Green for the frame, forks, tank and leg-shields, and Dover White for the front mudguard and side panels; the rims and bright parts were chromium-plated.

The Cruiser 84 was listed at £157 2s 3d, plus £38 17s 9d purchase tax. A chromium-plated tank was available for a total of £4 1s 1d.

The Trials No. 83

The Scrambler 82 continued into 1959 virtually unchanged, but it now had a partner in the Trials Model 83. Developed through factory participation in national trials, the engine was a modified version of the 249cc AMC 25T that powered the Cruiser 80, with a compression ratio of 9.25:1 and designed to run on premium fuel. The engine prefix in this instance was 25C.

The cylinder head had reduced finning, giving a flat appearance; the spark plug fitted vertically in the centre, with a release valve on the side. The cylinder was identical to that fitted to the road-going Cruiser 80. A four-speed wide-ratio gearbox was fitted as standard, and the AMAL monobloc carburettor type 376/138 was specified.

The frame was almost identical to the Scrambler 82, except that the right-hand rear suspension unit now had outriggers to clear the silencer mounted within the frame; the frame had a prefix of ACT. The forks were the Norton type, and there were Girling spring units on the rear. The full width hubs enclosed 6in front and 5in rear brakes. A 56T rear sprocket was fitted as standard, with 58T and 60T available as extras.

Equipment included a Dunlop trials saddle, ball-ended clutch and brake levers, Smith's speedometer, inflator and bulb horn. The frame, forks, tank and leg-shields were finished in Arden Green; the tank was dull chromium to resist fuels, and lined green; the rims and bright parts were chromium-plated, and the model had polished alloy mudguards. A direct lighting set was also available as an extra, for £6 11s.

The basic price for the Trials 83 was £159 plus £39 7s purchase tax, making a total of £198 7s.

The 1960 Season

In 1960 the Plover 78, the Falcon 81 and the Trials 83 were deleted from the catalogue and replaced with the Plover Model No. 86, the Falcon Model No. 87 and the Trials Model No. 85. The four remaining models continued as before.

During the year an alteration was made to the front wheel of the Light Cruiser 79, the Cruiser 80 and the Cruiser 84. The original fitment was a centre spindle threaded at both ends, to which the spindle nuts were screwed. In the new arrangement a knock-out spindle was used, sometimes referred to as the QD spindle, which was inserted or withdrawn from the left-hand side. A hole was drilled through the head of the spindle to enable a tommy bar to assist in the insertion or withdrawal of the spindle. The frame number prefix for the Light Cruiser 79 was BD and BBD for the one using the QD spindle; likewise the Cruiser 80 was BC and BBC, and the Cruiser 84 BE and BBE. In each case the latter model was referred to as the Series II model.

The other alteration to the Cruiser 80 and Cruiser 84 was a change in the engine number prefix, which now became M25T-80 and M25T-84. The Scrambler 82 had the QD spindle fitted as original in 1959.

The 1960 prices of the two Cruisers were the Cruiser 80, £149 plus £30 14s 8d, a total of £179 14s 8d; and the Cruiser 84, £158 10s plus £32 13s 10d, a total of £191 3s 10d.

Both the Series I and II of the Light Cruiser were continued for 1960, the Series I presumably until stocks of the obsolete cylinders and pistons were exhausted. The purchaser had several options regarding the colour finish. These were Arden Green throughout with white motifs on the tank and side covers; or Arden Green frame, forks and Dover White mudguards, tank and side covers (frame suffix W); or Arden Green frame, forks and Burma Red mudguards, tank and side covers (frame suffix R).

It was priced at £132 10s plus £27.67 purchase tax, a total of £158 16s 7d.

1960 Plover Model 86. (Courtesy FBOC)

Machine Specifications

❖

Model	Cruiser 84	Trials 85	Plover 86
Manufacturing year	1959–61	1960–62	1960–62
Engine	AMC 25T, single-cylinder, air-cooled two-stroke	AMC 25T, single-cylinder, air-cooled two-stroke	AMC 15/T, single-cylinder, air-cooled two-stroke
Number prefix	25T84, M25T84	25C, M25C	15T
Bore and stroke	66 × 73mm	66 × 73mm	55 × 62mm
Capacity	249cc	249cc	149cc
Compression ratio	8.1:1	9.25:1	7:1
Lubrication	Petroil	Petroil	Petroil
Carburettor	AMAL monobloc 389	AMAL monobloc 376	AMAL monobloc 375
Ignition	Wipac alternator with coil	AC generator	Flywheel magneto
Primary drive	Renold chain 110038	Chain	Renold chain 110038
Final drive	Renold chain 110046	Chain	Renold chain 110044
Gearbox	Four-speed	Four-speed	Three-speed
Gearbox ratios	6.2; 8.1; 11.5; 19.4; 18.3:1	8.0; 11.5; 19.4; 28.6:1	6.9; 9.1; 17.7:1
Frame	Similar to Cruiser 80 frame with moulded side panels	Heavy gauge loop, brazed and welded; 1.5in section down tube with bolt-on top and bottom stays; with offside outrigger for silencer	Welded box section forward member with bolt-on duplex loop tubes
Number prefix	AE, BE, BBE, CE	BCT, CCT, DCT	AB, B, C, D
Front suspension	Telescopic fork	Norton Road Holder type telescopic fork	Telescopic fork
Rear suspension	Swinging-arm fork with Girling spring units	Swinging-arm fork with Girling spring units	Pivot fork with optional friction damper unit
Rim size: front rear	WM2-18 WM2-18	WM1-21 WM2-19	WM1-18 WM1-18
Tyres: front rear	3.25 × 18in 3.25 × 18in	2.75 × 21in 4 × 19in	3 × 18in 3 × 18in
Hubs: front rear	Full width 6in Full width 6in	Full width 5in Full width 5in	Full width 4in Full width 5in
Brakes: front rear	6in drum 6in drum	5in drum 5in drum	4in drum 5in drum

General Specifications

Fuel tank capacity	3.75gal (17ltr)	2.25gal (10ltr)	2.25gal (10ltr)
Overall length	81in (2,057mm)	80.5in (2,045mm)	76.5in (1,943mm)
Overall width	26in (660mm)	29.5in (750mm)	26.5in (673mm)
Overall height	39in (990mm)	43in (1,092mm)	37.5in (953mm)

Wheelbase	52.25in (1,327mm)	52.75in (1,340mm)	49.5in (1,257mm)
Ground clearance	6in (152.4mm)	8.5in (216mm)	5in (127mm)
Seat height	30in (762mm)	31in (787mm)	29.5in (750mm)
Dry weight	307lb (139kg)	271lb (123kg)	171lb (78kg)

The Trials No. 85

The Trials 85 was almost identical to the Trials 83 it replaced, with a few exceptions. The brakes were 5in front and rear, and a padded seat was fitted. The option of a 58T or 60T rear sprocket was available as an extra, as was a QD direct lighting set. The Trials 85 was priced at £160 plus £33 purchase, a total of £193.

The Plover No. 86

The frame of the Plover Model No. 86 had a lot in common with that of the Plover 78 which it replaced. Most of the differences arose through the replacement of the Villiers Mark 30C engine by the AMC 15T engine. The AMC engine had a bore and stroke of 55 × 62.69mm and a capacity of 149cc; a three-speed gearbox was bolted to the crankcase. The frame number prefix was B, and the direct lighting was by flywheel magneto. The colour finish options were Arden Green with Dover White side panels, or Burma Red with Dover White side panels. The rims and bright parts were chromium-plated. The front wheel did not use the QD spindle.

The Plover 86 was priced at £94 10s plus £19 9s 10d purchase tax, a total of £113 19s 10d.

The Falcon No. 87

The other touring model added for 1960 was the Falcon Model No. 87, which continued in production until the company closed down in 1966. It replaced the Falcon 81 and was similar in looks. The latest version of the AMC engine, the 20T, was fitted to the Falcon 87; it had bore and stroke of 59 × 72mm giving a capacity of 199cc, a four-speed gearbox was bolted to the rear of the crankcase, and the carburettor was the AMAL monobloc type 376/23. The ignition, electrics and so on were identical to those of the Cruisers 80 and 84.

The frame consisted of a brazed and welded tubular loop main frame with bolt-on duplex cradle-type loop tubes forming rear stays; its prefix was 'BF'. The front forks were as those used on the Cruisers, except for the bridge piece, as was the Girling rear suspension units; the bottom chromium dirt shield was omitted on the Cruiser 84. The full width hubs, with journal bearings, contained 5in brakes. The front wheel had a knock-out spindle.

1960 Falcon Model 87. (Courtesy FBOC)

Machine Specifications

Model	Falcon 87	Fulmar 88	Cruiser Twin 89
Manufacturing year	1960–66	1962–65	1962–65
Engine	AMC 20/T, single-cylinder, air-cooled two-stroke	AMC 15/T, single-cylinder, air-cooled two-stroke	Villiers Mark 2T, twin-cylinder, air-cooled two-stroke; 1964: Mark 4T twin
Number prefix	20T, V20T	V15T	429D, 687E, 688E
Bore and stroke	59 × 72.8mm	55 × 62mm	50 × 63.5mm
Capacity	199cc	149cc	250cc
Compression ratio	8.5:1	7:1	8.2:1
Lubrication	Petroil	Petroil	Petroil
Carburettor	AMAL monobloc 376	AMAL monobloc 375/37	Villiers S.22/2
Ignition	Wipac alternator with coil	Flywheel magneto	Flywheel magneto
Primary drive	Renold chain 110038	Renold chain 110038	Renold chain 110038
Final drive	Renold chain 110046	Renold chain 110044	Renold chain 110046
Gearbox	Four-speed	Three-speed	Four-speed
Gearbox ratios	6.5; 8.6, 12.0; 19.1:1	6.7; 10.2; 17.2:1	6.2; 8.2; 11.8; 19.0:1
Frame	Brazed and welded main frame with bolt-on duplex cradle-type loop tubes forming rear stays	Front frame tube welded to steering head; bolted on straight tubing in triangulated formation	Oval section forward member and bolt-on duplex loop tubes
Number prefix	BF; CF; DF; EF; FF; HF; IF	DGR	DH, EH, FH, HH
Front suspension	Telescopic fork	Telescopic fork	Telescopic fork
Rear suspension	Swinging-arm fork with adjustable spring units	Swinging-arm fork with spring units	Swinging-arm fork with adjustable spring units
Rim size: front	WM2-18	WM1-18	WM2-18
rear	WM2-18	WM1-18	WM2-18
Tyres: front	3.25 × 18in	3 × 18in	3.25 × 18in
rear	3.25 × 18in	3 × 18in	3.25 × 18in
Hubs: front	Full width 5in	Full width 5in	Full width 6in
rear	Full width 5in	Full width 5in	Full width 6in
Brakes: front	5in drum	5in drum	6in drum
rear	5in drum	5in drum	6in drum

General specifications

	1965 specification	1965 specification	1963 specification
Fuel tank capacity	3.25gal (15ltr)	2.5gal (11ltr)	3.5gal (16ltr)
Overall length	78in (1,981mm)	76in (1,930mm)	80in (2,032mm)
Overall width	26in (660mm)	29.5in (750mm)	26in (660mm)

Overall height	39in (990mm)	36.5in (927mm)	39in (990mm)
Wheelbase	49.75in (1,264mm)	49.5in (1,257mm)	51.5in (1,308mm)
Ground clearance	6in (152.4mm)	5in (127mm)	5.5in (140mm)
Seat height	30.5in (775mm)	29in (737mm)	30in (762mm)
Dry weight	267.5lb (121kg)	225lb (102kg)	299lb (136kg)
Power	Not known	Not known	15bhp @ 5,500rpm

The colour finish was either Arden Green throughout with white motifs on the tank and toolbox covers, or Arden Green frame, forks and so on, and Dover White mudguards and tank; the rims and bright parts were chromium-plated. It was equipped with a Smith's speedometer, Lucas electric horn, inflator and toolkit.

The Falcon 87 was priced at £139 plus £28 13s 4d, a total of £167 13s 4d.

Perhaps some of you watched the Yorkshire TV series *Heartbeat* in the early 1990s starring Nick Berry, Niamh Cusack and Derek Foulds, with a supporting cast of two Falcon 87s bearing the same registration: LEF 296. One was bright and shiny for dull days, and the other not so bright and shiny for sunny days; however, the two were fairly easy to distinguish as only one had chromed upper fork shrouds.

The Light Cruiser 79, the Cruisers 80 and 84 and the Falcon 87 all had the option of a chromium-plated tank for £3 18s 5d. White-wall tyres for the Cruisers 80 and 84 and the Falcon 87 cost £1 10s 2d.

Falcon Model 87 in unusual black and red finish. (Courtesy FBOC)

The 1961 Season

The Plover 86, Cruisers 80 and 84, Falcon 87, Scrambler 82 and the Trials 85 continued as before, leaving only the Light Cruiser 79 to be deleted from the range. Comments had been made that the Light Cruiser 79 was unstable, allegedly due to the steering head angle. There were no additions to the range for 1961. The frame number prefix for the Plover 86 was C; for the Falcon 87, CF; for the Scrambler 82, CCS; for the Trials 85, CCT; and the commencing engine and frame numbers for the Cruiser 80 were M25T-20243 and CC15706, and for the Cruiser 84, M25T/84-20070 and CE15634. The colour finish on all models was as the 1960 season.

The 1962 Season

During the 1961 calendar year, the assembly of the AMC engines was transferred to the Villiers works, with the engines becoming available during the 1962 season. Only two engines were in fact affected, the 17T having already been discontinued, and the 25T and its variants ending their production run at the end of the season, leaving only the 15T and 20T engines to continue in production until 1966. These two engines can be identified by the engine number prefix, which became V15T and V20T. 1962 was the year that Francis-Barnett moved from Lower Ford Street and its other premises in Coventry, to Birmingham to share the James factory at Greet.

The six machines continued in production for the 1962 season. The Competition Models 82 and 85 remained unaltered; the Scrambler 82 had an engine number prefix of 25S and a frame number prefix of DCS. For the Trials 85, the engine and frame number prefixes were M25C and DCT. The prices were as follows: the Scrambler 82, £145 plus £29 purchase tax, a total of £174; the Trials 85, £146 10s plus £29 6s purchase tax, a total of £132 6s.

The Plover 86 engine and frame number prefixes were 15T and D. The colour finish was either Arden Green with a white-panelled tank, or Tartan Red with white-panelled tank. It was priced at £110 5s plus purchase tax of £22 1s, a total of £132 6s.

The Cruiser 80 engine and frame number prefixes for the year were M25T and DC. Although the Cruiser appeared in the 1963 season brochure, its production in fact ceased in April of 1963. The frame number prefix for 1962, DC, continued to be used into 1963. The Scrambler variants of the 25T, such as the 25S and the M25S, were fitted into some standard Cruiser 80 frames, probably because the frame continued to be manufactured until such time as all the variants of the 249cc engines were used up.

Available colour finishes consisted of all Arden Green with white tank flashes or Arden Green frame, forks, front mudguard and top half of tank, white bottom half of tank, centre section, tool box and rear mudguard, with this colour combination the frame number suffix was W; or with black in lieu of Arden Green the suffix was BW. The Cruiser was

1961 Falcon Model 87. (Courtesy FBOC)

*1961 Trials Model 85.
(Courtesy FBOC)*

*BELOW: 1961 Plover Model 86.
(Courtesy K.Young)*

priced at £148 plus £29 12s purchase tax, a total of £177 12s.

According to the sales brochure for the 1962 season, the Cruiser 84 now came without safety bar and leg-shields, but remained the same in all other respects. Glasses *Motorcycle Check Book 1961–68* quotes that the commencing engine and frame numbers for 1962 were M25-84-20133 and DE15892, whereas the *FBOC Register* has no Cruisers listed with the frame prefix of DE, and the frame numbers listed from 15904 to 16732 all have the prefix CE for 1961. It was priced at £155 12s 6d plus £31 2s 6d purchase tax, a total of £186 15s.

The Falcon 87 remained unchanged from 1961. Four colour finishes were available: Arden Green with white tank flashes; Arden Green frame, forks, front mudguard, top half of the tank and bottom half of the toolbox covers; or the bottom half of the tank, top half of tool box covers and the rear mudguard white, frame suffix W; or as before but black and white and a frame suffix of BW; or black and red. The engine and frame number prefixes commenced 20T-7071 and DF91046BW. It was priced at £135 15s plus £27 3s purchase tax, a total of £162 18s.

The Fulmar No. 88

New for 1962 was the Fulmar Model No. 88; it was very modern-looking for the time and totally dissimilar from the machines that preceded it. Fitted into the frame was the 149cc AMC 15T engine, with a three-speed gearbox bolted to the rear of the crankcase. The engine number prefix V15T signified that it was built by Villiers Ltd.

The main frame member consisted of 1.25in- (32mm-) diameter, twelve-gauge tubing welded near to the top of the steering head, and looked like a reversed letter 'J', leaning forwards at an angle of approximately 45 degrees. The bottom half of the 'J' curved round the back of the gearbox and under the engine to which it was attached. The rest of the frame was built up using 0.75in- (19mm-) diameter, sixteen-gauge straight tubing in a triangulated formation. Two top frame tubes ran from where they were bolted at the base of the steering head to the rear, past the top rear mudguard support assembly, which sat between the two tubes. The centre frame stud held the top mudguard support assembly in place; on either side of this, and on the inner side of the top frame tubes, were the rear frame tubes, and on the outside were the rear suspension mounting brackets. The rear frame tubes were

1962 Cruiser Model 80 fitted with the Villiers 2T engine in place of the AMC 25T. (Courtesy J. Baker)

1962 Falcon Model 87 in black and white finish. (Courtesy FBOC)

inclined downwards and forwards to meet the front frame tubes at the swing fork pivot stud. The forward ends of the front frame tubes were bolted to the steering head, utilizing the same bolt as the top frame tubes.

The forks were a new design of the leading link type, with Girling springing units enclosed in a pressed-steel fairing. The centre rods of the Girling units were locked to the fork crown arms, which were also bronze-welded to the pressed-steel stanchion tubes. The leading links carrying the wheel spindle pivoted on Silentbloc bushes; the linkage was specially designed to prevent interference with the fork movement on braking. The rear suspension unit consisted of an orthodox swinging fork employing Silentbloc bushes and Armstrong spring units.

Pressed-steel streamlining swept back from the 6in (15cm) headlamp to the rear mudguard, and enclosed a toolbox in front of the rider. A dual seat, hinged at the rear, had a trigger-release mechanism to give instant access to the fuel tank, battery and so on. The fuel tank was mounted low in the centre of the frame. A lifting handle was provided on the left rear of the bodywork.

1962 Falcon Model 87 in Arden Green finish. (Courtesy FBOC)

The frame numbers commenced DGR or DGB. Ignition was flywheel magneto, and the lighting was by a flywheel generator. The full width hubs contained 5in brakes front and rear. The colour finish was either Tartan Red or black for the frame, forks and front mudguards, with Dover White for the streamlined panelling and the rear mudguard.

The Fulmar 88 was the final model to come out of Lower Ford Street, Coventry. The total price of the standard model was £143 8s, £119 10s plus £23 18s purchase tax. Rectified lighting and a stoplight were an additional £5 12s 3d.

TOP LEFT: 1963 Fulmar Model 88 in black and white finish. (Courtesy D. Carr)

TOP RIGHT: 1962 Fulmar Model 88 in red and white finish. (Courtesy FBOC)

MIDDLE LEFT: Fulmar at speed. (Courtesy FBOC)

LEFT: 1962 Fulmar Model 88 restored by Des Heckle. (Courtesy Des Heckle)

ABOVE: *1962 Cruiser Twin Model 89 purchased for £5 in 1974. (Courtesy FBOC)*

LEFT: *1962 Cruiser Twin Model 89. (Courtesy J. Baker)*

1962 Cruiser Twin Model 89 and a 1954 Trials Falcon Model 62. (Courtesy FBOC)

1962 Cruiser Twin Model 89 in black and white finish. (Courtesy R. & R. Baxter)

The Cruiser No. 89

Another model appeared on the scene in 1962, but it was not entirely new as such. This was the Cruiser Twin, Model No. 89, which married the Cruiser 80 frame, suspension and so on, but with a revised centre stand with the Villiers Mark 2T engine, prefix 429D. The twin cylinders with a bore and stroke of 50 × 63.5mm had a capacity of 250cc and a compression ratio of 8.2:1. The carburettor was the Villiers type S.22/2. Ignition was flywheel magneto, and the lighting, flywheel generator. A stoplight was included in the specification. The frame number had the prefix DH. According to the 1962 sales brochure, two colour finishes were available to the buyers: the frame, forks, front mudguard and the top half of the tank in Arden Green or black and the remainder in Dover White. It was priced at £158 5s plus £31 13s purchase tax, a total of £189 18s.

The prices quoted for the 1962 season were those applicable from 6 April 1962. The Falcon and Cruiser models had the option of a chromium-plated tank for £4 6s 5d, and white wall tyres for £1 13s. Stoplights were now fitted as standard.

The 1963 Season

A lot of errors appeared in the 1963 season advertising brochures, from referring to the Cruiser Sports Twin 91 as the Model 93, and incorrectly converting imperial dimensions to metric. Was this an indication of the beginning of the end where no one cared any more, or maybe there wasn't anyone left from the past to care? Perhaps AMC management were more involved in their pending tie-up with the Japanese firm of Suzuki than with their British motorcycle firms.

The Falcon 87, Fulmar 88 and the Cruiser Twin 89 continued in production for 1963 much the same as they were for the previous year. The Cruiser 80 was also available for a short period before being discontinued; details are under the 1962 season.

The new features for the 1963 Falcon 87 were lowered headlamp, fully adjustable handlebars, number plates on either side of the front mudguard, and a 'cleaned up' lower fork. Colour finishes available were Arden Green with tank lined in gold; or Arden Green frames, forks, front mudguard, the bottom half of the tank and the top half of the toolbox covers, with the remainder in Dover White. The second option was indicated by the frame number suffix of 'W'.

The Cruiser 89 continued as before, but with lowered headlamp and fully adjustable handlebars. Colour finishes were Arden Green with tank lined in gold; or Arden Green frame, forks, front mudguard and the top half of the tank, with the remainder in Dover White.

The Cruiser Twin Sports No. 91

Making its debut this year was the Cruiser Twin Sports Model No. 91, which carried on the fashion of badge-engineered machines coming out of the Birmingham factory. There was little input from the Francis-Barnett side of the design team as the Cruiser was based on the same frame as that used by the James M25S Sports Superswift 250 Twin.

The frame was formed in the shape of a cradle and consisted of two 1.25in- (32mm-) diameter tubes brazed and welded at the front to the steering head. The top tube was joined at a junction to the rear by two short tubes from which the suspension units hung, and the bottom tube – which started at the steering head – came down and around the engine, then up to the junction with the top tube.

It is debatable whether the frame, prefix E91, was robust enough to cope with the 15bhp of the 2T engine, let alone the 17bhp of the 4T. Most parts of the two machines were identical – the Mark 2 front forks, the fuel tank, mudguards and so on. The engine was a high compression, tuned version of the 250cc Villiers Mark 2T, prefix 300E; the carburettor was the Villiers S.25/6. The specification included sports handlebars, fly screen and polished mudguards.

According to the 1963 sales brochures, the Fulmar 88 remained unchanged from the 1962 model except for the colour finish. Options were silver frame, forks, rear mudguard and chain guard, with the front mudguard and panels in Arden Green or Tartan Red in lieu of silver, and Dover White in lieu of Arden Green. Interestingly there are only 1962 season models with the frame prefix of DG recorded in the *FBOC Register*, and some were actually registered in 1963, 1964, 1965 and one even as late as 1968, well after the end of Francis-Barnett.

ABOVE RIGHT: 1965 Cruiser Sports Twin Model 91 with a rolling chassis. (Courtesy N. Clarke)

1963 Cruiser Sports Twin Model 91. (Courtesy FBOC)

Machine Specifications

Model	Fulmar Sports 90	Cruiser Twin Sports 91	Cruiser Twin Sports 91
Manufacturing year	1963–65	1963	1964–66
Engine	AMC 15/T, single-cylinder, air-cooled two-stroke	Villiers Mark 2T, twin-cylinder, air-cooled two-stroke	Villiers Mark 4T, twin-cylinder, air-cooled two-stroke
Number prefix	V15T	300E	687E, 688E
Bore and stroke	55 × 62mm	50 × 63.5mm	50 × 63.5mm
Capacity	149cc	250cc	250cc
Compression ratio	7:1	8.2:1	8.75:1
Lubrication	Petroil	Petroil	Petroil
Carburettor	AMAL 375	Villiers S.25/6	Villiers S.25/6
Ignition	Flywheel magneto	Flywheel magneto	Flywheel magneto
Primary drive	Renold chain 110038	Chain	Chain
Final drive	Renold chain 110044	Chain	Chain
Gearbox	Four-speed	Four-speed	Four-speed
Gearbox ratios	6.87; 8.72; 12.23; 20.20:1	6.21; 8.3; 11.79; 19.0:1	6.21; 8.3; 11.79; 19.0:1
Frame	Front frame tube welded to steering head; bolted-on straight tubing in triangulated formation	1.25in diameter single tube, cradle type brazed and welded	1.25in diameter single tube, cradle type brazed and welded
Number prefix	E.90, H90	E.91	F.91, H.91, I.91
Front suspension	Telescopic fork	Telescopic fork	Telescopic fork
Rear suspension	Swinging-arm fork with spring units	Swinging-arm fork with spring units	Swinging-arm fork with spring units
Rim size: front	WM1-18	WM2-18	WM1-19
rear	WM1-18	WM2-18	WM2-18
Tyres: front	3 × 18in	3.25 × 18in	2.75 × 19in
rear	3 × 18in	3.25 × 18in	3.25 × 18in
Hubs: front	Full width 5in	Full width 6in	Full width 6in
rear	Full width 5in	Full width 5in	Full width 6in
Brakes: front	5in drum	6in drum	6in drum
rear	5in drum	5in drum	6in drum

General Specifications

	1965 specification	1963 specification	1965 specification
Fuel tank capacity	2.25gal (10ltr)	2.75gal (12ltr)	2.75gal (12ltr)

Machine Specifications *continued*

General Specifications

	1965 specification	1963 specification	1965 specification
Overall length	73in (1,854mm)	79in (2,007mm)	79in (2,007mm)
Overall width	23.5in (587mm)	25.5in (648mm)	26in (660mm)
Overall height	42in (1,067mm)	45in (1,143mm)	45in (1,143mm)
Wheelbase	49.5in (1,257mm)	51.25in (1,302mm)	51.25in (1,302mm)
Ground clearance	5in (127mm)	5in (127mm)	5in (127mm)
Seat height	29in (737mm)	30in (762mm)	30in (762mm)
Dry weight	223lb (101kg)	290lb (131kg)	295lb (134kg)
Power		15bhp @ 5,500rpm	17bhp @ 6,000rpm

The Fulmar Sports No. 90

Joining the Fulmar 88 this year was the Fulmar Sports Model No. 90, the prototype of which was given a gruelling test in the 1962 Scottish Six Day Trial, gaining its rider a first class award. Although the Sports model was based on the standard model, there was quite some difference between the two. The 149cc AMC V15T engine was used, but married up with a Villiers close-ratio four-speed gearbox. The AMAL 375 carburettor was retained.

The equipment included short, lowered handlebars with adjustable ball-ended clutch and brake control levers, racing screen, polished light alloy mudguards, special silencer, abbreviated chromium-plated chain guard, special twin seat and indented knee grips. The frame number prefix was E90.

1962 Fulmar Sports Model 90 displayed at the FBOC AGM, Gaydon. It was the best Villiers-engined machine at Stafford Show in 2010; the owner S. Elkes. (Courtesy FBOC)

Machine Specifications

Model	Trials 92	Scrambler 93	Scrambler 94 (Starmaker)
Manufacturing year	1963–66	1963–64	1964–66
Engine	Villiers Mark 32A, single-cylinder, air-cooled two-stroke	Villiers Mark 36A, single-cylinder, air-cooled two-stroke#	Villiers Starmaker single-cylinder, air-cooled two-stroke
Number prefix	326E	352E	826E
Bore and stroke	66 × 72mm	66 × 72mm	68 × 68mm
Capacity	246cc	246cc	247cc
Compression ratio	7.9:1	11.2:1	12:1
Lubrication	Petroil	Petroil	Petroil
Carburettor	Villiers S.25/5	AMAL monobloc 389	AMAL 389/39
Ignition	Flywheel magneto	Flywheel magneto	Flywheel magneto
Primary drive	Chain	Chain	Chain
Final drive	Chain	Chain	Chain
Gearbox	Four-speed	Four-speed	Four-speed
Gearbox ratios	6.88; 9.35; 16.5; 24.8:1	8.6; 10.9; 15.3; 25.3:1	10.75; 13.2; 17.6; 27.0:1
Frame	Heavy gauge loop, brazed and welded; 1.5in section down tube with bolt-on top and bottom stays	Heavy gauge loop, brazed and welded; 1.5in section down tube with bolt-on top and bottom stays	Heavy gauge loop, brazed and welded; 1.5in section down tube with bolt-on top and bottom stays
Number prefix	ECT; F92; H92; I92	ECS	H94, I94
Front suspension	Norton Road Holder type telescopic fork	Norton Road Holder type telescopic fork	Norton Road Holder type telescopic fork
Rear suspension	Swinging-arm fork with spring units	Swinging-arm fork with spring units	Swinging-arm fork with spring units
Rim size: front	WM1-21	WM1-21	WM1-21
rear	WM3-19	WM3-18	WM2-18
Tyres: front	2.75 × 21in	2.75 × 21in	2.75 × 21in
rear	4 × 19in	4 × 18in	4 × 18in
Hubs: front	Full width 6in	Full width 6in	Full width 6in
rear	Full width 6in	Full width 5in	Full width 6in
Brakes: front	6in drum	6in drum	6in drum
rear	6in drum	5in drum	6in drum

General Specifications

	1965 specification		1965 specification
Fuel tank capacity	2.25gal (10ltr)	1.5gal (7ltr)	1.5gal (7ltr)

Machine Specifications *continued*

	1965 specification		*1965 specification*
Overall length	80in (2,032mm)	Not known	80in (2,032mm)
Overall width	25.5in (648mm)	Not known	Not known
Overall height	Not known	Not known	Not known
Wheelbase	52.5in (1,334mm)	52.5in (1,334mm)	52.5in (1,334mm)
Ground clearance	8.5in (216mm)	8in (203mm)	8in (203mm)
Seat height	31in (787mm)	31in (787mm)	31in (787mm)
Dry weight	248lb (112.5kg)	235lb (107kg)	251lb (114kg)
Power	12.4 @ 5,000rpm	Not known	25bhp @ 6,500rpm
		# Parkinson square-barrelled cylinder	

The colour finish was frame and forks silver, and the panelling red with gold lining; there were no other options.

A maximum speed of 60mph (96.5km/h) could be expected, depending on the conditions, and a fuel consumption of approximately 85mpg (3.3ltr/100km) at 50mph (80km/h). It was priced at £149 inclusive of purchase tax.

The Trials No. 92

Two Villiers-engined competition machines were introduced in 1963. The Trials Model No. 92 prototype, with Mick Ransom riding, won the 250cc Cup and best two-stroke performance in the 1962 Scottish Six Day Trial. The production model was a replica of that ridden by Mick, fitted with a Villiers Mark 32A engine and a wide ratio four-speed gearbox, bore and stroke of 66 × 72mm, with a capacity of 246cc and a compression ratio of 7.9:1; the engine number prefix was 326E. The carburettor was the Villiers-type S.25.

The cross-braced tubular steel frame, being particularly rigid, was coupled with Norton front forks and Girling adjustable rear dampers. The frame number prefix was ECT.

The full Trials specification included alloy mudguards with tubular steel stays; special lightweight wheel hubs with 5in brakes; alloy chain cover with sturdy chain guide; small steel fuel tank with quick-action cap; trials seat of foam rubber covered with leather cloth; wide handlebars with ball-ended levers. The colour finish was Arden Green for the frame and forks, with a silver tank.

The Trials 92 retailed at £195 including purchase tax.

The Scrambler No. 93

The Scrambler Model No. 93 was the other new competition model for 1963. With similar frame and suspension specification to the Trials model, and frame prefix ECS, it used the Villiers Mark 36A engine fitted with Parkinson square-barrel conversion and close-ratio gearbox, prefix 352E. A 6in front brake and a 5in rear were fitted as standard. An abbreviated megaphone exhaust system completed the set-up. The colour finish was identical to that of the Trials 92.

The Scrambler was priced at £249, including purchase tax.

The 1964 Season

In mid-1963 rumours abounded that AMC were to be the import and distribution agents for Suzuki motorcycles.

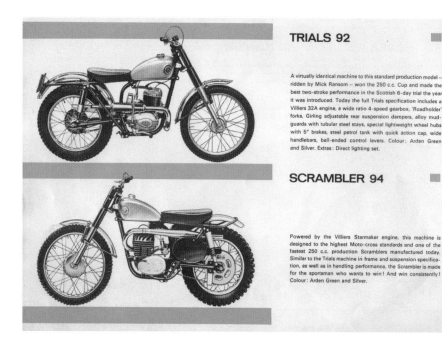

Trials Model 92 and Scrambler Model 94 advertisement.

In October 1963, the first Suzuki imports arrived at the James factory in Greet, Birmingham. AMC (the importers) organized a special test day for the British Press Corps at Crystal Palace on 23 October 1963. Between October 1963 and October 1964 about 18,000 machines passed through the back door of the James factory in Birmingham.

Little was done to update the current Francis-Barnett models or bring in new ones to compete with the pending invasion of foreign imports. The Falcon 87 introduced in 1960 could trace its ancestry back to the Falcon 70 of 1955; likewise, the Cruiser 89 could trace its roots back to the Cruiser 80 of 1957.

1963 Plover Model 86. (Courtesy FBOC)

1963 Trials Model 92. (Courtesy FBOC)

1964 Falcon Model 87, the owner J. Butler; FBOC East of England section meeting.

Seven machines were carried forwards in production from 1963 to 1964: first, the Falcon 87 was now fitted with the Villiers-built 199cc AMC engine, prefix V20T; frame prefix FF; colour finish Arden Green and Dover White, with the option of a chromium-plated tank

The Fulmar 88 continued unchanged, as did the Sports Fulmar 90. Colour finish for the Fulmar 88 was Arden Green and silver, and for the Fulmar Sports 90 red and silver with gold lining. The engine prefixes continued, and the FBOC records appear to indicate that the same frame prefixes continued from 1962.

The Cruiser 89 and the Cruiser Sports 91 had a change of engine, the Villiers Mark 2T being replaced by the Villiers Mark 4T engine; this year the James Mark 2 forks were adopted. The machines remained the same in all other features including gear ratios. Engine prefixes were now 688E for the Cruiser 89, and 687E for the Cruiser 91; frame prefixes were FH and F91. Colour finishes were Arden Green with tank lined gold, or Arden Green and white for the Cruiser 89 and Tartan Red and silver for the Cruiser 91. A chromium-plated tank was available for the Cruiser 89.

The two competition models, the Trials 92 and Scrambler 93, continued as before, although the Scrambler was discontinued in March 1964, being replaced by the Scrambler Model No. 94 introduced that year.

1964 Cruiser Sports Twin Model 91 with Villiers 4T engine. (Courtesy T. Allen-Ross)

This could not be described as an entirely new model as it was basically the Scrambler 93 with the Villiers Starmaker engine in place of the Villiers Mark 36A engine.

There were several unique features to the engine, as described in Chapter 6; not the least was the fact that it was a single-cylinder engine initially designed to have twin carburettors but changed to a single one for simplicity. Model 94 had a single AMAL 389 carburettor. The engine prefix was 826E, and the frame prefix H94.

The Plover No. 95

One other new model was introduced in1964: the Plover Model No. 95, again using the 149cc AMC V15T engine, with three-speed gearbox and AMAL 375/37 carburettor. The frame consisted of a single tube backbone with the prefix F95; telescopic front forks and swinging-arm rear suspension; a large capacity, short humped-back tank and a long foam-rubber twin seat that looked disproportionate with the rest of the machine. The colour finish was Arden Green with white tank panels. Extras were battery lighting and stop light.

1965 Cruiser Sports Twin Model 91 with Villiers 4T engine. (Courtesy J. Baker)

1965 Falcon Model 87 fitted with Villiers 2T engine instead of the AMC 20T. (Courtesy B. Oliver)

The 1965 Season

Nine models were in production during 1965, eight of which had been continued from 1964. These were:

- The Falcon 87, frame prefix HF, colour finish Arden Green and white
- The Fulmar 88, frame prefix HM88, colour finish silver frame and forks with Arden Green panels
- The Cruiser Twin 89, frame prefix HH, colour finish Arden Green and white
- The Fulmar Sports 90, frame prefix H90, colour finish silver frame and forks with red panels, gold lined
- The Cruiser Sports 91, frame prefix H91, colour finish red frame, forks and tank red with silver panels, chromium-plated toolbox and battery box lids, polished alloy mudguards
- The Trials 92, frame prefix H92
- The Scrambler 94, frame prefix H94
- The Plover 95, frame prefix H95, colour finish Arden Green with white tank panels.

Officially the Villiers 4T fitted to the Cruiser Twin 89 had the prefix 687E, and that fitted to the Cruiser Sports Twin 91 was 688E; in practice, however, they were both used on either machine during the last two years of production. It will be noted that the letter G was not used as the year prefix letter for 1965.

Model No. 96

Finally the last of the line, Model No. 96, was introduced in July 1965; they did not even bother to give

1965 Cruiser Sports Twin Model 91 with Villiers 4T engine. Rarely seen red and yellow colour finish; the owner N. Clarke.

1965 Plover Model 95 with AMC V16T engine; the owner Keith R. Clarke. (Courtesy FBOC)

it a name. Several names have been suggested over the years, and perhaps the most apt is the dodo, the phrase 'to go the way of the dodo' meaning to become extinct, or become a thing of the past.

This was the fourth model currently in production using the 149cc AMC V15T engine with three-speed gear box and AMAL 375/37 carburettor. The frame was of conventional tubular design, also used by the James model M16 and before that the 199cc James Captain. It had telescopic front forks and pivoted rear fork with Girling spring and hydraulic units. The frame number prefix was H96.

Electricity equipment included a Wipac 6-volt fly-wheel magneto with direct lighting coil, and a dry battery for a parking light; a 5.5in- (14cm-) diameter headlamp with a 24/24w bulb and a Wipac AC horn. Maximum speed was in the region of 55 to 60mph (88 to 96.5km/h), and fuel consumption about 90mpg (3ltr/100km) at 40mph (64km/h).

Colour finish was black frame and forks with metallic green tank, centre section and mudguards.

The 1966 Season

For 1966, three models were dropped from the range: the Fulmar 88, the Fulmar Sports 90 and the Plover 95, leaving six models to be carried forward; these were the Falcon 87, Cruiser Twin 89, Cruiser Sports Twin 91, Trials 92, Scrambles 94 and the Model No. 96. Apart from the Falcon 87 with the frame prefix of IF, all the other frame prefixes had the letter I following the model number. Colour finishes were as before. The Falcon 87 and the Cruiser Twin 89 were the only two machines that did not have a James equivalent.

The end finally came in 1966; various dates are given when all production ceased, ranging between August and October of that year. The insolvency of AMC brought to an end almost half a century of motorcycle manufacturing, covering over 100 models under the Francis-Barnett banner.

1965 Model 96. Seen at the FBOC AGM, Hagley. (Courtesy FBOC)

Machine Specifications

	Plover 95	Model 96
Model	Plover 95	Model 96
Manufacturing year	1964–65	1965–66
Engine	AMC 15/T, single-cylinder, air-cooled two-stroke	AMC 15/T, single-cylinder, air-cooled two-stroke
Number prefix	V15T	V15T, V16T
Bore and stroke	55 × 62mm	62.69 × 55mm
Capacity	149cc	149cc
Compression ratio	7:1	7:1
Lubrication	Petroil	Petroil
Carburettor	AMAL 375/37	AMAL 375/37
Ignition	Flywheel magneto	Flywheel magneto
Primary drive	Renold chain 110038	Renold chain 110038
Final drive	Renold chain 110044	Renold chain 110044
Gearbox	Three-speed	Three-speed
Gearbox ratios	6.7; 10.2; 17.2:1	5.84; 10.2; 15.1:1
Frame	Single tube, backbone frame	Simple loop frame of conventional design
Number prefix	F95, H95	HM96, I96
Front suspension	Telescopic fork	Telescopic fork
Rear suspension	Swinging-arm fork with spring units	Pivoted fork with Girling spring and hydraulic units
Rim size: front	WM1-18	WM1-18
rear	WM1-18	WM1-18
Tyres: front	3 × 18in	3 × 18in
rear	3 × 18in	3 × 18in
Hubs: front	Full width 5in	Full width 5in
rear	Full width 5in	Full width 5in
Brakes: front	5in drum	5in drum
rear	5in drum	5in drum

General Specifications

	1965 specification	1965 specification
Fuel tank capacity	2.75gal (12ltr)	2.25gal (10ltr)
Overall length	76.5in (1,943mm)	79in (2,007mm)
Overall width	24in (610mm)	28in (711mm)
Overall height	Not known	Not known
Wheelbase	49.5in (1,257mm)	51in (1,295mm)
Ground clearance	6.5in (165mm)	6in (152.4mm)
Seat height	29.5in (750mm)	29.5in (750mm)
Dry weight	165lb (75kg)	165lb (75kg)

CHAPTER SIX

Engines and Carburettors

The Villiers Engineering Company Ltd: Pre-World War II Engines

This part of the book covers those motorcycle engines specifically used by Francis-Barnett. For a more detailed account of the Villiers Engineering company look no further than the late Jack Sizer's book, *The Villiers Story*.

Originally named the Villiers Cycle Components Company, it later became the Villiers Engineering

Company Ltd when manufacturing cycle parts became less important to the business. In 1898 John Marston moved his cycle business to new premises in Wolverhampton, placing his son Charles Marston, later to be Sir Charles, in charge. As their factory was situated in Villiers Street they used Villiers as the name of their company.

The First Villiers Engines

Their first motorcycle engine was a 350cc four-stroke with built-in two-speed gear and clutch, introduced in 1912. The engine was of the single-cylinder type with a bore and stroke of 74.5 × 80mm, giving a capacity of 349cc. By the end of that year, their first two-stroke engine had been designed as having a non-detachable cylinder head, cast-iron deflector-type piston and fixed gudgeon pin. It was known as the Mark I and became available to motorcycle manufacturers in 1913. This was followed by the Mark II in 1916, the Mark III in 1920, the Mark IV in 1921 and the Mark V in 1922, all of which were made with a bore and stroke of 70 × 70mm, giving a cubic capacity of 269cc.

These first five two-stroke models are distinguishable by having flat fins on the cylinder head, while those that followed had fins placed radially on the cylinder head. The prefix letters of the engine numbers were O, A, B, C and D. The Villiers engine that was fitted to the first two-stroke Francis-Barnett was probably the Mark III or Mark IV, which would have had changes made to the driving shaft so as to allow a flywheel magneto to be fitted; from the Mark V onwards this became the norm for many years.

The 147cc Engine Series

The first 1.5hp or 147cc engine of this size was the Mark VIC, and it started a run of a new series of

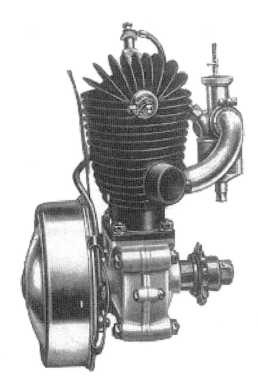

269cc Mark II engine.

engines. From time to time improvements and alterations were made, and these were denoted by an alteration in the mark number, which progressed from Mark VIC to VIIC, and then to VIIIC. These engines had a bore and stroke of 55 × 62mm, and the lubrication employed was petroil – the simplest method, but applicable only to the two-stroke engine. It was recommended that the petrol and oil were mixed before the fuel was placed in the tank, so there was no risk of the two fuels not mixing. The proportion advocated was one part oil to sixteen parts petrol, so half a pint of oil had to be mixed with each gallon of petrol.

The first 147cc engine to be used by Francis-Barnett in their three 1.5hp machines, new for the 1923 season, appears to be the Mark VIIC with engine prefix L. The engine had cast-iron pistons with fixed gudgeon pins, and a one-piece cylinder and head with compression release valve, and was only available for 1923 and 1924.

The next engine that appeared in the series, with the engine prefix W, was the Mark VIIIC fitted with a fully floating padded gudgeon pin. This engine was fitted to the Francis-Barnett Model No. 4 when it made its debut in the 1926 season, and eventually replaced the Mark VIC engine in the model numbers 1, 2 and 3 until they ceased manufacture.

The engine proved to be a very popular power unit for lightweight motorcycles, and was in continuous production until 1947. The Villiers carburettor was fitted as standard equipment. In 1931 Francis Barnett used it in the Merlin Model No. 19 and the Kestrel Model No. 20, and in 1932 in the Merlin Model No. 23 and the Kestrel Model No. 24. These were the last machines fitted with the long-running Mark VIIIC engine.

Villiers did not enter competitions as a company, but many of the individuals and some of the firms that did, used Villiers engines to great effect to win awards. One name that kept cropping up in this field was T. G. Meeten, the founder of the BTSC, who in 1923 used a 147cc-engined Francis-Barnett to win a three-lap handicap race and a five-lap event at Brooklands, and in so doing was awarded the Harry Smith Gold Cup.

The 172cc Sports Engine
In 1924 the 172cc Sports Engine was introduced to the range; it had a bore and stroke of 57.15 × 67mm

with a cast-iron cylinder and piston. Two exhaust pipes were used to obtain the most efficient scavenging and to enable the burnt gases to be expelled rapidly. It was an engine which had good road performance, a little faster than the 147cc engine, but made on the same simple basis. The first engine in the series used petroil lubrication, and the second used the Villiers patent automatic system, called 'autolube' for short.

THE VILLIERS $1\frac{1}{2}$ h.p.
TWO-STROKE ENGINE

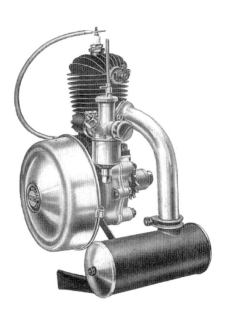

SPECIFICATION :

Bore and Stroke, 55 m/m × 62 m/m – 147 c.c.
Full Roller Bearing Big End.
Fully Floating Gudgeon Pin.
Extra long Bronze Gas-tight Main Bearings.
Flywheel Magneto with Cover.
Exhaust Pipe and Silencer.
Sparking Plug.
Release Valve.
Sprocket.
Villiers Single Lever Carburetter.

PRICE complete as above £10 : 2 : 6

PETROIL LUBRICATION,

147cc Mark VIIIC engine.

THE VILLIERS SPORTS
TWO-STROKE ENGINE

SPECIFICATION :

Bore and Stroke, 57.15 m/m : 67 m/m   172 c.c.
Full Roller Bearing Big End.
Fully Floating Gudgeon Pin.
Separate Induction Manifold.   Swan Neck or Angle.
Extra long Bronze Gas-tight Main Bearing.
Release Valve.
Sparking Plug.
Flywheel Magneto with Cover.
Twin Exhaust Pipes and Silencer with Long Tail Pipe.
Chain Sprocket.
Variable Ignition.
Villiers Single Lever Carburetter.

PRICE complete as above £11 : 5 : 0

AUTOMATIC or PETROIL LUBRICATION.

172cc Sports engine.

The Villiers Automatic Lubrication System

In the Villiers automatic lubrication system, variations in the crankcase pressure were utilized to supply oil direct to each bearing. The basis of the system was that the more the throttle was opened with a consequential heavier load on the engine, the greater was the supply of oil. The Mark I tended to be used by manufacturers who incorporated an oil compartment within the petrol tank, Mark II by those who used a separate oil tank, and Mark III where no sight feed was required.

The differences between the three types of lubricator was a matter of arrangement, with the working principle exactly the same.

Compressed air from the crankcase passed along the centre of the shafts to the holes J, and the air then passed through holes drilled in the crankcase to a union situated in front of the crankcase. It then passed through pipe A to the top of the oil tank and forced oil up through pipe B. The pressurized tank fed the oil to union D, via the sight feed except for the Mark III, with the flow of oil regulated by an adjustable screw F. Except in certain models where the oil passed straight to the crankcase, the oil was divided at union D, with part of it being sucked through a hole in the cylinder wall and the rest passed down to the crankcase. Here it was again divided between the two main bearings, with grooves in these married up with ports K in the crankcase when the piston descended, any surplus being sucked though oil-way E to the big end. It is obvious that the system worked on pressure, and it was essential that this was maintained with no leakage at any of the joints or oil compartment.

The 172cc Engine Series

Several variants of the 172cc engine were eventually produced: the standard 'Sports' with either petroil or autolube that used the engine prefix T and TL; the 'Super-Sports' with the prefix Y for 1925 and XY for 1926; the 'TT Super-Sports' from 1926 with the prefix BZ; and the 'Brooklands' from 1925, which was a derivative of the 'Super-Sports' and retained the prefix Y. All versions of the Super-Sports and Brooklands engines used the automatic lubrication system.

The 'Sports' engines were identical except for the lubrication system. The 'Super-Sports' engine was able to produce higher maximum and average speeds and to assist with the cooling; a special aluminium piston and detachable cylinder head were employed. The Brooklands engine used a similar set-up but was purely for racing, and was not suitable for normal road use. The cylinder barrel had a shrunk-on, heavily finned aluminium jacket, high compression cylinder head and padded crankshafts, and a large bore carburettor was used. The power output was given as 8.25bhp at 4,900rpm. The Francis-Barnett Model No. 5 was available with either of the two types of lubricated Sports engines, and Model No. 8 and No. 9 with the TT Super-Sports engine.

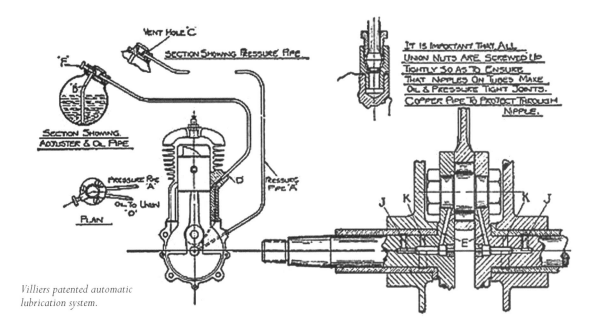

Villiers patented automatic lubrication system.

The Twin-Cylinder Two-Stroke Engine

In 1927 the first Villiers twin-cylinder two-stroke engine was introduced. Each cylinder had a bore and stroke of 57.15 × 67mm, giving a capacity of 344cc. Like the 172cc engines, it used aluminium pistons, it had three large plain bearings, and the

Brooklands engine in situ. Seen at the Stafford Show 2010.

THE VILLIERS T.T. SUPER-SPORTS ENGINE

247cc Mark IXA engine.

SPECIFICATION :

Bore and Stroke 57.15 m/m × 67 m/m = 172 c.c.
Aluminium Alloy Cylinder Head.
Aluminium Alloy Piston.
Fully Floating Gudgeon Pin.
Full Roller Bearing Big End.
Flywheel Magneto and Cover.
Twin Exhaust Pipes and Large Silencer.
Variable Ignition.   Release Valve.
Sparking Plug.   Chain Sprocket.
Villiers Two-Lever Carburetter.

PRICE complete as above £12 : 3 : 9

AUTOMATIC LUBRICATOR 15/- extra.

172cc TT Super-Sports engine.

three-speed clutch and gear were incorporated within the unit; it used automatic lubrication and was fitted with the flywheel magneto. The engine number prefix was TW. Francis-Barnett built its Model No. 10, the Pullman, to use this engine, but it was only manufactured for two years, 1928 and 1929, because although the Pullman was highly rated in the Press, it wasn't popular with the buying public.

The 247cc Engine Series

The next Villiers engine to be used by Francis-Barnett was the Mark IXA. The original model in this series of 247cc engines was the Mark VIA, with a cast-iron cylinder and piston; it was produced in 1922. The Mark VIIA followed in 1924, and the VIIIA in 1925. The Mark IXA was an improvement on the previous engines in the series in that it had a special aluminium piston and a detachable cylinder head similar to that on the 172cc Super-Sports engine. The bore and stroke was 67 × 70mm. To obtain increased smoothness in the running of the engine, particularly at low road speeds, an auxiliary flywheel was fitted on the crankshaft on the opposite side to the flywheel magneto.

The engine number prefix was DZ for the Mark IXA, which was fitted to the 1929 Francis-Barnett Model No. 12, the Empire. 1929 was the last year of manufacture of the Mark IXA engine; the Mark XA, a slightly changed engine, became available for 1930 to 1932. It is assumed that this latter engine was fitted to the 1930 Empire machine.

196cc Mark IE engine.

196cc MARK IE Super-Sports engine.

The Mark IE

In 1928 a new engine, the Mark IE, was introduced; apart from the bore its specification was similar to that of the 172cc Sports, the bore and stroke being 61 × 67mm, giving a capacity of 196cc. Initially this engine was introduced for use in Germany, where motorcycles with engines under 200cc were tax free. British manufacturers were soon fitting it to their machines as it was a very reliable engine, required a minimum of attention, and gave good petrol consumption. Variable ignition timing was fitted, and the cylinder and head were a combined casting with a twin exhaust port; in addition a de-compressor was fitted. The IE could be supplied with either petroil or automatic lubrication; in both instances the engine prefix number was IE, the same as the Mark number; this was the only occasion that this occurred.

A Super-Sports version was introduced in 1929: the bore and stroke was identical to the IE, but it was designed to give higher performance. It had a deeply finned cylinder with large twin-exhaust ports, a detachable alloy head, and an aluminium piston with

an inertia ring fitted. The automatic lubrication system was used. The Villiers magneto and the Villiers middleweight carburettor were fitted as standard equipment. The prefix letters were KZ or KZS. Francis-Barnett used the Mark IE engine in Model No. 13

of which there is little known, except a brief statement to say that it was based on the 172cc Sports – and Model No. 14, the '200'.

The Super-Sports version was used in the 1930 Super-Sports '200' Model No. 15 and the 1930 Falcon Model No. 18 – which also had the option of the 172cc Super-Sports engine being fitted – also the 1932 No. 22, the 1933 No. 31 and the 1934 No. 38. A further version of this engine came on to the market in 1930: the Mark IIE with the prefix XZ or XZA. The Mark IIE used petroil lubrication only, had a single exhaust port and, in common with the Mark IE, a cast-iron piston fitted with an inertia ring, detachable inlet manifold and variable ignition.

The following Francis-Barnett models all used the Mark IIE engine: No. 17 of 1931, No. 21 of 1932, No. 29 and No. 30 of 1933, No. 36 and No. 37 of 1934, and No. E36 of 1935.

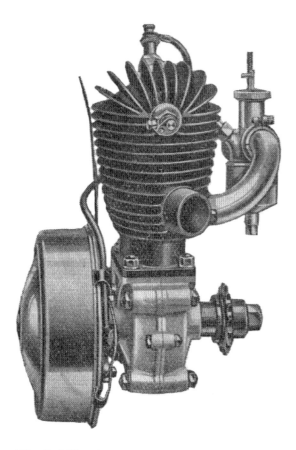

196cc Mark IIE engine.

TWO-STROKE ENGINE

SPECIFICATION:
Bore and Stroke, 79 m/m × 70 m/m = 342 c.c.
Aluminium Alloy Cylinder Head.
Aluminium Alloy Piston.
Patent Automatic System of Lubrication.
Fully Floating Gudgeon Pin.
Full Roller Bearing Big End.
Flywheel Magneto and Cover.
Twin Exhaust Pipes and Large Silencer.
Variable Ignition.   Release Valve.
Sparking Plug.   Chain Sprocket.
Front Engine Plates.
Separate Induction Manifold.   Swan Neck or Angle.
Villiers Two-lever Carburetter.

PRICE complete as above £13 : 17 : 6
AUTOMATIC LUBRICATOR 15/- extra.

342cc Mark IXB engine.

The 342cc Series of Engines

Commencing in 1922, a new series of engines was produced with a bore and stroke of 79 × 70mm, giving a capacity of 342cc. They were the models Mark VIB and VIIB, which were similar to the Mark VIA and VIIA 247cc engines, with the prefix letters K and M. The Mark VIIIB of 1925/26 became the Mark IXB of 1926–29; the prefix letters were AZ and CZ, and for the Mark IXBA of 1929–32, CZA. According to Sizer, the CZ engines were fitted with automatic lubrication, and the CZA engines petroil lubrication. However, the Francis-Barnett Dominion Model No. 16 was advertised as being supplied with automatic lubrication, and the surviving Dominions have an engine prefix of CZA.

The Mark XIIC engine

The Mark XIIC engine was introduced in 1931, with a prefix of GY or GYF; it had a bore and stroke of 53 × 67mm, giving a capacity of 148cc, and the piston was a cast-iron deflector type with floating gudgeon pin and inertia ring. Two exhaust ports were employed, and the carburettor was fitted to the manifold on the near side of the cylinder. Francis-Barnett referred to it as the '148cc Villiers long-stroke engine' in their advertisements.

From 1932 to 1940 it was fitted to several machines, the first being the 1932 Lapwing Model No. 25, the 1933 No. 27 and No. 28, and in 1934 numbers 33, 34 and 35. The Plover followed next, with 1935 Model No. E40 and E41, the 1936 F40 and F41, the 1937 G40 and G41, the 1938 H40 and H41, the 1939 J40 and J41, and finally the 1940 K40 and K41.

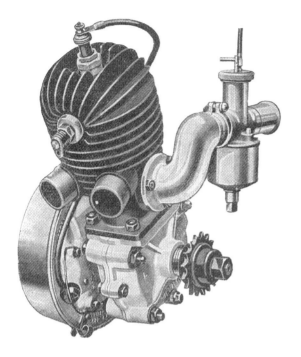

148cc Mark XIIC engine.

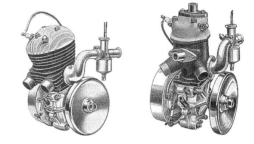

249cc Mark XIVA engine with water-cooled variant.

documentary evidence so far that Francis-Barnett supplied the Cruiser with the water-cooled engine as original equipment, however the FBOC have a photograph of one in a Cruiser showing the radiator; the engine may have been fitted at a later date. The Mark XIVA was also used in a run of Seagulls commencing with the 1935 Model No. E42 and E43, the 1936 F43, the 1937 G43, the 1938 H43, the 1939 J43 and the 1940 K43.

The compression-release valve on the Cruiser Mark XIVA engine was the first pattern that permitted the

The Mark XIVA

In 1932 the Mark XIVA became available; it was a long-stroke model with a bore and stroke of 63 × 80mm, giving a capacity of 249cc. It was available as air-cooled with automatic lubrication, air-cooled with petroil lubrication, or water-cooled with automatic lubrication. The prefix letters were BY, BYP and RY for the engines. A detachable cylinder head was fitted, and an aluminium deflector piston with a patent inertia ring. It had long plain bearings to the crankshaft, and lubrication was available by the automatic system or petroil.

Although not mentioned by Sizer or Browning, there were other prefix letters used, namely BYF and BYPF from around 1934/35. It may be coincidental, but it was around that period when the flat-top piston was first introduced.

The Mark XIVA was used by Francis-Barnett in their series of Cruisers that were in production from 1933 until 1940. The first one was the 1933 Model No. 32, followed by the 1934 Model No. 39, the 1935 E39, the 1936 F39, the 1937 G39, the 1938 H39, the 1939 J39 and the 1940 K39. I have not seen any

249cc Mark XVIIA engine.

compression to escape into the exhaust port. Hitherto the spring-loaded stem, seating against the body, screwed into the cylinder head and permitted only of compression release into the atmosphere; as a result there was invariably an oily deposit on the outside of the head. This was remedied by channelling the released compression through a hole drilled in the cylinder head connecting with a copper tube pressed into the cylinder barrel leading into the exhaust port. Providing this tube protrudes just above the top cylinder fin to butt against the cylinder head there is no oily mess, but quite often when this tube is shortened by misguided zeal, the exhaust will blow back – with no ill effect, of course, except that it is mistaken for a leakage of compression.

The Mark XVIIA

The Mark XVIIA engine came on to the market for 1935 with the prefix BYX. It had the same bore, stroke and capacity as the Mark XIVA but was fitted with a cylinder that had four transfer ports and a flat-top piston. The crankshaft was carried in a single row of bearings with the compression retained by bronze bushes on the shafts. Lubrication was by petroil. All motorcycle engines since then have used a cylinder with four transfer ports and a flat top piston. There were two main versions of the Francis-Barnett Cruiser: Models No. 39 and No. 45. The latter Cruiser, the F45 model with petroil lubrication, was introduced to the public in 1936, followed by the G45 in 1937. The 1938 H45 model, the 1939 J45 and the 1940 K45 had the Mark XVIIIA engine fitted.

The Mark XVIIIA

The Mark XVIIIA engine, prefix letters UU, retained the same bore, stroke and capacity of 249cc and the same cylinder and piston as the Mark XVIIA engine. A new crankshaft assembly was used with a double row of bearings and spring-loaded gland bushes to maintain the compression in the crankcase. Lubrication was by petroil. In addition to the Cruiser 45 models, the Mark XVIIIA engine was fitted to the 1938 Seagull Model No. H47, the 1939 J47 and the 1940 K47.

The Mark VIIID

The Mark VIIID unit was extremely compact, combining the engine and three-speed gearbox in one unit. It had a bore and stroke of 50 × 62mm, giving a capacity of 122cc. The aluminium cylinder head was detachable, and the piston was of the flat-top design, ball and roller bearings were used throughout, and the gearbox was of the sliding dog type with a very smooth single plate clutch. There were exhaust stubs on either side of the cylinder barrel, and the carburettor fitted to the off side. A hand gear-change lever was used to select the gears in the three-speed box. This unit was also made in a 98cc version with a bore and stroke of 50 × 50mm.

The Mark IXD

The Mark IXD engine, later referred to as the Mark 9D engine, replaced the Mark VIIID in 1938. It had the same bore, stroke and capacity as the Mark VIIID, the difference being in the better gear change and a six pole, eighteen watt flywheel magneto. The flywheel metal cover was domed, allowing for a hammertight nut which held the magneto on to the shaft. The Mark 9D engine, prefix letters AAA, was used by Francis-Barnett in the 1939 Snipe Model No. J48 and the 1940 K48. In 1946 Francis-Barnett introduced the Merlin Model No. 51, which used the Mark 9D engine.

Villiers Mark 9D engine fitted to a 1948 Merlin L51.

The engine number prefix now consisted of numbers or a combination of numbers and/or letters; in the case of the Mark 9D it was 597.

The 98cc Engines

The first engine of 98cc had a bore and stroke of 50 × 50mm; it was produced in 1931 and called the 'Midget', and used the prefix letters CY and CYA. It remained in production until 1940.

In 1934 an improved version known as the 'Junior' was introduced. The cylinder was a one-piece type with three ports, an inlet, an exhaust and a transfer. The aluminium piston was new but still retained the deflector head. In 1938 another version became available, and this was known as the 'Junior de Luxe', or JDL for short. The bore, stroke and capacity remained the same. Several of the assemblies were not interchangeable between the engines. The JDL engine had a detachable aluminium cylinder head, a flat-top piston and a seven-port cylinder barrel: one inlet, two exhaust and four transfer. The prefix letters for the Junior were SH, and those for the JDL were XX and XXA.

The 1946 Powerbike Model No. 50 was a continuation of the pre-war machine using the same name and model number. The JDL engine was used, the prefix letters were XXA, and from 1947/8 the numbers were 434.

98cc Midget engine.

The Villiers Post-World War II Engines

The first two post-war engines used by Francis-Barnett have already been discussed as they were a continuation of pre-World War II engines, the Mark 9D and the JDL used in the Merlin and Powerbike respectively, both of which were produced between 1946 and 1949. The JDL engine was succeeded by the Mark 1F and the Mark 2F engines in 1949; the difference between these two engines was that the Mark 1F was a two-speed unit and the Mark 2F was a single-speed unit. The bore and stroke were 47 × 57mm, giving a capacity of 98cc. The cast-iron cylinder had one exhaust port and two transfer ports, a detachable head, and a flat-top piston. Francis-Barnett used the Mark 2F engine in the 1949/50 Powerbike Model No. 56. The prefix was 801, then 189A.

The engine coding system was changed from the prefix being mainly letters to a numerical system. In about 1951 the system was changed again so that the prefix consisted of three numbers followed by a letter, with each type of engine having more than one prefix. The new coding system was introduced so that a prefix for a type of engine could be allocated to one firm, and a different prefix for the same type of engine to another firm. Therefore by quoting the engine number Villiers would immediately know which firm had purchased the engine. Unfortunately there were times when more than one firm was supplied with engines with the same prefix. Under the latter system a Mark 6E engine supplied to Ambassador had a prefix 139A, and to Francis-Barnett 158A, amongst others.

The 'E' Series Engines

The Mark 5E was the first new post-war engine to be produced; it had a bore and stroke of 59 × 72mm and a capacity of 197cc. A new trend was started with the gearbox being built as a separate unit and bolted on to the crankcase with four bolts, and the gears changed by foot control. This meant that various gearboxes could be used – for example, a three-speed or a four-speed as required, and either close- or wide-ratio gears. It was manufactured between 1946 and 1948.

The Mark 6E followed in 1949 with the same bore, stroke and capacity as the Mark 5E; it could be supplied with either direct lighting or rectified lighting to charge a battery. The cylinder head was detachable, and the original metal-to-metal joint was later modified by the specification of a soft aluminium washer. The crankshaft assembly ran on three journal bearings, and the big end comprised a double row of 0.25 × 0.25in rollers. A two-plate clutch was used running in oil, with fifteen corks fitted to each plate.

The Mark 7E replaced the Mark 6E for competition use, and the Mark 8E came in for general road use in 1953. The Mark 7E cylinder head increased compression ratio from 7.25:1 to 8.25:1 and developed 8.5bhp at 4,500rpm. A more efficient ignition coil was fitted to the magneto, and the flywheel had a slightly different cam.

With the Mark 8E, a different primary chain case and clutch assembly were required for the three-speed gearbox than for the four-speed gearbox. The four-speed gearbox could be fitted with wide-ratio gears if required. For improved ignition in competition models, higher-powered magnetos were available. The standard direct lighting system could be replaced by a battery and rectifier system on both the D and E engines.

The Mark 6E engine was fitted to the 1949 Francis-Barnett Falcon models No. 54 and No. 55 with the prefix 824, the 1950/53 No. 54 and No. 55 with the prefix 946 and then 207A, and the 1952/53 No. 58 with the prefix 209A.

The Mark 7E was fitted to the 1952 No. 60 with the prefix 158A, the 1953 No. 62 and the 1956/57 No.

197cc Mark 6E engine.

77 with the prefix 375A; the 1953 No. 64, the 1955 No. 62, the 1955 No. 72 and the 1956/57 No. 76 with the prefix 374A; and the 1954 No. 62 and No. 64 with the prefix 387A.

The Mark 8E engine was fitted to the 1953 No. 54, the 1953/54 No. 58 and the 1954 No. 67 with the prefix 387A; the 1953/54 No. 65 with the prefix 688A; the 1955 No. 70 and the 1956/57 No. 74 with the prefix 070B for the three-speed version, and 071B for the four-speed version.

The Mark 6E, 7E and 8E engines are in the main what could be described as competition engines, and not all were supplied in standard form. In addition it appears that a prefix could be used on more than one type of engine. This also applies to the Mark 10D, 11D and 12D engines, as all three are recorded as having the same prefix on at least one occasion. As several sources of information appear to contradict each other, it is impossible to give a definitive list of what engines went into which frame, and so a consensus of opinion has been used. While the sources of information appear to contradict each other, and knowing what we do about the differing requirements of individual riders in the competition arena and the multiple use of the prefix, it would be incorrect to say that one source is right and the other wrong. The loss of Villiers records with the closure of the Norton Villiers Triumph combine has not helped in any way.

The 'D' Series Engines

The bore, stroke and capacity of the Mark 10D engine remained the same as its predecessor the Mark 9D, but had a cylinder barrel with one exhaust port. In addition, a foot-change system instead of a hand gearchange system was employed. The Mark 10D was fitted to the 1949/53 Merlin Models No. 52 and No. 53 using the prefix 824 or 206A, and the 1952/53 No. 57 (TLS) with the prefix 208A. Competition riders pressurized Villiers to provide an engine for them, and so they developed the Mark 10D engine, offering a close-ratio box and/or a four-speed gearbox. The 1953 Merlin Trials Model No. 61 was fitted with a Mark 10D or a Mark 12/4D engine with the prefix 420A and 402A. The 1953 Merlin Scrambler Model No. 63 was fitted with either the Mark 10D or Mark 12/4D engine with the prefix 403A.

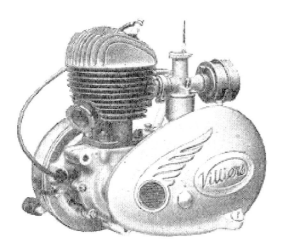

122cc Mark 10D engine.

225cc Villiers Mark 1H engine.

The Mark 11D, 12D and 13D engines all became available in 1953, and each had the same bore and stroke of 50 × 62mm and a capacity of 122cc. The Mark 11D was introduced as the next stage in supplying a competitive competition engine, following the improved Mark 10D. This had a cylinder with developed ports, a larger carburettor, and an improved flywheel with the magnets being much more powerful. The option of a four-speed gearbox continued. The Mark 12D was a replacement for the Mark 10D road model, and the Mark 13D was a hybrid of a 12D bottom half married with a 10D cylinder; these latter two engines were only supplied with three-speed gearboxes. A 'D' suffix to the engine number denoted that it was fitted with a close-ratio gearbox. Francis-Barnett took up the Mark 13D for only one of its machines, the 1954 Kestrel Model No. 66 with the prefix 618A.

The Mark 1H Engine

For 1954 one of the new engines introduced was the Mark 1H engine, with a bore and stroke of 63 × 72mm, giving a capacity of 225cc. It had a compression ratio of 7:1 and a four-speed gearbox. The feature of this engine was that the carburettor was fully enclosed within a cover which had a built-in air filter. The primary chain tensioner was omitted after engine No. 2929, and a felt washer was replaced by a rubber seal after engine No. 13257; an alteration was needed to the chaincase to accommodate this modification.

The Mark 1H engine was fitted to three Francis-Barnett Cruiser models: the 1954 No. 68, the 1955 No. 71 and the 1956/57 No. 75, all with the prefix 842A.

The 'C' Series Engines

The other new engines introduced in 1954 were the Mark 29C and the Mark 30C, with a bore and stroke of 55 × 62mm, giving a capacity of 147cc. This was the first time that a 150cc class engine had become available to motorcycle manufacturers since the Mark VIIIC was withdrawn after 1947.

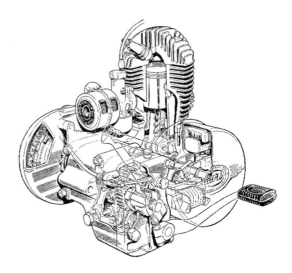

Sectional illustration of the Villiers 30C engine.

The Mark 29C was a 'tuned' engine with special porting and a different inlet pipe for the larger S25-type carburettor. A four-speed gearbox, the 'S'-type, was available, with the standard gears or an option of the wide range 'V'-type gearbox. The Mark 30C was fitted with a three-speed gearbox and an S19 carburettor. Both marks of engine had the option of direct or rectified lighting.

Of these two engines, only the Mark 30C was used by Francis-Barnett, firstly in the 1955 Kestrel Model No. 69, prefix 958A, and then two Plover models, the 1956 No. 73 and the 1957/59 No. 78, all with the prefix 295B.

The Mark 10E engine
The Mark 10E engine was introduced in 1957, having the same bore, stroke and capacity as had all previous 'E' models from the 1939 Mark 3E to the 1955 Mark 9E. The cylinder was mounted vertically on the Mark 10E. The flywheel magneto had been redesigned to reduce its size, and this produced a corresponding reduction in weight. Instead of being on the outside, it was now enclosed in the right-hand engine casing. The reduction in weight allowed the internal sizes of the crankshafts to be increased, and as a consequence this provided a smoother running engine.

Francis-Barnett fitted the Mark 10E engine to the 1958/59 Falcon Model No. 81 with the prefix 662B. This was the last Villiers engine used in a Francis-Barnett motorcycle until 1961, although they did have an input by taking over the assembly of the Piatti-designed engines (*see* Chapter 1).

The Mark 'T' Series Engines
In 1956 Villiers brought out the Mark 2T, a side-by-side twin-cylinder engine of unit construction. It had been a long time coming: the last one produced was the 344cc in-line twin of 1927, almost thirty years earlier. The bore and stroke of the cylinders was 50 × 63.5mm, giving a capacity of 249cc.

It was similar in style to the 'H' series engines, with an enclosed carburettor, the separate four-speed gearbox, and the ignition key switch on the upper contact breaker cover. It had cast-iron cylinder barrels, with each barrel having its own crankcase, the barrels being separated by a central disc. The stated compression ratio was 8.2:1, which produced 15bhp at 5,500rpm. Two gearboxes were available, a standard and a wide ratio. A carburettor-type S22/2 was fitted for motorcycle use.

The Mark 3T engine of 324cc was basically a bored-out version of the Mark 2T, and became available to motorcycle manufacturers in 1958. The Mark

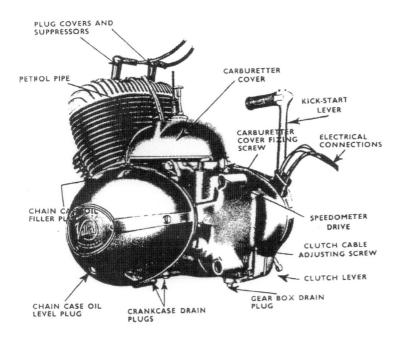

250cc Villiers 2T engine-gear unit left-hand side.

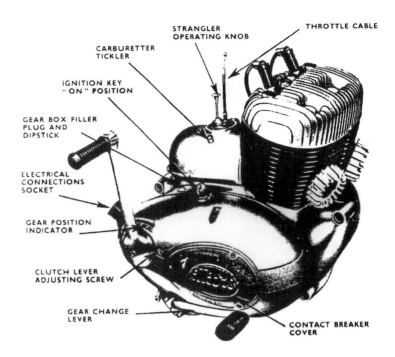

250cc Villiers 2T engine-gear unit right-hand side.

4T replaced the 2T in 1963, and was very similar to it. The transfer ports had doubled from two to four, and a different type of piston was used. It had a stated compression ratio of 8.75:1, and was recorded as developing 17bhp at 6,000rpm. There were basically three versions of the engine: one for motorcycles, and the other two for scooters and three-wheelers.

The Mark 2T engine was fitted by Francis Barnett into their 1962/63 Cruiser Model No. 89 and the 1963 Cruiser Sports Model No. 91, with the prefix 429D. From 1964 the Mark 4T was used in these machines, with the prefix 687E or 688E.

Trials and Scrambler Engines

In 1956 the Mark 31A engine was produced with the intention of it being used in three-wheelers, but it was quickly adapted as a Trials engine and used in motorcycles. This was followed by the Mark 33A, produced as a Scrambles engine. The 31A and 33A had a bore and stroke of 66 × 72mm, giving a capacity of 246cc, and both had a four-speed gearbox fitted. The Mark 33A turned into the Mark 32A as a Trials engine, and the Mark 34A as a Scrambles engine. The Mark 35A was only intended for scooters. The Mark 36A engine followed in 1962.

The Mark 32A had a compression ratio of 7.9:1 and was fitted with a Villiers S25/5 carburettor; the Mark 36A had a compression ratio of 12:1 and was fitted with the AMAL carburettor 389/39. All were fitted with a four-speed gearbox, with a wide-ratio gearbox fitted to Trials models which was available to other models if required. The Mark 32A was fitted to the Francis-Barnett 1962/66 Trials Model No. 92 with the prefix 326E, and the Mark 36A to the 1962/64 Scrambler Model No. 93 with the prefix 352E. This engine had a special Parkinson barrel, piston and head fitted.

The Starmaker

The final engine to consider is the Starmaker, initially known as the Star Maker. The Starmaker engine designer was Bernard Hooper, and on the transmission was John Favill. Manufactured from 1963, it had a bore and stroke of 68 × 68mm, giving a capacity of 247cc, a compression ratio of 12:1, and it developed 25bhp at 6,500rpm in standard form. The cylinder was constructed of light alloy with a spun-cast austenitic iron liner. The combustion chamber shape was again unorthodox, with a mushroom-shaped recess in the cylinder head and the spark plug centrally positioned. The barrel and cylinder head had widely spaced, large cooling fins; the wide spacing was to prevent the fins becoming clogged up and their cooling effect impaired.

A novel feature of the design was the proposal to mount two splayed AMAL monobloc carburettors on the light-alloy inlet manifold via rubber hoses. This system was later replaced by a single AMAL monobloc carburettor for simplicity.

This engine was originally intended as a Scrambler, but it soon became used as a Road Racing engine. Three variants quickly became available: a Road Racing version and a Trials version besides the original Scrambler version. Lighting varied from 6 volt direct to 12 volt rectified, depending upon the engine, as did the gear ratios and the carburettors used.

The Starmaker was fitted to one Francis-Barnett machine, the 1964–66 Scrambler Model No. 94 with the prefix 826E.

Carburettors

The carburettor has one main function, and that is to regulate the engine speed. This is done by metering the amount of fuel and air required to sustain combustion at a given throttle action. With the engine at idle speed a small amount of air and fuel is required in the combustion chamber; this lessens the engine power and reduces the revolutions per minute (rpm) of the engine. As the throttle is opened it allows more air and fuel into the combustion chamber, thus increasing engine power and the rpm. Varying engine temperature and load conditions make the problem of carburation rather complex, and even a more modern instrument is really a compromise – but nevertheless an efficient one.

The action of a carburettor causes petrol to be delivered through a jet orifice into a stream of rapidly moving air, by which process it is converted from liquid fuel into a highly atomized vapour. The upward stroke of the piston sucks this air stream through the carburettor, and the amount that is allowed to pass into the engine is controlled by the throttle slide. It is obvious that the strength of the mixture depends upon the proportion of fuel emerging from the jet, and the air passing through the carburettor.

In the early carburettors the size of jet was fixed, so that a set quantity of petrol with air, giving a specific ratio, was constantly fed to the engine. This specific ratio was determined for average running, but there was a need to be able to vary the mixture according to the different engine conditions; at times there would be a requirement for a much richer or leaner mixture – for example, a greater or lesser proportion of petrol in the air may be needed.

The Villiers Carburettors

The Mills Carburettor Co. was purchased by Villiers in 1926, who renamed the Mills carburettor 'the Villiers'. Prior to 1926, Francis-Barnett machines were advertised as mostly being fitted with the Mills carburettor; from 1926 it was the Villiers. Up until then, in most of the carburettors, the size of the jet was fixed so that the quantity of petrol with air was constantly fed to the engine. The proportion was determined by average running, but because on occasions a richer mixture was required, it would be beneficial that the proportion could be altered when needed.

In the Villiers carburettor, the amount of air allowed to enter into the engine automatically controlled the amount of fuel that issued from the jet. There was only one lever to operate it, which opened and closed the throttle, and at the same time enlarged or reduced the size of the jet by use of a taper needle attached to, and working with, the throttle. This was known as the single-lever carburettor, to distinguish it from the two-lever carburettor, the difference being that the adjuster to give a 'rich' mixture when starting from cold was part of the carburettor on the single-lever model, and on the handlebars for the two-lever model.

The taper needle could be adjusted independently to give an especially rich mixture at times when it is required, such as when starting a cold engine. This independent adjustment is provided on some models by means of a rod having a quick-thread in the throttle, which is arranged to raise or lower the needle 0.25in by one complete turn of the bar; this is referred to as the Villiers single-lever carburettor. On other models the needle is raised and lowered in the jet by means of a separate control operated from the handlebar; this is referred to as the Villiers two-lever carburettor. The handlebar lever is marked 'rich' and 'weak' to indicate how the jet size is set.

The action of the carburettor is very simple: depressing the float tickler creates a well of petrol which, with the throttle open only a little, is drawn

Sectional drawing left and right of the Villiers single- and double-lever carburettor.

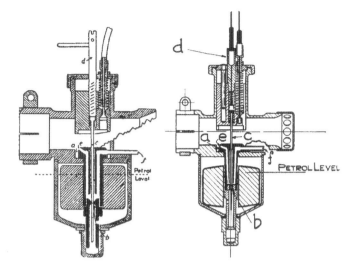

into the cylinder at the first kick, so giving very easy starting. The opening and closing of the throttle, as already explained, enlarges and reduces the size of the jet, *b*, by means of the taper needle. The size of the jet may be enlarged independently of the throttle opening to give a rich mixture when starting from cold, the 'rich' and 'weak' positions being marked on the top disc of the carburettor, or on the handlebar lever top plate. When the engine is warmed up the needle is again lowered in the jet, to weaken the mixture as much as is consistent with good running. The position of the needle will then not require to be altered again until the engine is started from cold.

When on the road, the automatic compensating action of the carburettor is as follows:

- Mixture is delivered by the carburettor in two different ways: first, by the suction of the engine on the orifice *e*, and second, by the force of the head of petrol through jet *b*. Since the jet *b* is below petrol level, petrol is always issuing from it.
- The suction of the engine on the orifice *e* draws in a stream of air through the compensating tube *f* across the top of the jet *b*, where it mixes with and breaks up the petrol, and so issues from *e* into the main air stream as a partially atomized vapour.
- If the load on the engine is increased, so reducing the engine speed – as, for instance, when hill climbing – the suction on the orifice *e* is reduced. This would weaken the mixture but for the fact that the

VILLIERS CARBURETTERS

Single Lever Model

Automatic in Action
Economical
Suitable for
Two-Strokes and
Four Strokes.

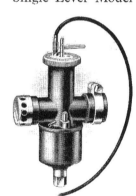

It is impossible to get a choked Jet in the Villiers Carburetter.

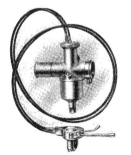

Two Lever Model

Exactly the same as the Single Lever instrument in operation but has Jet Control on Handlebar.

An Air Filter is recommended for use with every Villiers Carburetter.

Villiers carburettors, single- and two-lever models, 1928.

petrol issuing from jet *b* is constant, thereby enriching the partially atomized vapour coming through *e*, the combined effect being that the mixture strength is maintained constant, irrespective of engine speed or load.

The lightweight model was suitable for most single-cylinder engines under 250cc, and twin-cylinder engines under 500cc with induction pipe diameters not exceeding 1in (25mm). The middleweight was suitable for most single-cylinder machines under 400cc and

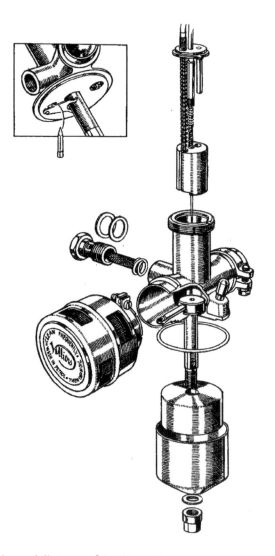

Sectional illustration of the Villiers 4/5 carburettor.

twin-engined machines under 800cc with induction pipe diameters not exceeding 1.125in (28mm).

Air filters, which are regarded as essential today to stop grit, dirt and dust from entering the engine, were originally an optional extra costing approximately 4s 6d, and must have been a good investment considering the state of the roads at that time.

Other types of carburettor were used, and as they are basically the same in principle, only three types are illustrated here.

AMC Engines

AMC announced in 1956 the production of their own Vincent Piatti-designed, single-cylinder two-stroke engine and gearbox, to be used by James and Francis-Barnett. Piatti, as the name suggests, was an Italian who designed the Piatti scooter, which was built under licence in the UK by Cyclemaster Ltd. In the same year, Villiers introduced the Mark 2T engine, which was a development from the Mark 1H engine. The Mark 2T was taken up by many small companies, but not initially by Francis-Barnett.

The first AMC Piatti engine to be used had a bore of 66mm and a stroke of 72.8mm to give a capacity of 249cc, driving a four-speed gearbox, and was known as the 25T. This engine was fitted to the 1957 Cruiser 80 on its debut, whose frame evolved from the Cruiser 68 through the Cruisers 71 and 75, all of which had the Villiers 1H engine. The majority of the engine internals followed conventional practice, where the difference lay in the transfer ports, which were just two shallow depressions or troughs in the cylinder wall.

The cylinder head and the piston were more complicated, with the head having a pair of deflectors pointing down which matched the cutaways in the sides and the crown of the piston. The theory was that when the piston moved towards top dead centre, the gas stream from the transfer troughs was squeezed by the head wedges and deflected by the cutaways in the piston, and this action would ram the fuel mixture into the combustion chamber. This 'squish' effect was claimed to improve efficiency and scavenging, and early tests appear to substantiate these claims. The engine was similar in looks to the Villiers 1H engine, with a streamlined appearance and an enclosed carburettor.

AMC 20T cylinder head showing downward projecting deflectors.

AMC 20T cylinder and piston showing cutaways in the piston.

Sectional drawing of the Villiers S24 carburettor.

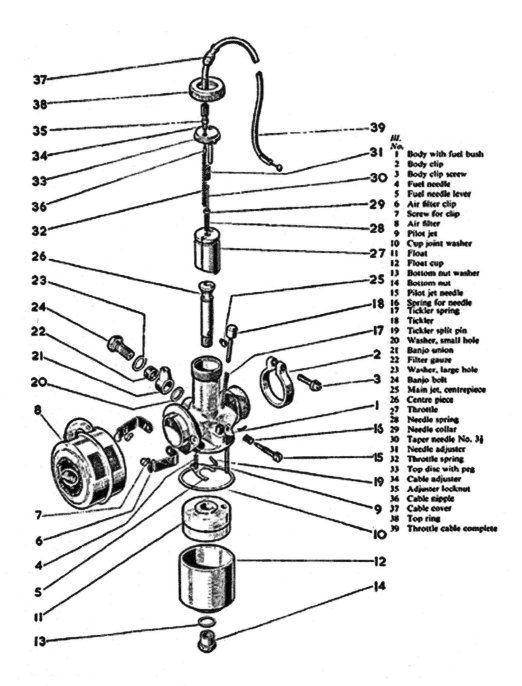

Ill. No.	
1	Body with fuel bush
2	Body clip
3	Body clip screw
4	Fuel needle
5	Fuel needle lever
6	Air filter clip
7	Screw for clip
8	Air filter
9	Pilot jet
10	Cup joint washer
11	Float
12	Float cup
13	Bottom nut washer
14	Bottom nut
15	Pilot jet needle
16	Spring for needle
17	Tickler spring
18	Tickler
19	Tickler split pin
20	Washer, small hole
21	Banjo union
22	Filter gauze
23	Washer, large hole
24	Banjo bolt
25	Main jet, centrepiece
26	Centre piece
27	Throttle
28	Needle spring
29	Needle collar
30	Taper needle No. 3½
31	Needle adjuster
32	Throttle spring
33	Top disc with peg
34	Cable adjuster
35	Adjuster locknut
36	Cable nipple
37	Cable cover
38	Top ring
39	Throttle cable complete

Sectional drawing of the Villiers S25 carburettor.

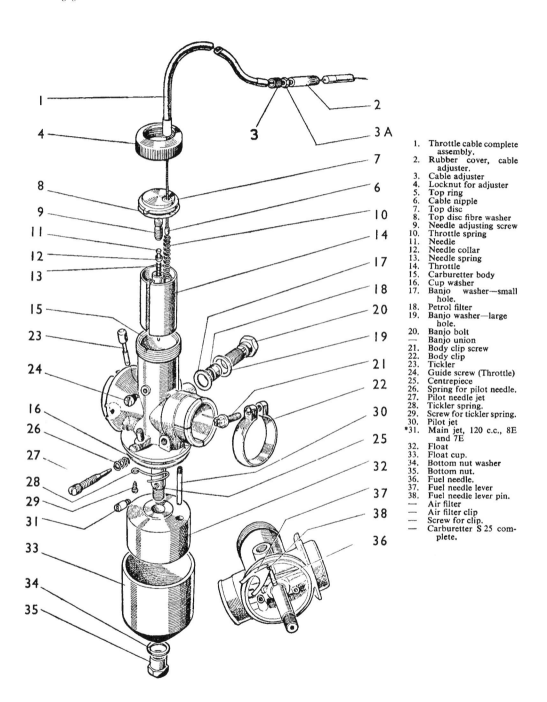

1. Throttle cable complete assembly.
2. Rubber cover, cable adjuster.
3. Cable adjuster
4. Locknut for adjuster
5. Top ring
6. Cable nipple
7. Top disc
8. Top disc fibre washer
9. Needle adjusting screw
10. Throttle spring
11. Needle
12. Needle collar
13. Needle spring
14. Throttle
15. Carburetter body
16. Cup washer
17. Banjo washer—small hole.
18. Petrol filter
19. Banjo washer—large hole.
20. Banjo bolt
— Banjo union
21. Body clip screw
22. Body clip
23. Tickler
24. Guide screw (Throttle)
25. Centrepiece
26. Spring for pilot needle.
27. Pilot needle jet
28. Tickler spring.
29. Screw for tickler spring.
30. Pilot jet
*31. Main jet, 120 c.c., 8E and 7E
32. Float
33. Float cup.
34. Bottom nut washer
35. Bottom nut.
36. Fuel needle.
37. Fuel needle lever
38. Fuel needle lever pin.
— Air filter
— Air filter clip
— Screw for clip.
— Carburetter S 25 complete.

AMC 25T engine, left-hand side, showing the smooth outline similar to the Villiers 1H.

Other engines followed with various capacities, including a 171cc (17T), 149cc (15T), 199cc (20T) and also a 16T, although there appears to be no record of the latter one, only a number stamped on the engine to indicate that it was manufactured. The 16T engine was used mainly for the James M16 machines, although a handful of the equivalent Francis-Barnett Model 96s also had them fitted. Both these models were only in production for a short period before the demise of AMC.

The new AMC engine brought many warranty claims from customers and a loss of confidence in the machines. The majority of the complaints related to broken piston rings and engine seizures, and some concerned condensation in the engine. The main problem appears to have been the lack of precision in machining the transfer troughs. The width of the trough was critical, because if only slightly too wide it would enable the piston ring to spring into the trough, with disastrous results. Other factors aggravated the situation, including the high development costs of the new engine.

In 1961, AMC announced that they were to cease assembling their engines, and this would be carried out in future by Villiers. The engines assembled by Villiers were denoted by having the letter 'V' included in the engine prefix – V15T, V20T – and were much more reliable.

The 147cc 15T engine was altogether different from the other AMC engines, having a more conventional

AMC engine casing stamped V16T fitted to a Plover Model 95. (Courtesy Keith R. Clarke)

cylinder barrel with fully cored transfer ports and a simple domed piston with a flat top. It had a reputation for reliability and for its simplicity of construction. A further variant of the engine with a prefix of V16T appeared in James and Francis-Barnett machines in 1966. Unfortunately no specification for the engine has yet been found to enable a comparison to be made between that and the V15T.

The problems with the AMC engines also affected the off-road competition machines. Up to 1957, Francis-Barnett had featured as a winner in road racing, trials and scrambling, but these successes were threatened with the introduction of the modified 25T engine. The 25S was fitted in the Scrambler 82 and the 25C in the Trials 83 when they were introduced in 1958; however, as well as the engine failures there was also the problem of weight and size.

Amal Carburettors

The spelling of the word 'carburettor' has changed over time. In the early Francis-Barnett manuals it was spelt as 'carburetter', and later changed to 'carburettor'. The AMAL Carburetter Company still retains the earlier spelling version in both their name and their literature. The company and trademark 'AMAL' was formed from the 'amal'gamation of two or three organizations following World War I in order to manufacture and market carburettors and associated products.

In the 1960s AMAL became part of the IMI group of industries before being sold in 1993 to Grosvenor Works Ltd in North London, a family-run business specializing in supplying components to various fuel systems companies. Grosvenor then began revitalizing the AMAL product range by commencing a programme of reintroducing some of the more popular ranges of obsolete products.

In 2003 the business was sold yet again, this time to the current manufacturers, Burlen Fuel Systems Ltd (BFS), who also produced SU, Solex and Zenith products, and over recent years gained a high reputation for continuing to produce carburettors and spares, thereby keeping a vast range of classic British vehicles running. BFS have continued to invest in AMAL by further increasing the range of popular obsolete carburettors back into production.

The 'AMAL' and 'AMAC' trademarks have been in constant use since their initial conception, and now cover a range of products including carburettors (principally, but not exclusively, for motorcycle engines), controls such as brake and clutch levers, cables, and so on.

Francis-Barnett used a range of AMAL products following World War II, with both pre-monobloc and monobloc carburettors being used in conjunction with Villiers and AMC engines. The pre-monobloc carburettor type 276 was used mainly in the competition machines of the 1950s, and the monobloc carburettors such as the types 376 and 389 were used in conjunction with the AMC-designed engines and the Trials and Scrambler machines.

Sectional drawing of the AMAL-type 370 carburettor.

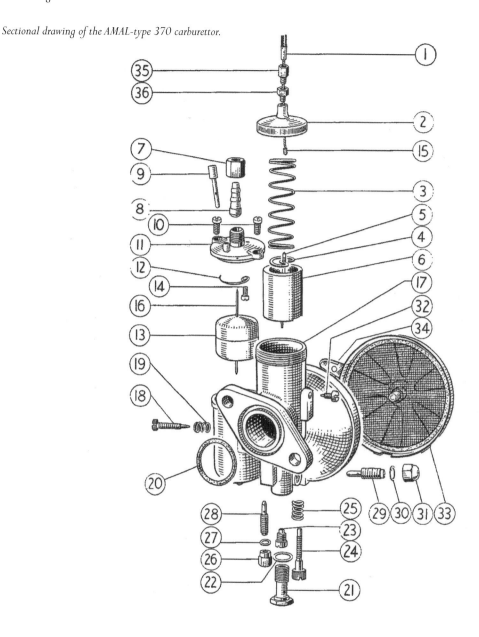

1	Cable.	13	Float.	25	Spring.
2	Mixing chamber top cap.	14	Spring securing screw.	26	Pilot jet nut.
3	Throttle spring.	15	Cable nipple.	27	Washer.
4	Needle clip.	16	Float needle.	28	Pilot jet.
5	Jet needle.	17	Carburetter body.	29	Main jet.
6	Throttle slide.	18	Pilot air adjusting screw.	30	Washer.
7	Petrol feed union nut.	19	Spring.	31	Cover nut.
8	Petrol feed union.	20	"O" ring.	32	Slide locating screw.
9	Tickler.	21	Jet plug.	33	Filter and strangler unit
10	Float chamber cover screws.	22	Fibre washer.	34	Guide screw.
11	Float chamber cover.	23	Needle jet.	35	Cable adjuster.
12	Tickler spring.	24	Throttle stop screw.	36	,, ,, nut.

Sectional drawing of the AMAL-type 389 carburettor.

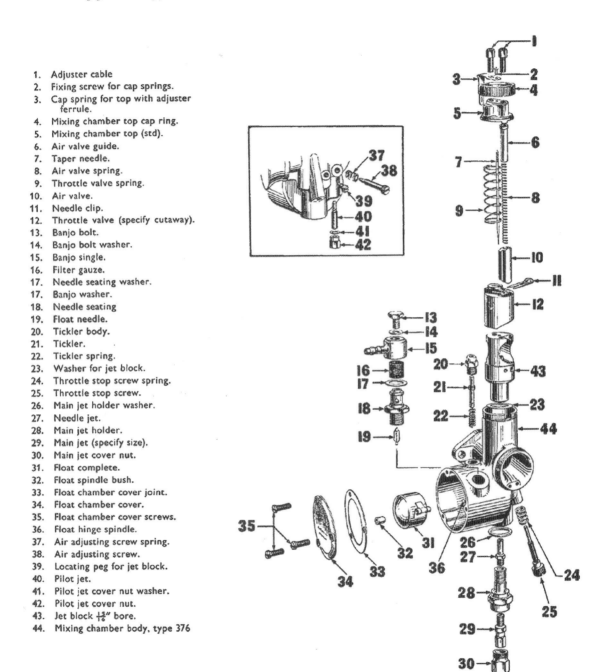

1. Adjuster cable
2. Fixing screw for cap springs.
3. Cap spring for top with adjuster ferrule.
4. Mixing chamber top cap ring.
5. Mixing chamber top (std).
6. Air valve guide.
7. Taper needle.
8. Air valve spring.
9. Throttle valve spring.
10. Air valve.
11. Needle clip.
12. Throttle valve (specify cutaway).
13. Banjo bolt.
14. Banjo bolt washer.
15. Banjo single.
16. Filter gauze.
17. Needle seating washer.
17. Banjo washer.
18. Needle seating
19. Float needle.
20. Tickler body.
21. Tickler.
22. Tickler spring.
23. Washer for jet block.
24. Throttle stop screw spring.
25. Throttle stop screw.
26. Main jet holder washer.
27. Needle jet.
28. Main jet holder.
29. Main jet (specify size).
30. Main jet cover nut.
31. Float complete.
32. Float spindle bush.
33. Float chamber cover joint.
34. Float chamber cover.
35. Float chamber cover screws.
36. Float hinge spindle.
37. Air adjusting screw spring.
38. Air adjusting screw.
39. Locating peg for jet block.
40. Pilot jet.
41. Pilot jet cover nut washer.
42. Pilot jet cover nut.
43. Jet block $\frac{13}{16}$" bore.
44. Mixing chamber body, type 376

Acknowledgements

Although my name appears on the cover as the author, this book really has been a team effort, and the sources of information are threefold: my initial research as the club registrar and librarian; the not inconsiderable notes of J. H. Goddard, Francis-Barnett service manager, generously given to the Francis-Barnett Owners' Club by his family; and the club members, ex-employees and works riders, with their knowledge and use of personal photographs.

There are several club members who have given more than a little help on the project: Sue Dorling, the current club chairlady and her husband William; John Harding, the club technical officer; Trevor Wells, past club chairman; John Baker, past club secretary and events organizer; Norman Clarke, past events organizer; Peter Anderson, Keith Clarke; Des Heckles, Mick Ransom, ex-works rider; Triss Sharp, ex-works rider; and Colin Dean, chief works tester, who was invaluable in putting names to faces in old photographs.

Sources of Information

The notes of J. H. Goddard, service manager, and Francis & Barnett Ltd, kindly donated to the Francis Barnett Owners' Club by his family.

Bacon, Roy *Villiers Singles & Twins* 1983, Niton Publishing.

Browning, B. E. *The Villiers Engine* 1950 (C. Arthur Pearson Ltd).

British Cycles and Motor Cycles Overseas, June–July 1951.

FBOC magazine, *The Directory.*

Francis-Barnett, James and Villiers literature.

Glasses *1961–1968 Motorcycle Guide.*

Goddard, J. H. *Francis-Barnett Motor Cycles 1957* (C. Arthur Pearson Ltd).

Goddard, J. H. *Francis-Barnett* 1961 (C. Arthur Pearson Ltd).

Grange, Cyril *The Book of the Villiers Engine 1929* (Pitman's Technical Books).

Motor, Marine and Aircraft Red Book 1917: Motor Cycles.

Sizer, Jack *The Villiers Story.*

The Motor Cycling.

The Motor Cycle.

Index